Discourse
A Series on Architecture

Ellie Abrons
Lucia Allais
Frank Barkow and Regine Leibinger
Marshall Brown
Peter Eisenman
Hal Foster
Curt Gambetta
Sylvia Lavin
Thom Mayne
Antoine Picon
Florencia Pita and Jackilin Bloom
Jesse Reiser
Julian Rose
Eda Yetim

Princeton University
School of Architecture

Distributed by
Princeton University Press

Discourse

a mode of organizing knowledge, ideas, or experience that is rooted in language and its concrete contexts (such as history or institutions).
—Merriam-Webster Dictionary

Today the world is at our fingertips: images and facts are immediately available, constantly streaming into our living rooms, desktops, and back pockets. And yet, it is fair to say that this proliferation of information has made it difficult to ascertain knowledge. It is hard to sort through the avalanche of images, given there are no standards to measure what truly matters. At the same time, the not-so-new media has also provided an equal platform to voices that historically were not present at the table; with this new access comes the potential to expand knowledge. *Discourse* capitalizes on the dissonance of this moment in order to construct a new mode of organizing knowledge. By focusing the dialogue on a single topic, *Discourse* seeks to understand the impact of architecture on contemporary culture. Acknowledging the impossibility of a canon and its corollary dissenting argument, *Discourse* thrives on presenting multiple points of view—including misinterpretations and counter narratives—as reflected in the format of each issue.

Authorship, the first issue of the series, critically examines the discipline of architecture by revisiting the seemingly defunct notion of design authorship. As we revel in the death of the master architect, how do we come to terms with the shifting role of creativity on architecture's cultural production? In *Authorship,* a cross-disciplinary group of designers and scholars explore this topic through a myriad of lenses. From the impact of digital tools and computational scripts on the making and conception of buildings in the age of robotics; to the current climate of appropriation and sampling as a counter-form of authorship; to contemplations of re-authored materials in a post-digital age. These emerging inquiries are cast against a repositioning of the history of architecture through alternative ideas of authorship. Featured essays investigate the separation between the personal and the authored; while others expose meaning, symbolism and iconography as the subjects of authority—not forms of authorship. Ultimately, this volume dismantles, realigns, and reassembles disparate architectural conditions to form a new legibility.

—Mónica Ponce de León

Contents

Author after Author

Ellie Abrons

We are, undoubtedly, in a postdigital age. This is not to say that we are after or beyond the digital, but simply that The Digital has shifted from something novel and exceptional to something banal and ubiquitous[1]. It's almost cloying to say it. Digital technology and media have transformed nearly every aspect of our lives. Digital apps and instruments lubricate the world—reducing the frictions that slow things down or require physical labor. Lines between the digital environment and the physical world are difficult to detect. It's no longer the case that digital stuff is an abstract representation of more real physical stuff—digital stuff is simply other, real stuff. These shifts have profound impact on the nature and status of authorship, in architecture and culture at large. Authorship is hardly dead (although The Author likely is), but its persistence cannot be mistaken for stability. Authorship is undergoing radical transformation in the postdigital world.

First, there is no original anymore, neither instance nor format. One can't claim a singular original from which all instances are mere copies. Nor can one claim that the drawing comes first and the physical object second (or, was it the other way around?) or that renderings are representations of another, more "real" thing. The distinctions are flattened, irrelevant, quaint.[2] Originality is now distributed—atomized across various media and instances as images and ideas are adopted, combined with others, altered, and re-presented. This circumstance discards singular origins in favor of a new sociality. It produces a collective enterprise where we are simultaneously consumers and producers of the same content.

Distinctions between original and copy aren't the only things flattened in the postdigital age. Divisions between physical and digital materiality, between the concrete and the abstract, between the real and the representational also collapse. Digital-ness has crept into material things, fusing with the physical in ways that make it almost impossible to detect. This ranges from new ways of seeing the world around us conditioned by digital processes and techniques to aesthetic expressions that are digitally native; from embedded technologies to the internet of things. The grain of computation has erupted, sometimes undetected, into our physical world. A characteristic example of this blurring can be seen in the popular use of photogrammetry. Highly detailed digital models derived from photographs are readily available for download or can be custom-created with an app on your mobile phone. These models separate form and surface articulation from material and image (three-dimensional polygon mesh models and texture map image files), presenting an opportunity to work on each as a distinct set of raw materials to be manipulated. Rather than approaching photogrammetry as a means of replicating "real" things

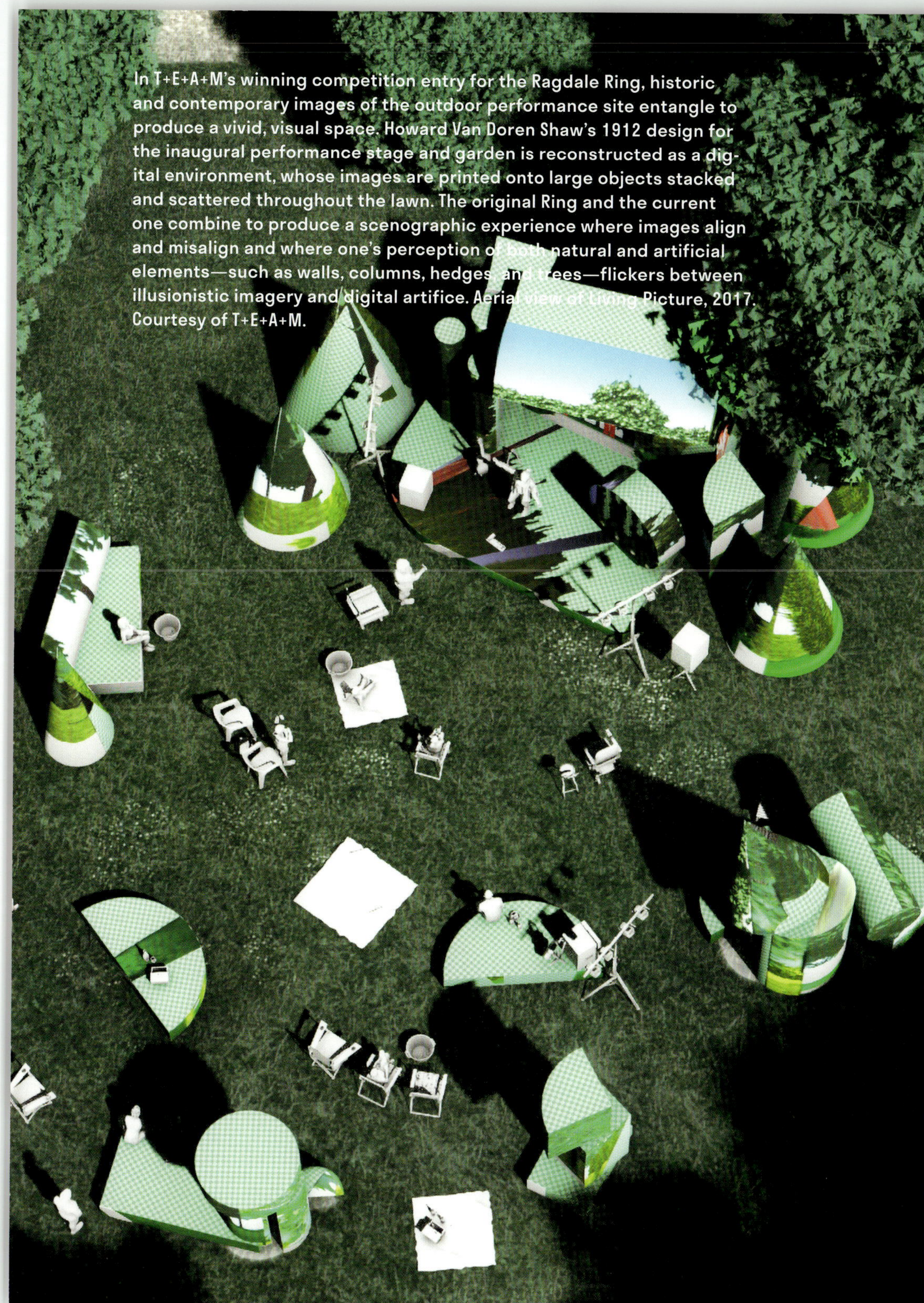

In T+E+A+M's winning competition entry for the Ragdale Ring, historic and contemporary images of the outdoor performance site entangle to produce a vivid, visual space. Howard Van Doren Shaw's 1912 design for the inaugural performance stage and garden is reconstructed as a digital environment, whose images are printed onto large objects stacked and scattered throughout the lawn. The original Ring and the current one combine to produce a scenographic experience where images align and misalign and where one's perception of both natural and artificial elements—such as walls, columns, hedges, and trees—flickers between illusionistic imagery and digital artifice. Aerial view of Living Picture, 2017. Courtesy of T+E+A+M.

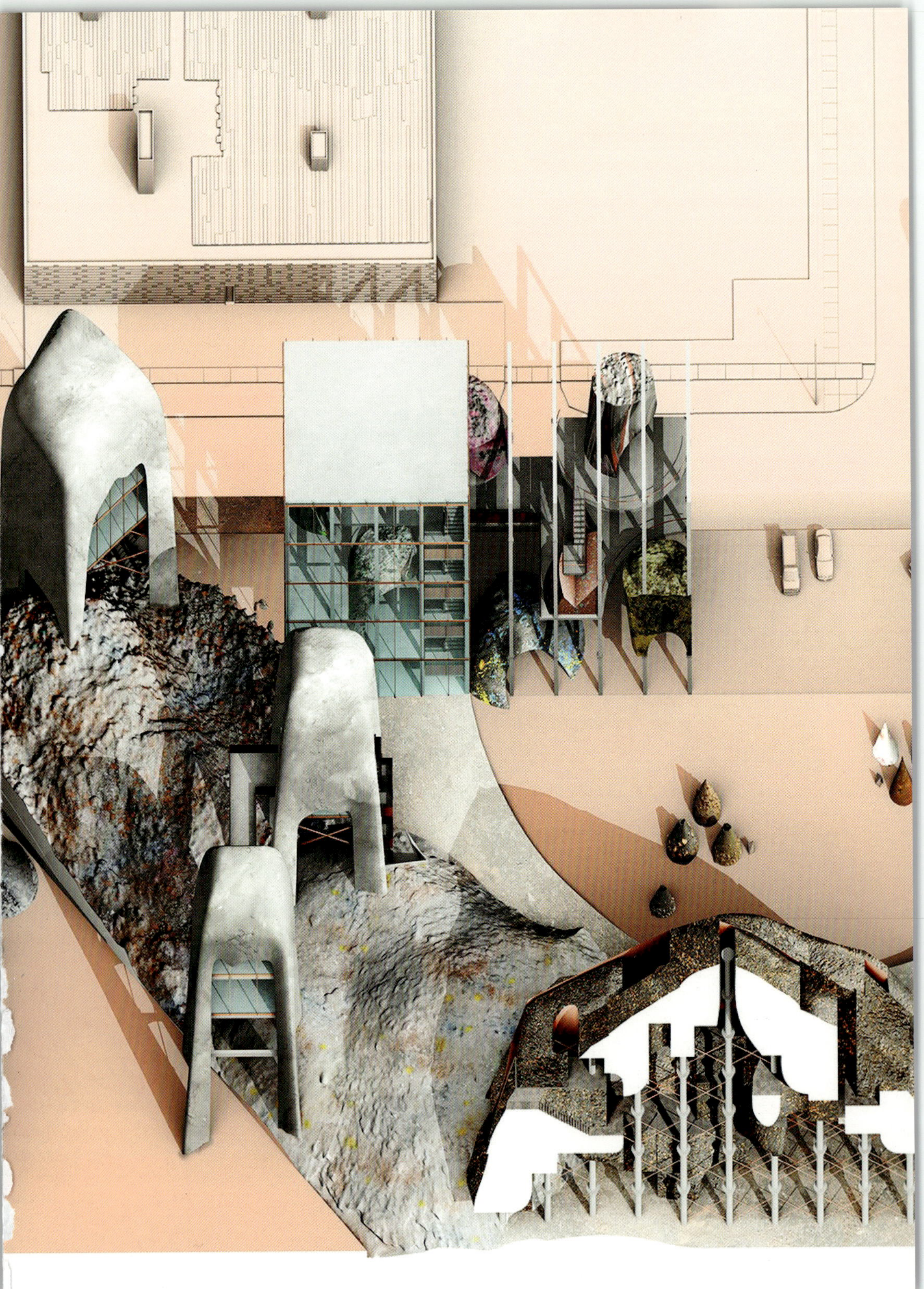

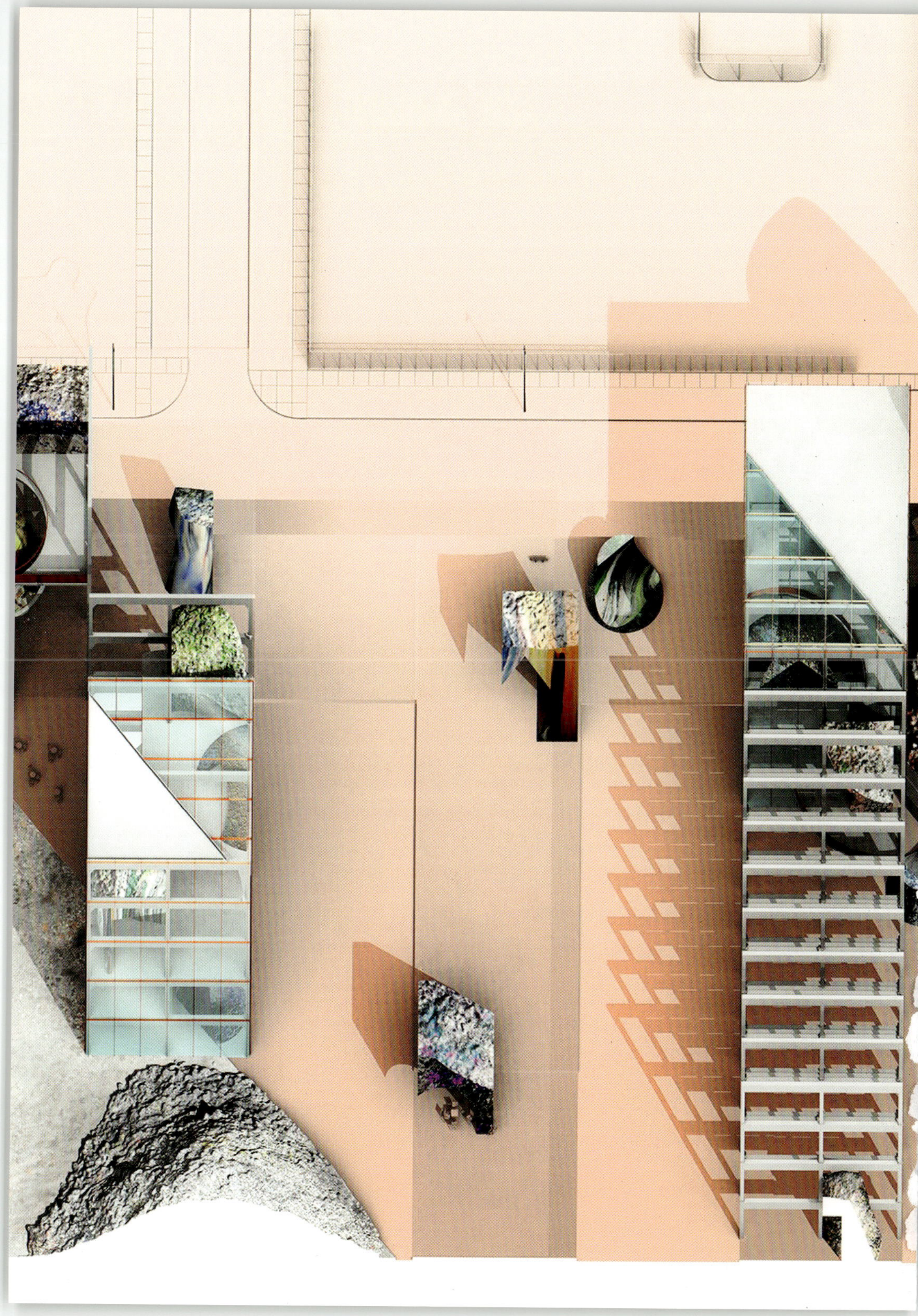

In Another Rock (facing page), a rendered two-dimensional image of a digital model is used to produce a new, three-dimensional, physical rock. This new rock is comprised of stacked horizontal and vertical planes printed with digital imagery. The rendered image is sliced into rows of pixels and stretched across each layer to produce another, more optically blurry, version of the rock's surface, now reduced to swatches and stripes of color. The authority of the "original" is dismantled, as copies of copies take on the status of authenticity in our post-digital moment. Materiality is no longer tied to the physical world and can now be digitally authored. The project isn't a model of a "real" rock, but is itself another rock. Winning competition entry exhibited in "Objects" at the Secret Life of Buildings Symposium, Another Rock, 2016. Photograph by Ellie Abrons and Adam Fure, courtesy of the author.

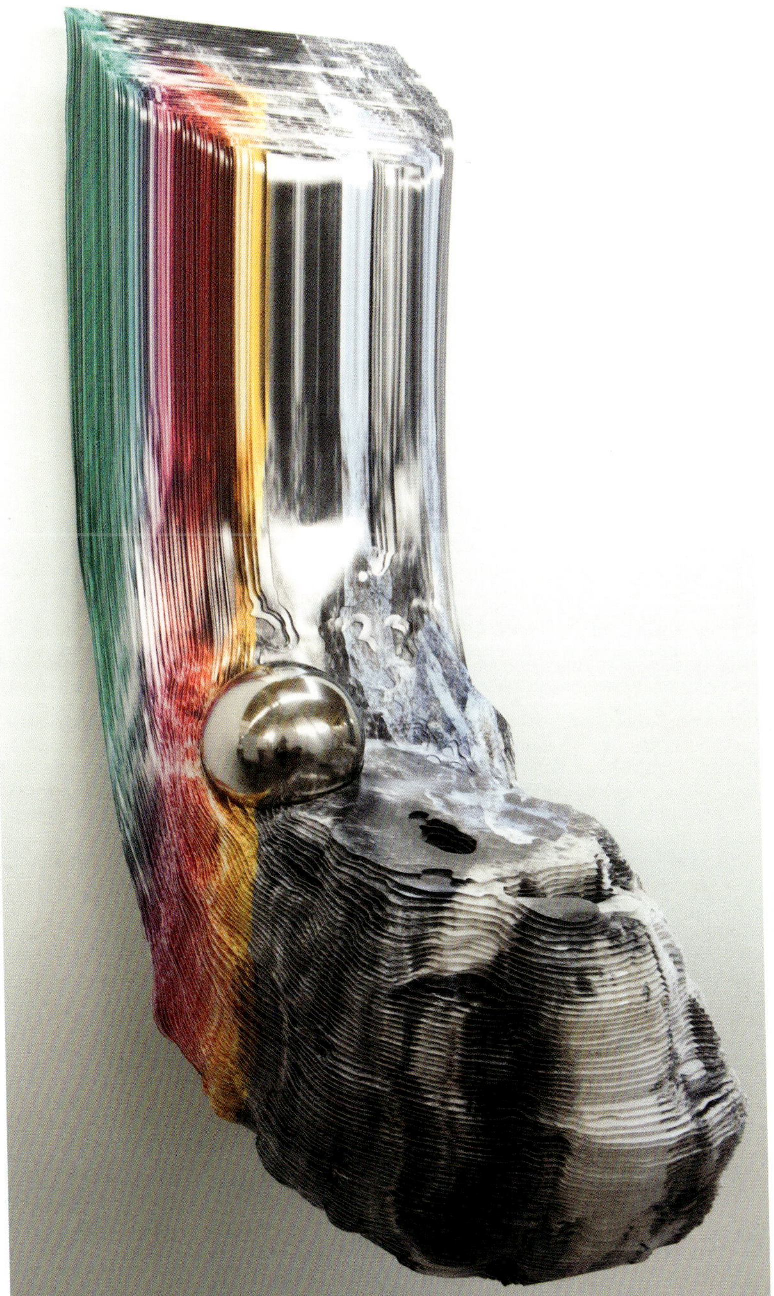
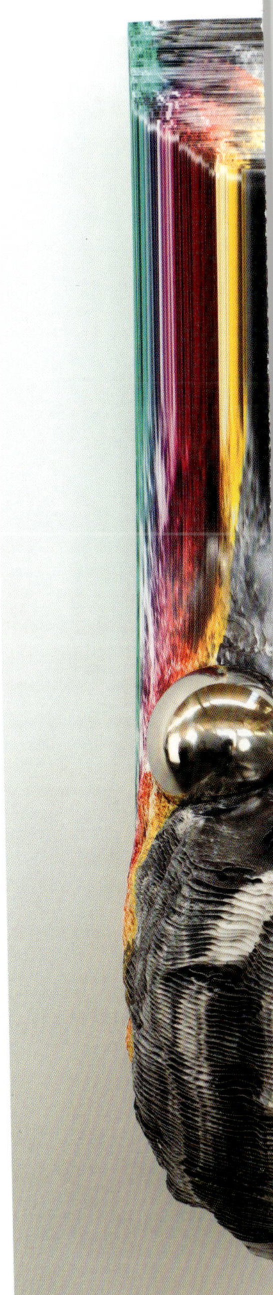

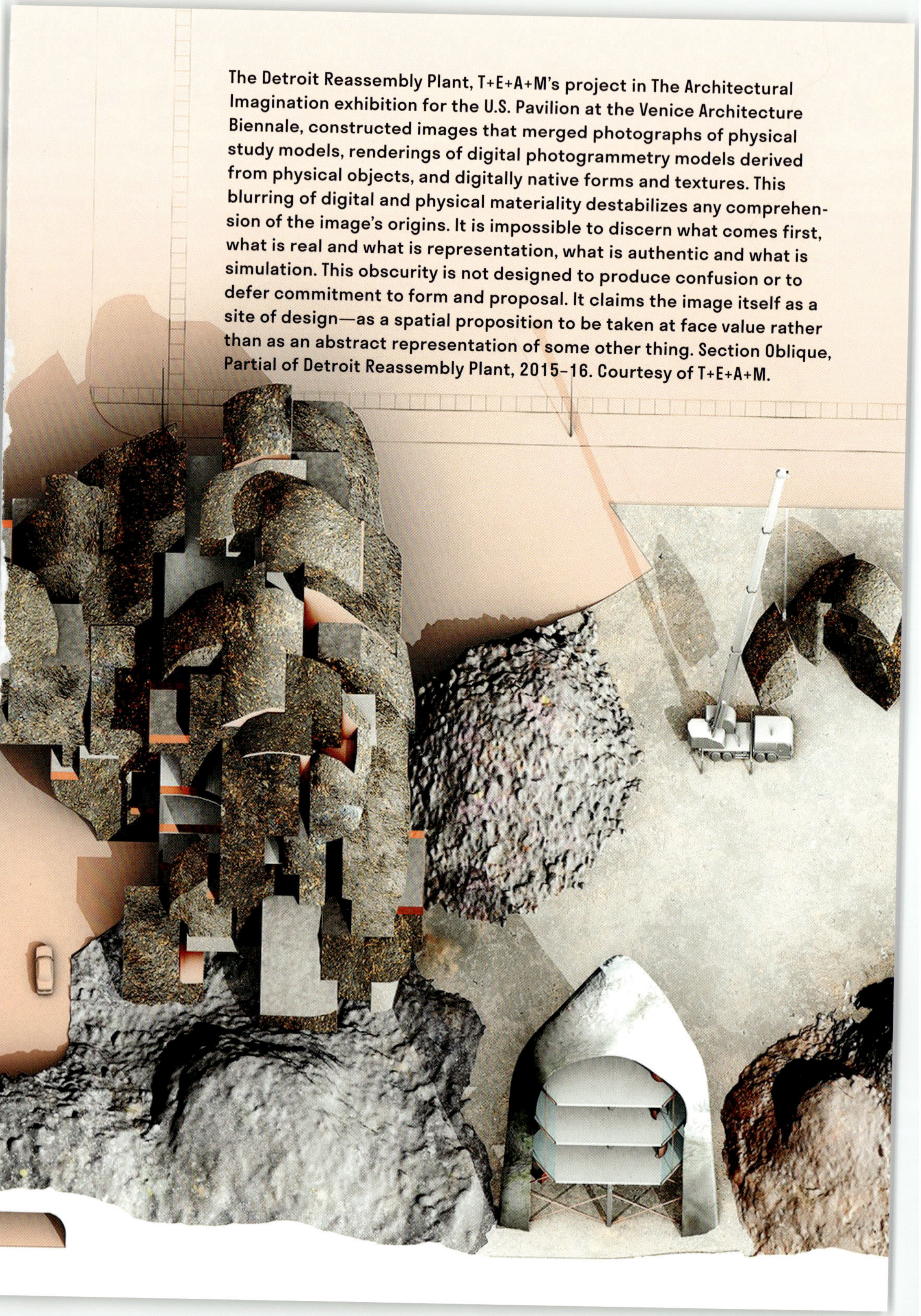

The Detroit Reassembly Plant, T+E+A+M's project in The Architectural Imagination exhibition for the U.S. Pavilion at the Venice Architecture Biennale, constructed images that merged photographs of physical study models, renderings of digital photogrammetry models derived from physical objects, and digitally native forms and textures. This blurring of digital and physical materiality destabilizes any comprehension of the image's origins. It is impossible to discern what comes first, what is real and what is representation, what is authentic and what is simulation. This obscurity is not designed to produce confusion or to defer commitment to form and proposal. It claims the image itself as a site of design—as a spatial proposition to be taken at face value rather than as an abstract representation of some other thing. Section Oblique, Partial of Detroit Reassembly Plant, 2015–16. Courtesy of T+E+A+M.

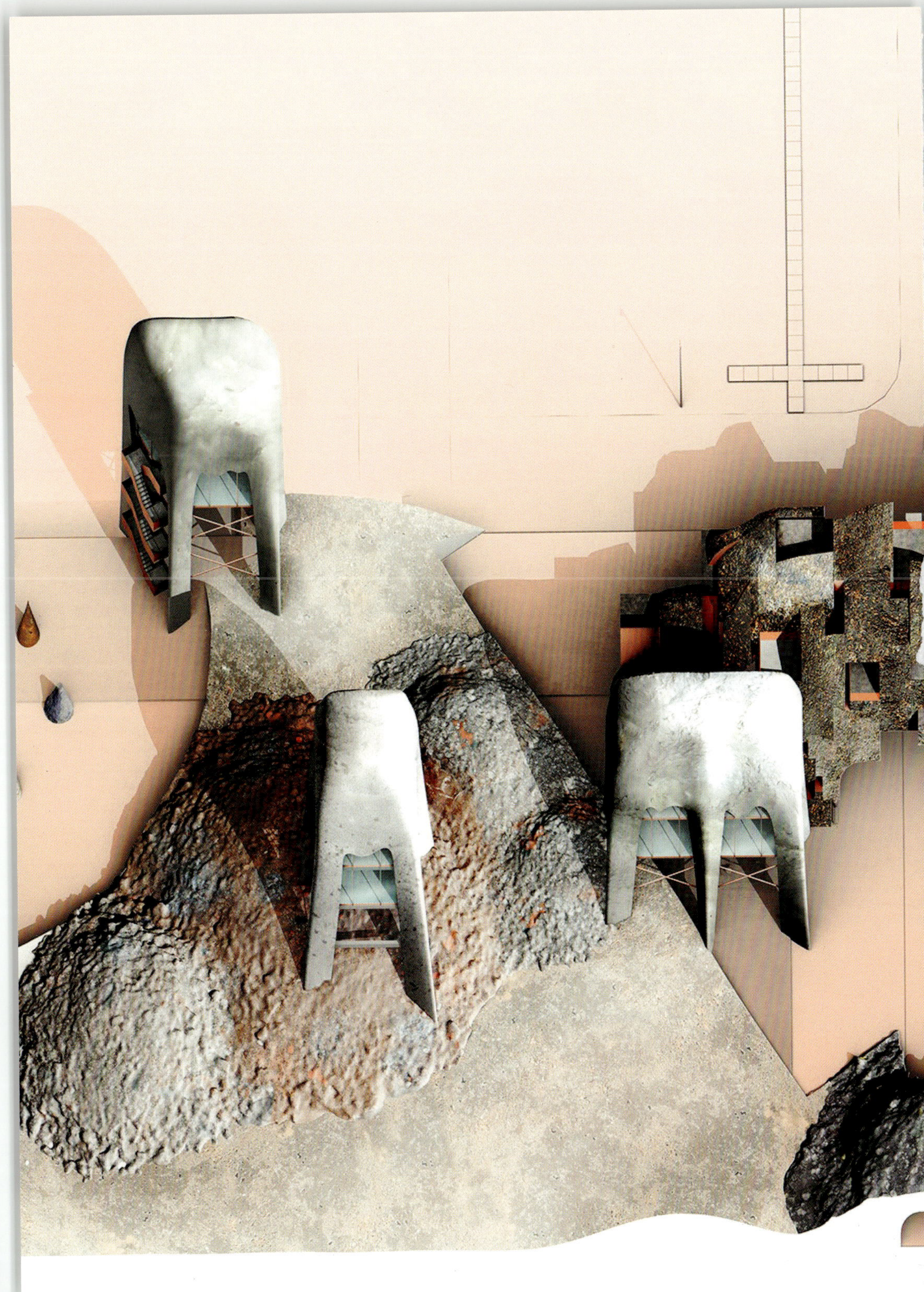

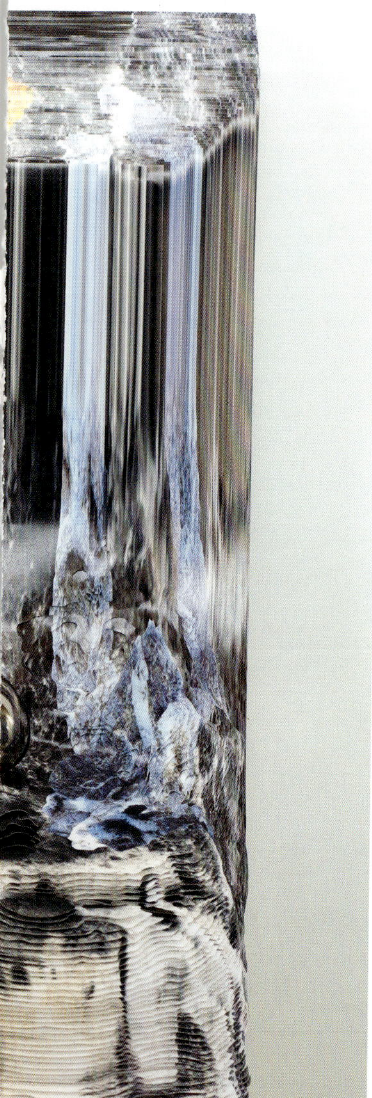

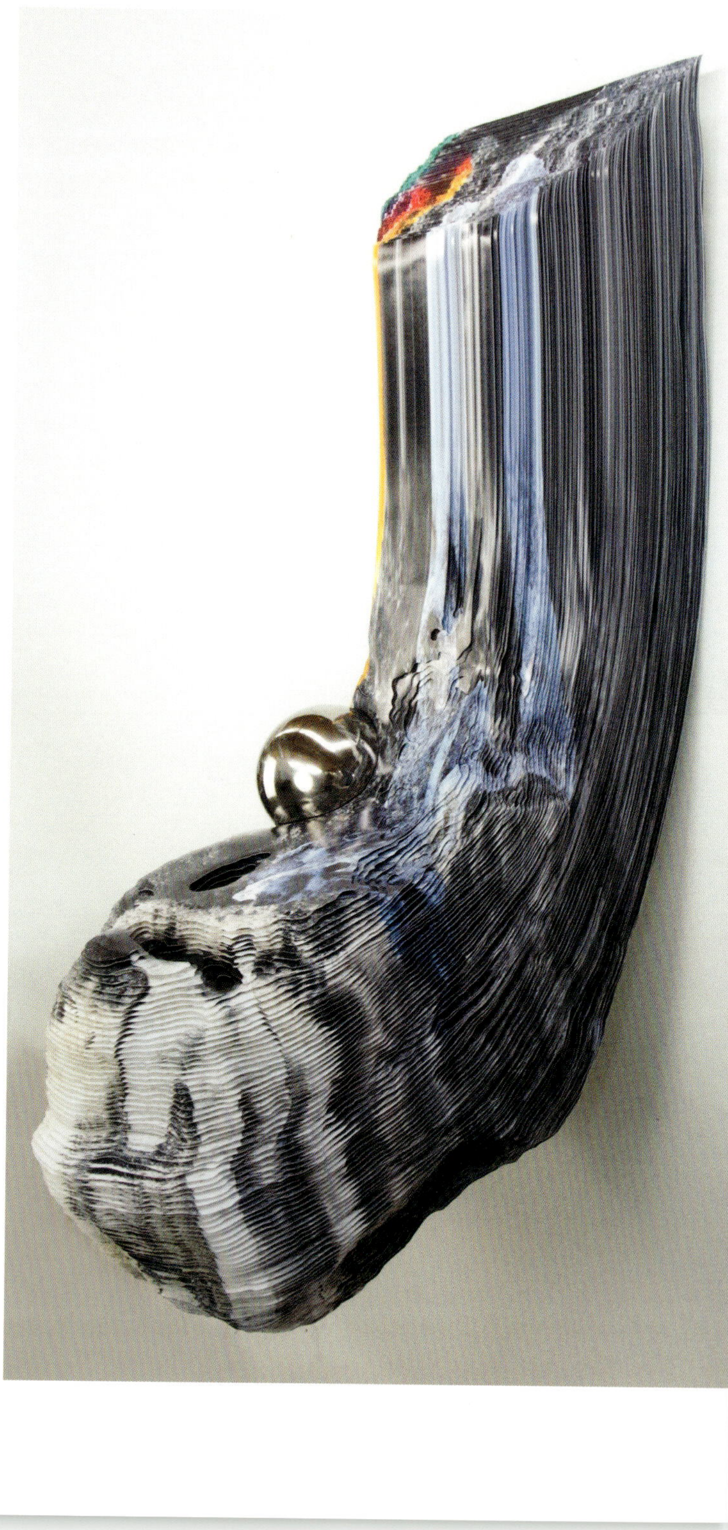

in a digital environment, each layer of information becomes a material in and of itself, ontologically equivalent in terms of design. Suddenly, it becomes nearly instinctual to move smoothly between hyper-realistic digital instantiations of physical things and highly mannered, plastic manipulations of digital material. Once inherent qualities and characteristics of physical materials are up for grabs, able to be authored and reimagined through new aesthetic registers.

These altered forms of authorship implicate creative propriety and ownership. As Artie Vierkant describes in his essay, "The Image Object Post-Internet," the shift from physical, fixed forms of media to networked, infinitely reproducible, digital ones reorganizes our cultural value system. A "one to many" distribution system based on a scarcity of creative production controlled by systems of power moves towards a "many to many" model where we collectively participate in cultural construction and transmission[3] This ethos of collectivity isn't utopian or uniform; the messiness of our pluralist moment is unavoidable. It is rife with contradictions as we struggle with opportunism and narcissism, defiance and appropriation, conformism and exploitation.[4] Nonetheless, it erodes the historical exclusivity and elitism of cultural production and provokes the creation of "reader-authors" who regard all cultural output as a work in progress to be taken up and continued by any of us.

These outputs of creative production are beholden to a new set of values. Transience is acceptable and permanence is questionable. Circulation and acceleration surpass close attention and perpetuity. Small file sizes, universal formats, and common aspect ratios all contribute to a new form of temporality where meaning and association are destabilized through constant re-contextualization of the work. Images jump from small screens to big screens to paper to digital environments to physical surfaces and back again.

The effects are this: relieved of a duty to authenticity, originality, or even stable referents, architects work in a collage culture of mixed media, messages, signs, and materials. Authorship doesn't disappear but disperses into a cloud of influence that seeps and infiltrates layers of imagery, materiality, and form. Found objects combine with new digital textures, repurposed materials are formed into unfamiliar shapes, historic images bleed into fictional ones. Unquestionably, this form of collage should be distinguished from the postmodern collage of the 1970s and 80s where architecture could be considered an accumulation or composition of signs that held stable cultural meaning. Now, meaning and association shift continuously as we move away from compositions of fixed parts, quotations of historical types, or formal expressionism that works through metaphor. This architecture "builds alliances as it travels, provokes translation or mistranslation, and creates new publics and debates."[5] Postdigital sensibilities consider all material and imagistic qualities to be ripe for authorship and design and use the agency of images and visual culture to gain traction for architecture with a diverse audience.

1 The capitalization of "The Digital" refers to its canonization as an entity in architecture with its own history, protagonists, and discourse.
2 For more on the disappearing distinction between originals and copies and a discussion of "post-original originals," see Douglas Davis, "The Work of Art in the Age of Digital Reproduction," *Leonardo*, Vol. 28, No. 5 (The MIT Press, 1995), 381–86.
3 Artie Vierkant, "The Image Object Post-Internet," (2010), accessed May 9, 2017, http://jstchillin.org/artie/pdf/The_Image_Object_Post-Internet_us.pdf
4 Hito Steyerl discusses this at length in an essay on the political and social agency of poor images. See Hito Steyerl, "In Defense of the Poor Image," *e-flux journal #10* (November 2009), accessed May 9, 2017, http://www.e-flux.com/journal/10/61362/in-defense-of-the-poor-image
5 Ibid.

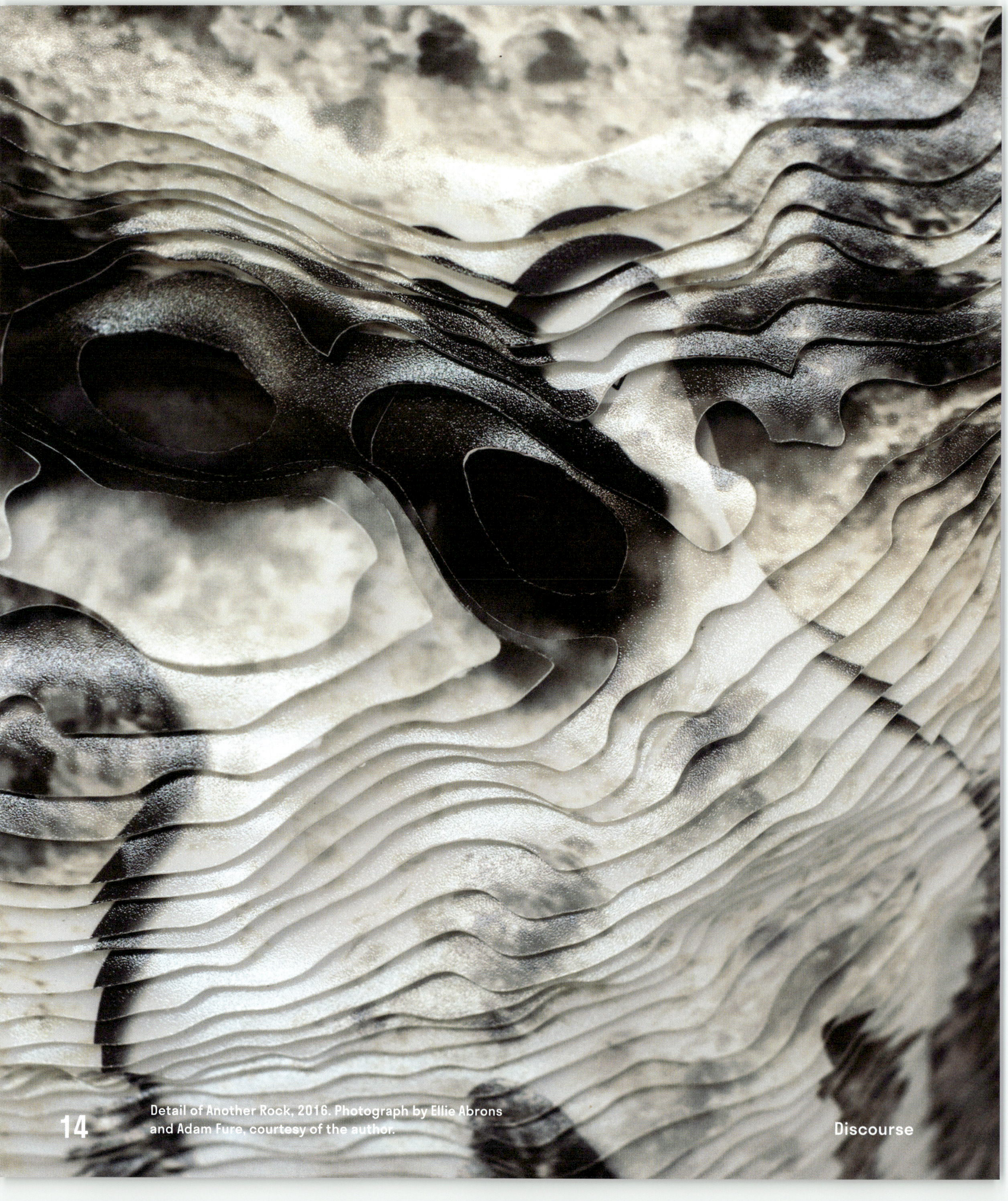

Detail of Another Rock, 2016. Photograph by Ellie Abrons and Adam Fure, courtesy of the author.

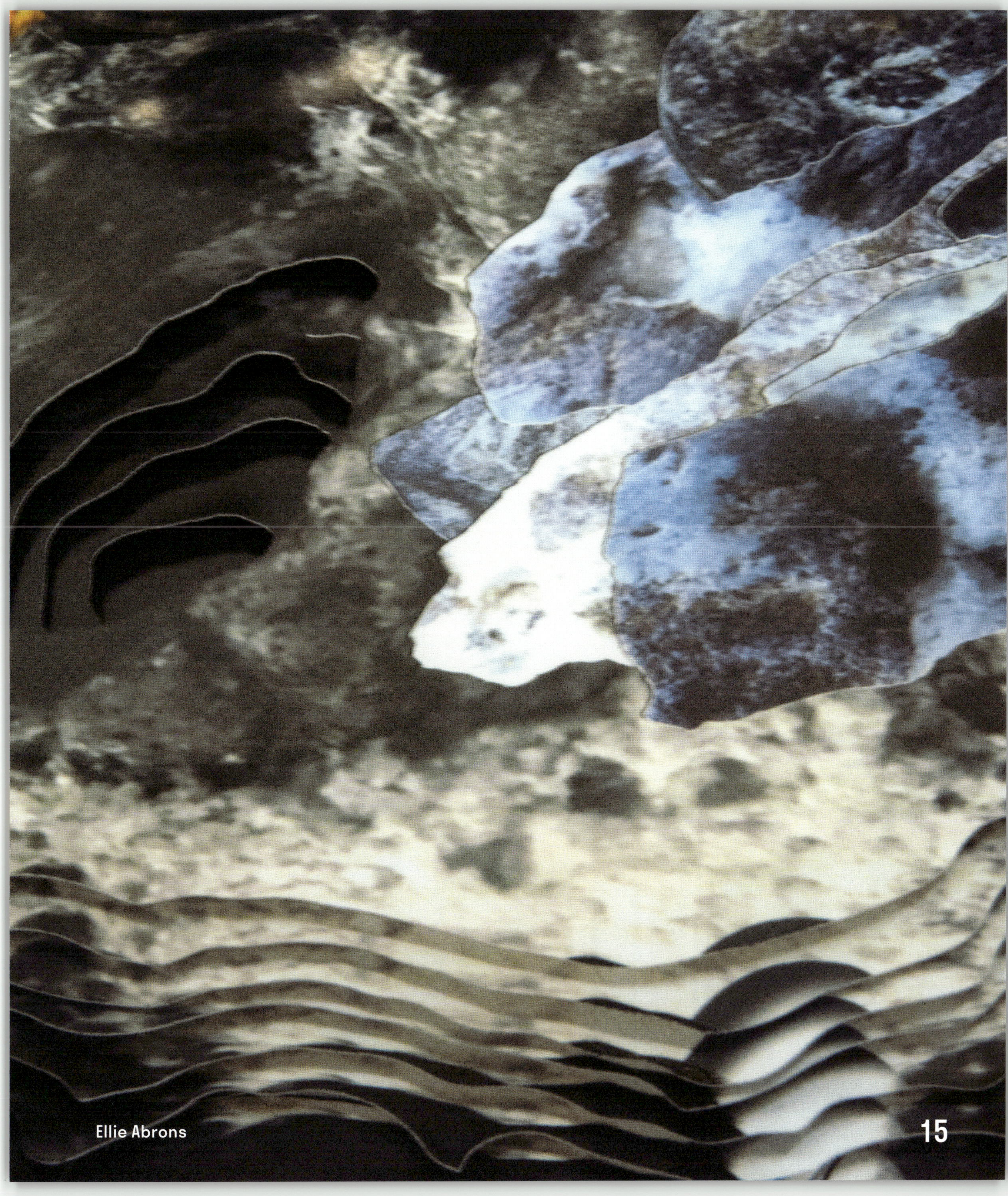

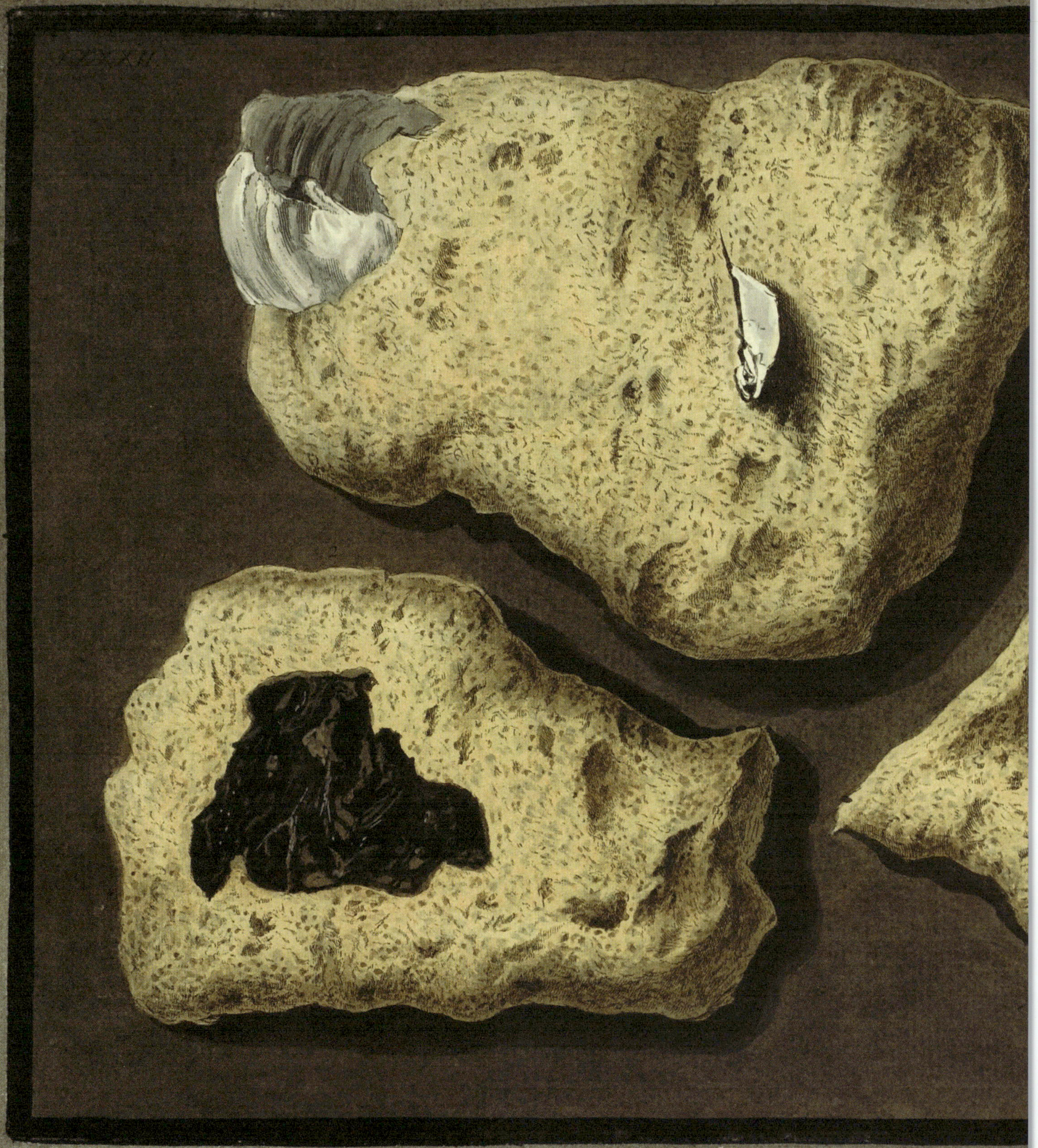

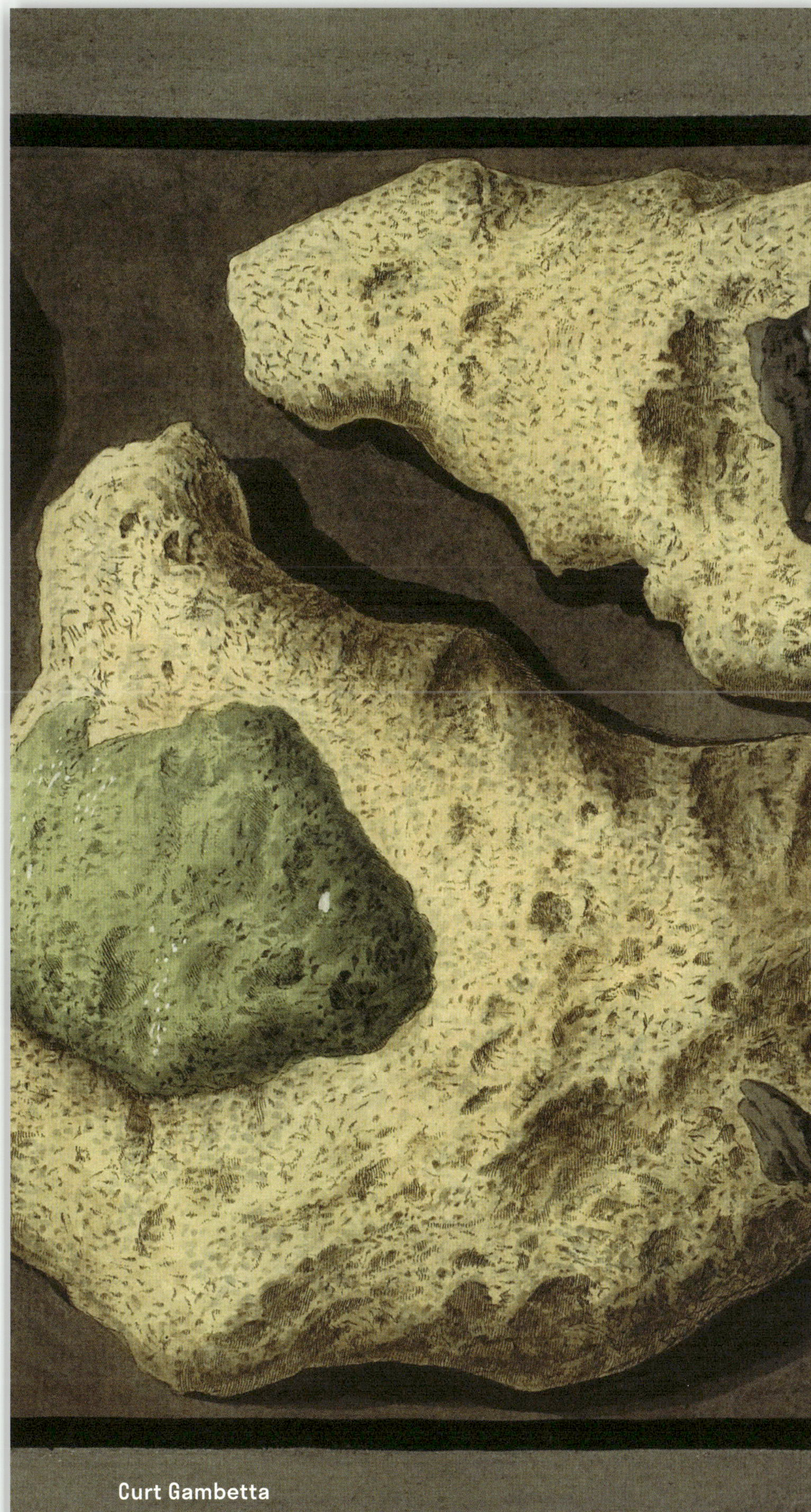

Curt Gambetta

Authoring Materials

Curt Gambetta

What is "Another Rock"? Is it a rock? Is it plastic? Paper? An image? All of the above? Its authors, Ellie Abrons and Adam Fure, meticulously preserve its manifold provenance, mixing its sources but preventing them from dissolving into homogenous substance. "Another Rock" bears traces of its means of production, showing the handiwork and irresolution entailed in managing the translation from one form of media (a digitally rendered image) to another (printed surfaces, which comprise a rock-like object). Abrons describes its effects by way of visual approach. From certain vantage points, she explains, its "hue and saturation" evoke the visual qualities of a rock. Look closely, and it reveals itself as a series of layered, printed contours that "interfere" with its appearance as a rock.[1]

Abrons wants "Another Rock" to be scrutinized, if only to obscure its signification and provenance. Citing exhaustion over the "positivism" of architectural representation in the 2000s, Abrons and her collaborators interject digital workflows and platforms with physical constructs, preferring outcomes that sit uneasily in the strictures and goals of contemporary image production and materials research.[2] Projects such as "Another Rock" resist the cozy relationship of architectural production with knowledge, misusing techniques otherwise reserved for producing and retrieving knowledge about buildings, cities and landscapes, such as photogrammetry. To BIM, a counterproposition: information mismanagement?

Much as the transmutation of plastic into different forms is a "spectacle to be deciphered," as Roland Barthes put it, so-called "postdigital" inquiries into weird and otherworldly forms are eager to explain their inputs and methods. But only to a point. While they expose hints and traces of their production, they stop short of workflow diagrams and transparent explanations.[3] Barthes imagines plastic as infinitely malleable, musing that "the whole world can be plasticized."[4] Abrons and her collaborators embrace the material constraints of a plastic method. "Another Rock" insists on expressing traces of use, reveling in digital and material vestiges not unlike those that accompany the circulation of bad copies of video and images on the internet. The malleability of a work such as "Another Rock" resides less in the material as such than it does in deforming, patching up or expressing the gaps between users, materials and computational platforms. Abrons and Fure arrest, in other words, not the formation of a material but its translation between one medium and another.

In this, contemporary preoccupation with conglomerate and composite materialities (if not materials) points to a renewed tension between enduring appeals to the origin of materials (how they are authored, by what or whom), and their resistance to any such identification with origins. After all, as Sylvia Lavin argues, authenticity to materials was an alibi for medium specificity in mid-20th century architecture, a way of closing ranks around the disciplinary malleability witnessed in insurgent experimentation with plastics and "soft materials."[5] Do conglomerates summon the ghosts of medium specificity, now resuscitated under a mantle of architecture's commitments to sustainability? Think, for instance, of the growing market for recyclable composites, a world of feel good and LEED-certified terrazzo. Or do composite materials point to new conditions of architectural work—a composite process, irreducible to a whole—as Abrons seems to suggest?

Abrons and Fure photograph "Another Rock" in a white gallery space, culling the object from its manifold origins. Its mise-en-scène recalls the depiction of rock specimens in non-places such as wooden cabinets and blank tableaus in studies of natural history during the 18th and 19th century. But where Abrons and Fure use the isolation of the gallery space to obscure the origins of "Another Rock," historical depictions of conglomerate rocks invited scrutiny of their origins. For instance, Enlightenment-era reports such as William Hamilton's "Campi Phlegraei, Observations on the Volcanoes of the Two Sicilies" (1776) sought to read natural and cultural origins off of earthen materials and architectural ruins.[6] Hamilton took great pains to describe and illustrate the craggy byproducts of a landscape under construction, employing the painter Pietro Fabris to depict rock samples and the ongoing eruptions of Mount Vesuvius. Fabris' painting of tufa stones featured agglomerations of oyster shells, lava and different kinds of stone with "soft" and "light" volcanic tufa stone.[7] Hamilton proposed that the oyster-laden stones were proof that the region's volcanoes rose from the sea, and that other hybrid stones were evidence of origins in earlier and multiple volcanic eruptions, not a singular catastrophic event. Against theories of catastrophism or the earth's ruination and decay, tufa stones showed instances of the earth's gradual formation.

Homogenous materials confounded verification of their origins. As Roberto Gargiani observes, the material origins of Egyptian architectural antiquities was a subject of considerable debate in Europe during the 1700s, owing to conflicting reports that explained their apparent homogeneity as cement or *pierre fondue*.[8] By the 19th century, the undifferentiated quality of new materials such as rubber complicated their position in new theories of architectural modernity. Gottfried Semper's history of style (1860), for instance, struggled over rubber's alleged lack of history. Whereas other materials and techniques bore traces of use or natural origin, rubber disguised its origins in industrial manufacture, let alone Equatorial forests and colonial plunder.[9] Semper excoriated its deployment as the "ape of useful materials" at the World Exposition in Paris and the Great Exhibition of 1851 in Hyde Park, which featured rubber imitations of industrial products, such as boats, walking sticks and tassels.[10] Ultimately, Semper redeemed rubber, arguing that the idiosyncrasies of its use made it available to techniques familiar to an evolutionary history of ceramics or textiles. Exposed seams from molds and soldering preserved the vestiges of its use, he argued, inviting further elaboration and encrustation on a material that had "no natural grain."[11]

Semper hedged that for rubber to participate in processes of historical change, it had to be acted upon. Otherwise, rubber risked devolving into a mere "factotum" of industry.[12] Hamilton's observations of rocks and antiquities were also a way of acting on them.[13] Fabris' paintings extracted rocks from the landscape and arranged them for a lettered public of readers. Tufa and other stones served as evidence of natural and cultural antiquity, propelling Hamilton into competition with other savants over the collection and classification of rocks, pots and geological formations.[14]

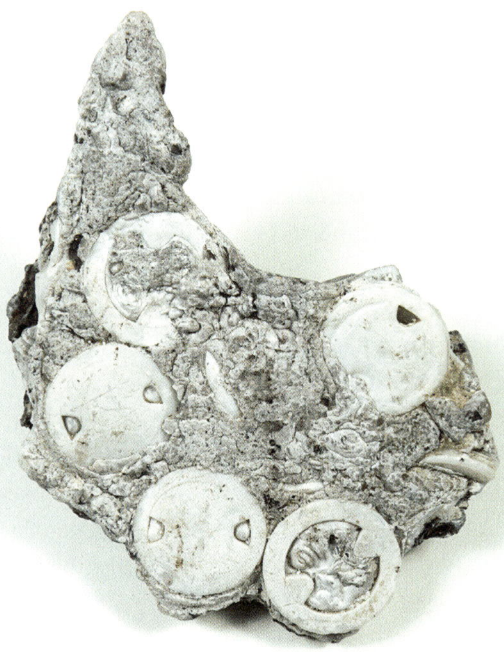

Plastiglomerate sample/ready-made collected by Patricia Corcoran and Kelly Jazvac at Kamilo Beach, Hawai'i, 2012. Photograph by Jeff Elstone, courtesy of Kelly Jazvac.

Contemporary studies of conglomerates resist the taxonomic goals of historical studies. Contemporary art and architectural practices profess ambivalence about their status as knowledge. Consider the plastiglomerate, a material type that is, quite literally, lost at sea.[15] Named by sculptor Kelly Jazvac, oceanographer Charles Moore and geologist Patricia Corcoran after an evidence-gathering mission to Kamilo Beach in Hawaii in 2012, plastiglomerates include gnarly mashups of deformed and degraded plastic, rock, sand and other itinerant ocean waste.[16] Beach combing for plastic mash-ups explodes historical ideas about the everyday discovery of consumer detritus. Whereas Alison and Peter Smithson envisioned the "as found" as a "new way of seeing the ordinary" from the vantage point of a pedestrian in London, the oceanic furling of the Pacific Gyre indexes forces whose vast scale and complexity make the ruins of postwar London seem like a minor hiccup.[17]

Like Abrons and Fure's "Another Rock," Jazvac's plastiglomerates elicit an overwhelming sense of déjà vu: the rock samples are isolated from their context and photographed on a white background. If Hamilton and Semper found common ground in efforts to locate materials in the origin narratives of their time, contemporary discourse about plastiglomerates mobilize their origins to different ends. Their presentation without context makes them amenable to a contemporary economy of evidence about the Anthropocene. But Jazvac cautions their use as data. Rather than classify plastiglomerate "stones" according to material or morphological types, Jazvac and her collaborators present them as complex objects that resist classification by type, origin, location or time. For their purveyors, plastiglomerates are epistemically and materially inflexible: they cannot be broken down and separated. As writers Kirsty Robertson and Heather Davis observe, the durability of plastic embodies the "obduracy" of forces that bring it into being, such as colonialism and capitalism.[18]

Recent architectural studies of plastiglomerates reinforce their opacity. Meredith Miller, a regular collaborator of Abrons, proposes that plastiglomerates and other anthropogenic rocks resist their abstraction into data. Instead, Miller writes, they make "sensible those scattered inputs and distant geographies without *explaining* their contingencies."[19] An alternative, she proposes, to the information heavy rhetoric of architectural work during the 2000s, which sought to represent the complex entanglement of cities, landscapes and planetary systems. Rather than construe plastiglomerates as a system or model (think, for instance, of a map of their origins and trajectories around the Pacific), Miller suggests that architects participate in their manifold relations and construction.

For example, in their contribution to "The Architectural Imagination," a series of architectural proposals for Detroit exhibited in the American Pavilion at the Venice Biennale in 2016, Miller, Abrons, Fure and Thom Moran (known by their collaborative moniker "T+E+A+M"), envision plastiglomerates at an architectural scale.[20] Stating unequivocally that "Detroit doesn't have a material problem; its material has an image problem," they reimagine the ruins of the historic Packard Plant in Detroit as a resource for design, rather than an icon of decay.[21] After demolishing unviable parts of the plant, T+E+A+M propose to synthesize demolition waste with plastic and other consumer waste from contemporary Detroit, creating thick, multistory heaps and grottos out of resulting marbleized and composite material.

The use of plastiglomerate is a subject of emerging debate. Jazvac, for instance, holds firm against the production of new plastiglomerate materials. She informed me that she does "not endorse the manufacturing of plastiglomerate as a new resource of any kind," owing to the "toxicity of the process and the complicated logistics of ethically sourcing the plastics."[22] Instead, she prefers that research target "production and consumption habits from the beginning of the cycle, not at the end."[23] In response to plastic's refusal to go away, Jazvac asks that we refuse plastic.[24]

Jazvac's misgivings prompt a reassessment of plastic's impact on architectural production and thought. As concept and material, plastic releases architecture from the stranglehold of "material specificity, medium specificity and even semantic specificity," as Lavin puts it, challenging architectural norms and ideals.[25] But if we acknowledge its obduracy, plastic introduces a new problem set for architectural work that is different from earlier anxieties about its untamed malleability. In plastics, architecture finds itself stuck to intractable ethical dilemmas and environmental politics. Plastic gloms architectural production onto extra-disciplinary actors and processes, such as the production cycle for consumer items—itself a longstanding preoccupation of architectural experimentation.[26] Do new conglomerate materials threaten the plasticity of architectural work? Or do they explode it even further, redistributing its commitments and mediums in unexpected ways?

Much like the molten plastic that binds plastiglomerates together, Abrons envisions methods of working that absorb vestiges as they go, allowing images to deform to their means of reproduction, and vice versa. In her essay "Author After Author," Abrons hints at the possibility that the author, too, might get swept up in the amalgam. Abrons likens "postdigital" architecture to Hito Steyerl's paean to the circulation of degraded media, or what Steyerl calls "poor images."[27] Quoting Steyerl, Abrons imagines an architecture that "builds alliances as it travels, provokes translation or mistranslation, and creates new publics and debates."[28]

What alliances are generated by the production of conglomerate, lumpen artifacts of "postdigital" practice, such as "Another Rock"? Abrons' prolific collaborations offer a clue. Her involvement in collaborative work and ongoing pedagogical initiatives, such as T+E+A+M and Possible Mediums, relax authority over production, drawing materials into an ecosystem of high and low-res media production.[29] Their format is group work and workshops, displacing knowledge and expertise from expert roundtables and lectures to the scene of production.[30] The majority of its participants are producers, leaving open the productive and critical role of consumers.

For Steyerl, "poor images" upend authority over the distribution, ownership and image quality of cinema and video art, blurring the boundaries between producers and consumers of media. Do they have a correlate in composite materials? In ocean currents and the flood of digital image culture, materials downsample and degrade as they drift and pass from user to user. Circulation exposes their rites of passage: the ocean and the circuitry of image consumption and production, respectively, but also the economic and political infrastructures that carry them forth. While plastiglomerates bind together oceanographers, artists and geologists, can composite materials such as "Another Rock" open up space for new alliances with architectural production?

1 Ellie Abrons, "Another Rock," *A+U* 05 (2017): 113.
2 Ibid., 113.
3 Roland Barthes, "Plastic," in *Mythologies* (New York: Hill and Wang, 1957), 97.
4 Barthes, "Plastic," 99.
5 Sylvia Lavin, "Plasticity at Work," in *Architecture Words 13: A Flash in the Pan* (London: Architectural Association, 2015). See also Lydia Kallipoliti, "The Soft Cosmos of AD's 'Cosmorama' in the 1960s and 1970s," *AD* 80/6 (2010).
6 See Roberto Gargiani, *Concrete from Archeology to Invention: 1700–1769*, trans. Stephen Piccolo (Lausanne: EPFL Press, 2013).
7 William Hamilton, *Observations on Mount Vesuvius, Mount Etna, and other volcanos: in a series of letters, addressed to the Royal Society/from the Honourable Sir W. Hamilton...; to which are added, explanatory notes by the author, hitherto unpublished, Vol. 2* (Printed for T. Cadell, in the Strand, 1773), 42.
8 Gargiani, *Concrete*, 12–15.
9 Rubber was located outside the geography of civilizational development that underpinned Semper's *Der Stil*, which by and large focused on the antiquities of the West and near East.
10 Gottfried Semper, *Style in the Technical and Tectonic Arts; or, Practical Aesthetics* (Los Angeles: The Getty Research Institute Publications, 2004), 181–183.
11 Ibid., 184.
12 Semper, *Style*, 180.
13 Recall Sigfried Giedion's well-known refrain that "to observe something is to act upon and alter it." Sigfried Giedion, *Space, Time and Architecture: the growth of a new tradition* (Cambridge: Harvard University Press, 1982), 5.
14 Noah Heringman, *Sciences of Antiquity: Romantic Antiquarianism, Natural History, and Knowledge Work* (Oxford: Oxford University Press, 2013).
15 Meredith Miller, "Views from the Plastisphere: A Preface to Post-Rock Architecture," in *Climates: Architecture and the Planetary Imaginary*, ed. James Graham (New York: Columbia Books on Architecture and the City, 2017).
16 Patricia Corcoran, Kelly Jazvac, and Charles Moore, "An anthropogenic marker horizon in the future rock record," *GSA Today* 24: 6 (June 2016): 4–8.
17 Alison and Peter Smithson, "The 'As Found' and the 'Found,'" in *The Independent Group: Postwar Britain and the Aesthetics of Plenty*, ed. David Robbins (Cambridge: MIT Press, 1990), 201.
18 Kirsty Robertson, "Plastiglomerate," *e-flux journal* 78 (2016), 11; Heather Davis "Life and Death in the Anthropocene: A Short History of Plastic" in *Art in the Anthropocene: Encounters Among Aesthetics, Politics, Environments and Epistemologies*, eds. Heather Davis and Etienne Turpin (London: Open Humanities Press, 2015), 351–353.

19 Miller, “Views,” 78.

20 “The Architectural Imagination,” curated by Cynthia Davidson and Mónica Ponce de León, was exhibited at the 2016 Venice Biennale. See Cynthia Davidson and Mónica Ponce de León, *Log 37: The Architectural Imagination cataLog* (Spring/Summer 2016).

21 “Detroit Reassembly Plant,” T+E+A+M, accessed May 31, 2017, http://tpluseplusaplusm.us/reassembly.html

22 Kelly Jazvac, e-mail message to author, May 29, 2017.

23 Ibid.

24 Ibid. Referring to research by Samantha MacBride (*Recycling Reconsidered)* and Max Liboiron (https://discardstudies.com/2015/06/05/how-the-ocean-clean-up-array-fundamentally-misunderstands-marine-plastics-and-causes-harm/), Jazvac argues that production and consumption rates should be a focus for research, in order to ward off the perception that “the problem is being taken care of by technology.” She learns from a recent youth summit for ocean plastic pollution at the Algalita Marine Research Foundation in February 2017, where its teenage participants called for “refusing plastics in our lives.”

25 Lavin, “Plasticity at Work,” *Flash in the Pan* Kindle edition.

26 Studies of consumer products by John Habraken and Martin Pawley during the 1960s and 70s, for instance, proposed that consumer products be designed for their appropriation as materials for building, after their initial use. Pawley referred to the process as “secondary use.” See: Martin Pawley, *Garbage Housing* (London: The Architectural Press, 1975).

27 Hito Steyerl, “In Defense of the Poor Image,” in *The Wretched of the Screen* (Berlin: Sternberg Press, 2012).

28 Quoted from Ellie Abrons, “Author After Author,” 21.

29 See T+E+A+M http://tpluseplusaplusm.us/ and Possible Mediums http://www.possiblemediums.com

30 Balliet, Fure et. al. “Super Session 1: Possible Mediums and Studios,” Filmed April 2015 at the ACSA Annual Meeting in Toronto, YouTube video, 1:35:49, posted by ACSA National, May 6, 2015, https://www.youtube.com/watch?v=cyrhpPkuR4E

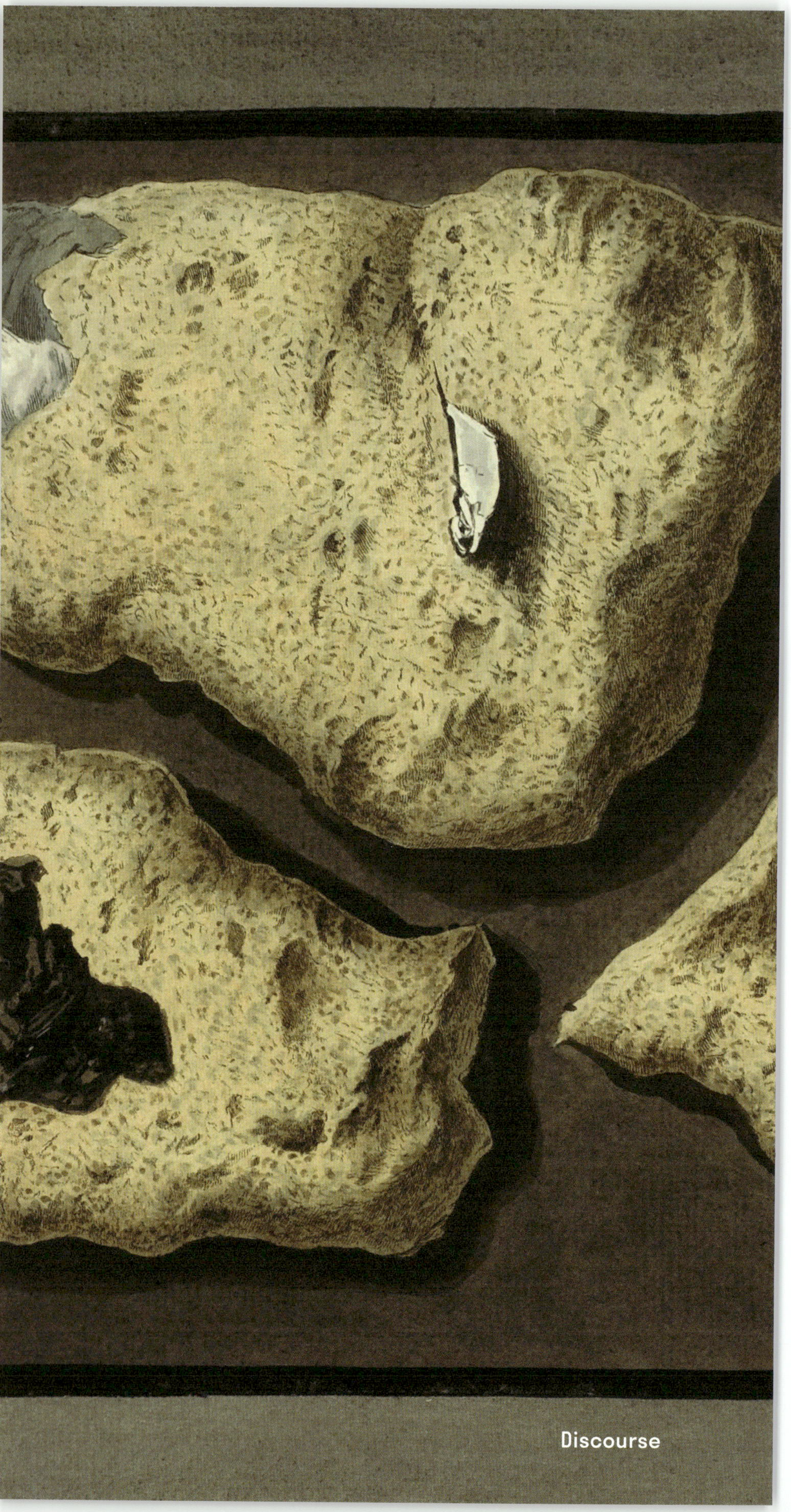
Discourse

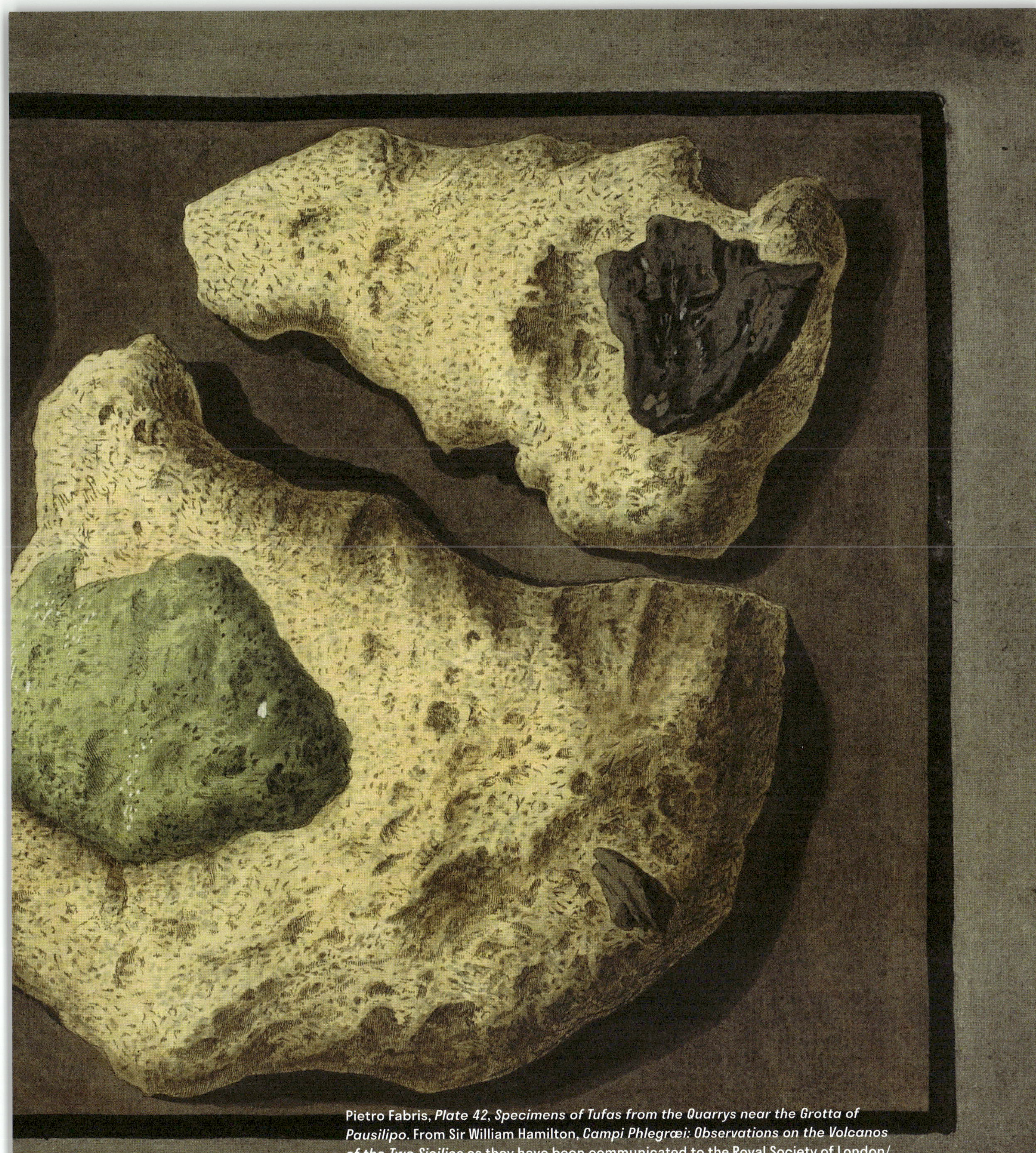

Pietro Fabris, *Plate 42, Specimens of Tufas from the Quarrys near the Grotta of Pausilipo*. From Sir William Hamilton, *Campi Phlegræi: Observations on the Volcanos of the Two Sicilies* as they have been communicated to the Royal Society of London/ Naples, 1776. Courtesy of Special Collections, The Claremont Colleges Library.

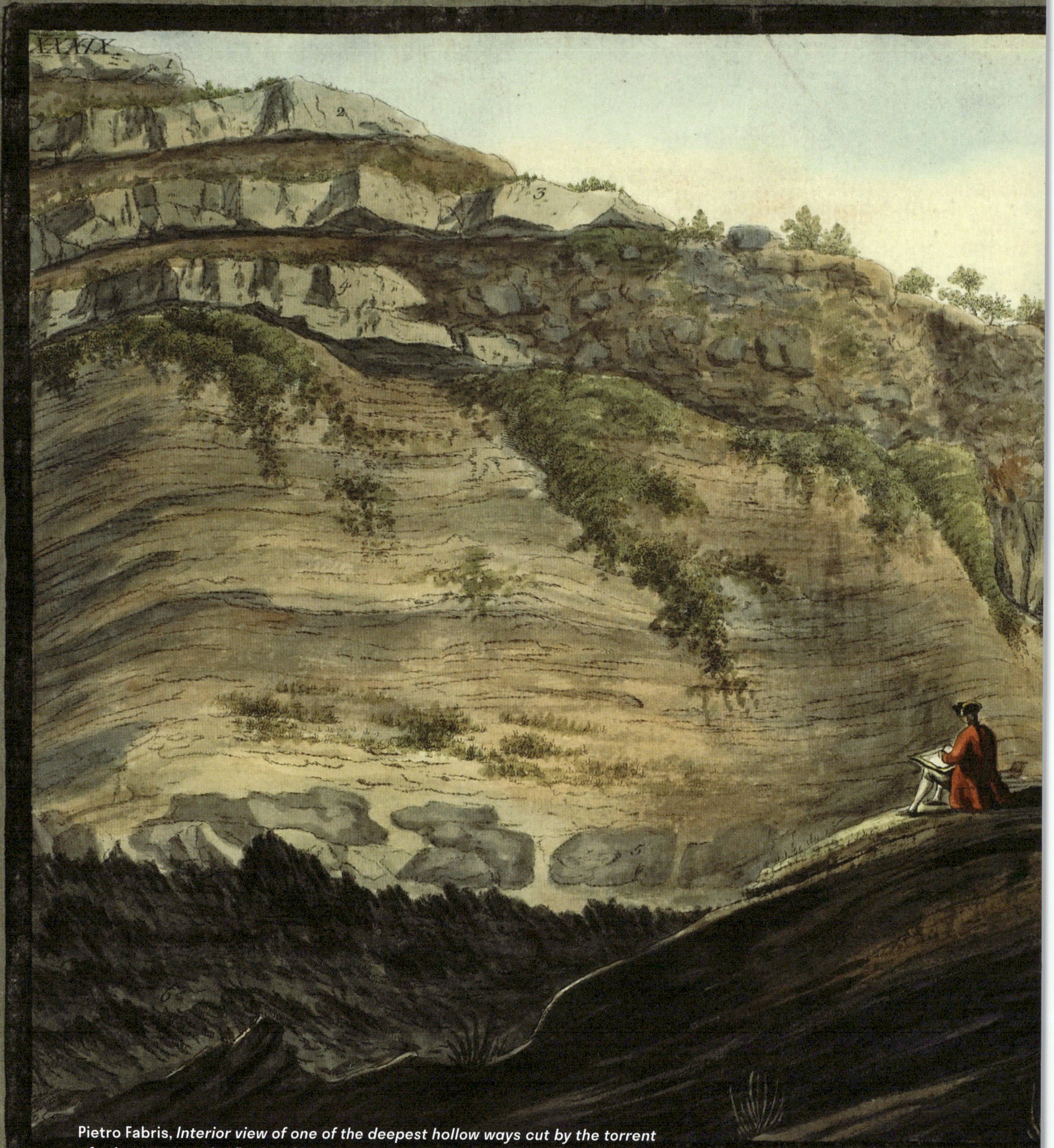

Pietro Fabris, *Interior view of one of the deepest hollow ways cut by the torrent of rain water, on the flanks of Mount Vesuvius, call'd the FOSSA GRANDE*. From Sir William Hamilton, *Campi Phlegræi*, observations on the volcanos of the two Sicilies as they have been communicated to the Royal Society of London/Naples 1776. Courtesy of Special Collections, The Claremont Colleges Library.

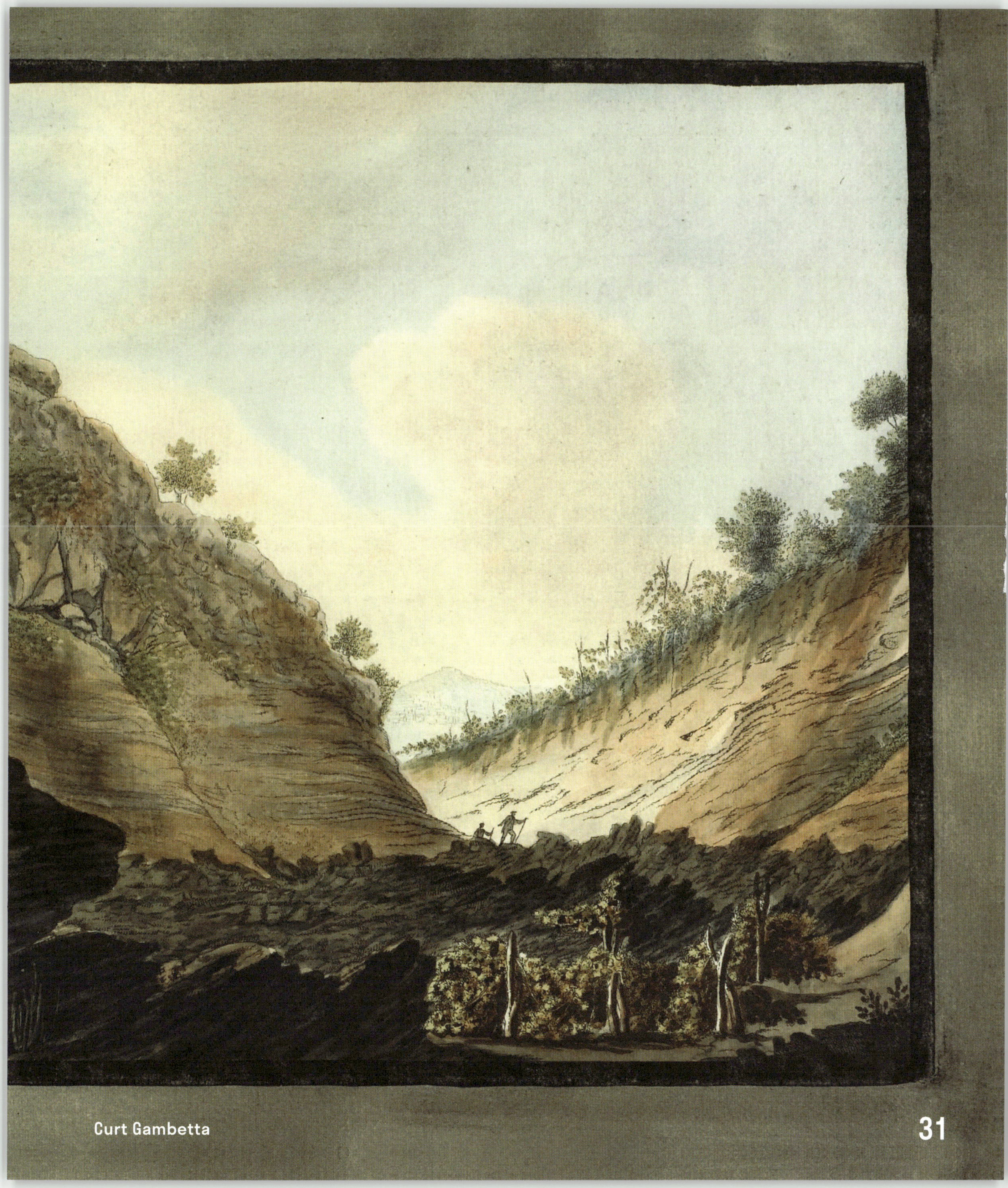

The Ownership Revolution: Digital Culture and the Transformation of Architectural Practice and Ideals

Antoine Picon

What has the digital done to architecture? Computers have been present as design tools for almost twenty years in the architectural field. An abundance of literature has been devoted to the consequences of their introduction on architectural form and on fabrication techniques. Theorists and historians, including myself, have dealt extensively with the cultural implications of the changes brought by the digital. This essay unpacks a different set of consequences of the digital, namely its impact on the organization of the profession. This is just the beginning, for despite its crucial importance, we do not know a lot about this issue—far from it. In many respects, this is more of an exploration rather than something grounded in definitive certitudes. The aim is to raise a certain number of questions.

Central to this inquiry is the possible shift from traditional questions of authorship to problems linked with the difficult question of ownership. Ownership—and justly compensating for the various inputs of a project or a product—is becoming central in the digital age. Architecture cannot escape this shift for a series of reasons, ranging from the overall organization of the profession, to the new perspectives revealed by the development of open source software and projects. This does not mean that authorship no longer matters, rather its definition is probably going to evolve in the near future. To understand where authorship is going, we need to intersect it with questions of ownership, which might provide a useful thread to rethink these fundamentals. Questions of creativity and copyright are becoming quite inseparable: in which direction will the evolution of authorship take place? Curiously, history might shed some light on this complex issue, as it presents us with a surprising variety and understanding of authorship.

Far from being a purely intellectual notion, authorship is actually inseparable from a set of cultural and economic practices. Even more than our understanding of authorship, the practices on which it is based have changed. They are going to change substantially in the near future and this is where ownership surfaces again. We might be facing a major turning point, something like a revolution. What will be its implications on architectural production itself? It is, of course, almost impossible to answer this question with certitude. This is a relatively new domain of investigation for me, although it is related to a series of threads in my recent work, such as the desire to inscribe the digital within an even broader historical frame than usual. This line of inquiry is based on reflections and materials used for a recent issue of *Architectural Design* I co-edited with my Doctorate of Design student, Wendy Fok, an alumnus of the Princeton University School of Architecture.

Changing Structures of Practice

The evolution in the structure of architectural practice is the first phenomenon to consider. A few years ago, I was at a Harvard faculty meeting sitting between two of our distinguished professors in practice. They were discussing the evolution of architectural practice and complaining, as we all do with colleagues. What was striking was their common assessment that their respective practices, by no means insignificant, were having more and more difficulty competing because of the presence of much larger fish in the pond. With something like 50 employees, they found themselves on the lower side of the ladder in terms of size. A rapid glance at what the 100 largest architectural firms in the world represent today is quite enlightening—this is a worldwide phenomenon. The same trend can be observed in a country like France, where the number of people has grown more slowly, while the share of the market held by the large firms has grown in a spectacular way.

The diffusion of the computer, and digital tools more generally, plays an important role in this evolution. Digital tools make collaboration easier; although, collaboration has generally triggered visions of horizontal networks and in many cases what seems to happen is the emergence or consolidation of practices based on a large number of architects. Large concentrations of architects have become highly efficient and, above all, manageable. These concentrations enable us to make heavier equipment investments more profitable than in the past. Computers and software are more expensive than the tools that came before them and most digital tools are about collaboration. While collaboration has been thoroughly explored, very little has been written about how it brings into question issues of control in design, the process itself and the actors involved.

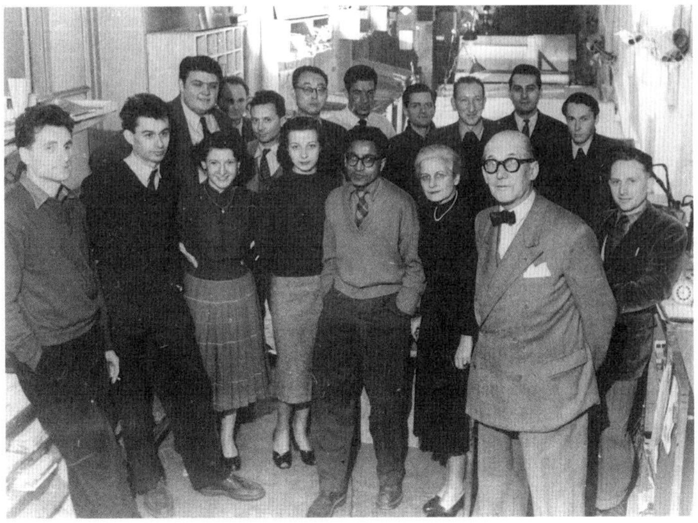

Le Corbusier and his collaborators in the Atelier de la Rue de Sèvres. Photograph by Willy Rizzo.

It is important to also note the diffusion of Building Information Modeling (BIM), which is probably one of the most important ongoing transformations. BIM is as much about control as it is about collaboration. Who is allowed to do what becomes a fundamental question in an interactive world. BIM is actually a potential battlefield as much as a cooperative opportunity and who will control it is one of the most crucial questions of the years to come. In France, where BIM was just made compulsory for large projects, building companies—which are very powerful—architects, engineers, and sometimes large institutional clients have begun to maneuver in order to gain control of the tool. The consolidation of architectural practice must be set against this background. Control and collaboration are vital in the digital world.

Digital equipment has made transcontinental practices possible and has even given them a competitive edge upon more localized ones in certain areas of architectural practice. In many respects, starchitecture is inseparable from this background as it is less and less about small or medium-sized practices. Starchitect forerunners, like Le Corbusier, often had small to medium-sized practices. The Atelier de la Rue de Sèvres was not especially large. Foster & Partners paved the way as the first star practice to employ more than 1,000 people and it counts more than 600 architects today. Zaha Hadid Architects employs 400 people with a pretty straightforward hierarchy. I remember vividly when Herzog and de Meuron told me that they would not go beyond 200 to 250 employees in order to maintain true control over the production of the practice. They now count something like 40 associates and 380 collaborators. Then there are the very specialized niches, as in someone who can master extremely complex geometries, or specific and highly-advanced knowledge on certain materials, or issues related to sustainability. In this context, it could be said that the future of the "in between" is becoming problematic. Of course, there are attempts to imagine alternative forms of network-like practices and this is what the open source movement hopes to achieve, to a large extent. So far, none have proved as efficient as the large, integrated firm. And this is a problem for architects aiming at authorship.

Large, so-called starchitect firms mostly hire relatively young employees. *The Competition*, a documentary which opened at the Rotterdam Architecture Film Festival in 2013, is quite telling in this regard. As suggested by the title, the documentary follows a competition in which Jean Nouvel, Zaha Hadid, Frank Gehry, Dominique Perrault, and Norman Foster are invited to compete for the design of the future National Museum of Art in Andorra. This is a competition between teams of young collaborators, most of which are 30 years old or younger with very few old designers present. As an aside, Le Corbusier was also surrounded by young people, but it was quite exceptional. Today, there is an accelerated obsolescence of architects due to the rhythm of production and the know-how linked to software evolution. These eponymous firms are like springboards for young designers, but many fail to make the proper jump.

It is difficult to remain an author in such a context. Either you succeed in creating your own firm and growing very fast, or you find a stable niche. This might explain why an architect like Peter Zumthor is so fascinating—a figure from another age it seems. We attribute part of the meditative quality of his famous baths in Vals to this preserved artisanal dimension. It does not mean that you cannot be an author in large, relatively anonymous firms. Take Gordon Bunshaft, who worked mainly for Skidmore, Owings and Merill, and how recognizable his creations are—from the famed Beinecke Library at Yale to the Albright Art Gallery in Buffalo—which perhaps is uncommon and becoming more and more so.

With its neo-avant-gardes, the digital has generated an ideological screen that prevents taking the full measure of what has really happened. We have iconic projects and installations, along with a lot of experimental pavilions since the beginning of the 2000s, though these might act as a decoy. Digital fabrication has further reinforced the opacity by popularizing the vision of the designer as a potential craftsman dealing only with 3-D printers and robots. This is not so much about a series of star theorists and designers or the rise of a new inspired craftsman than about a major reorganization of the architectural profession through the consolidation of its practices. It is a challenge for architectural education, perhaps more so for elite institutions (like Princeton) that educate a small number of students compared to larger institutions. In France, there are raging debates on whether one should train architects for an average practice or aspire to a higher destiny, but the meaning of average is no longer clear. As for a higher destination, is it really about authorship or about a complex mix of design intuition, entrepreneurial and communication skills, the latter taking more and more importance? What is the right combination to become Bjarke Ingels? And is this what (or who) we should to train students to become?

Many of these questions are foreign to the rising desire of saving the world, which permeates at many schools of architecture. It is preceisely this kind of inspiration that led to the 2016 Biennal and its "reporting from the front," which tended to ignore issues related to the organization of the profession. Ironically, it is an iconic author—who, to a large extent, is connected to and even part of the star system—that was the curator of this event. The political agency of architecture is actually inseparable from its professional organization. A large firm must first and foremost pay salaries, and this limits what it can actually invest in. Authorship is not the only dimension of architecture challenged by its current professional reorganization, but it reveals many other questions at stake.

Software Packages and Digital Models

If professional organization is synonymous with an important change, another set of transformations are linked to the use of digital tools themselves. Previsouly, tools were somewhat neutral in the production of architecture, as they were not inhabited by other people and their intentions. This is somewhat different with software packages, which are designed for certain purposes and tend to orient conception in specific directions. Software packages also propose the consideration of certain objects, to make particular operations possible and not others. What Patrik Schumacher calls "parametricism" is actually predetermined in many ways by the designers of the software. In short, software packages possess a certain agency. Even more striking is the variety of levels at which this agency is present: it goes from the software as a whole to the various extensions that can be designed, adding to its functionality. We are entering an age of intensive plug-in practices. Who is the author in such a context? Is it the isolated figure or the small group? The hive or the swarm?

Another factor is the development of digital models, something that digital fabrication is certainly going to accentuate. For example, since Thingiverse was started in 2008, it has accumulated more than 400,000 designs. Buildings are not yet concerned, but we are getting there with sites, such as Paperhouses, which propose "free, downloadable blueprints of residential architecture." Digital models can be customized at various levels and this will be the case more frequently. When fabrication finally does come, there are a lot of possible interventions that may claim partial authorship. A compelling example that superimposes various levels of authorship was offered by Dutch fashion designer Iris van Herpen in her Spring 2016 ready-to-wear collection, Quaquaversal. The show's dramatic centerpiece included the real-time, partial weaving of a dress around actress Gwendoline Christie, known for her role in *Game of Thrones*. In addition to Iris van Herpen, essential contributors to this piece were artist Jolan van der Viel, who designed the fabric covering the robots, and architect Marjan Colletti, who worked on the robotic 3D printing. Of course, all of this is not completely new and some historical perspective is useful.

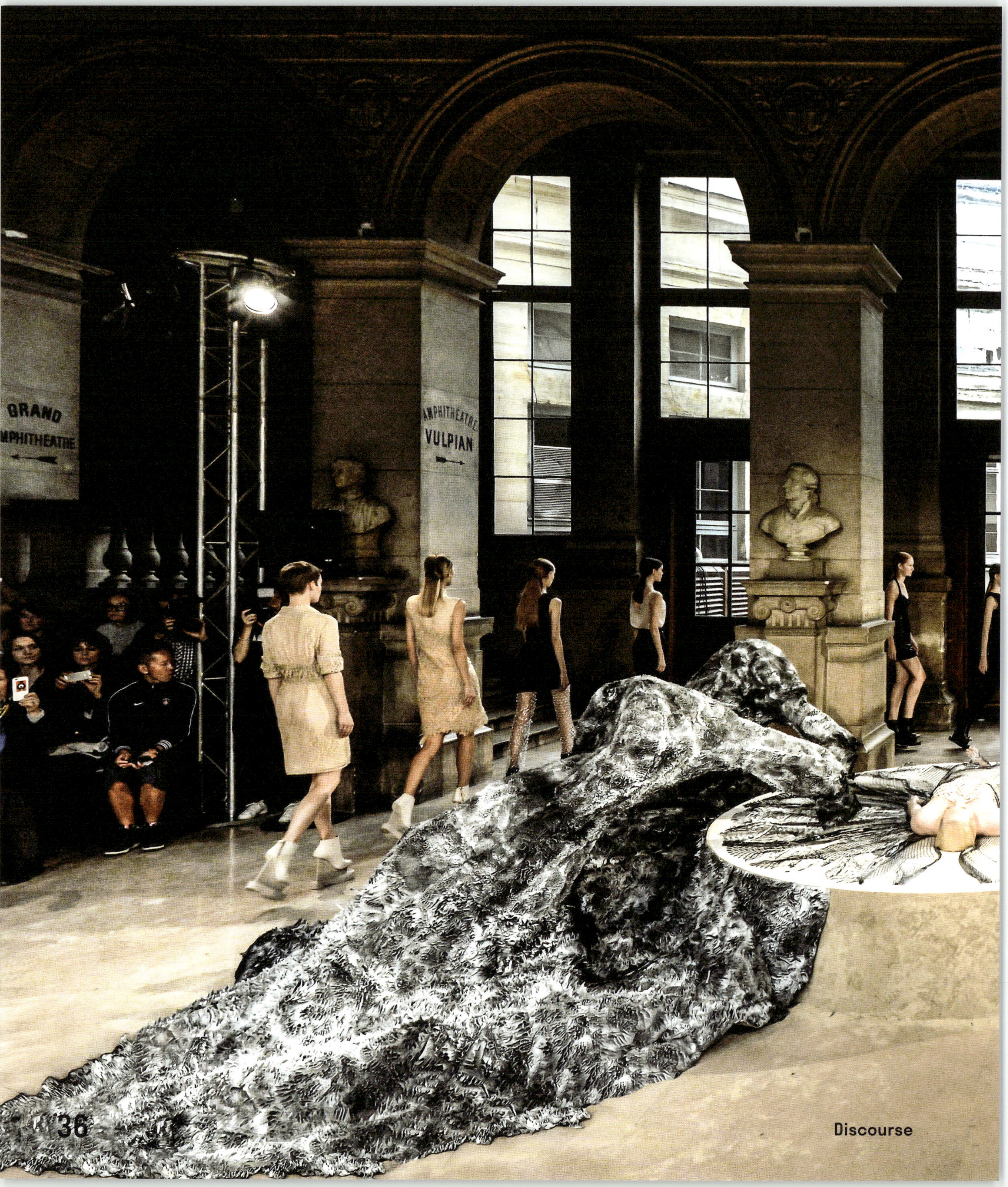
GRAND
AMPHITHEATRE
AMPHITHEATRE
VULPIAN

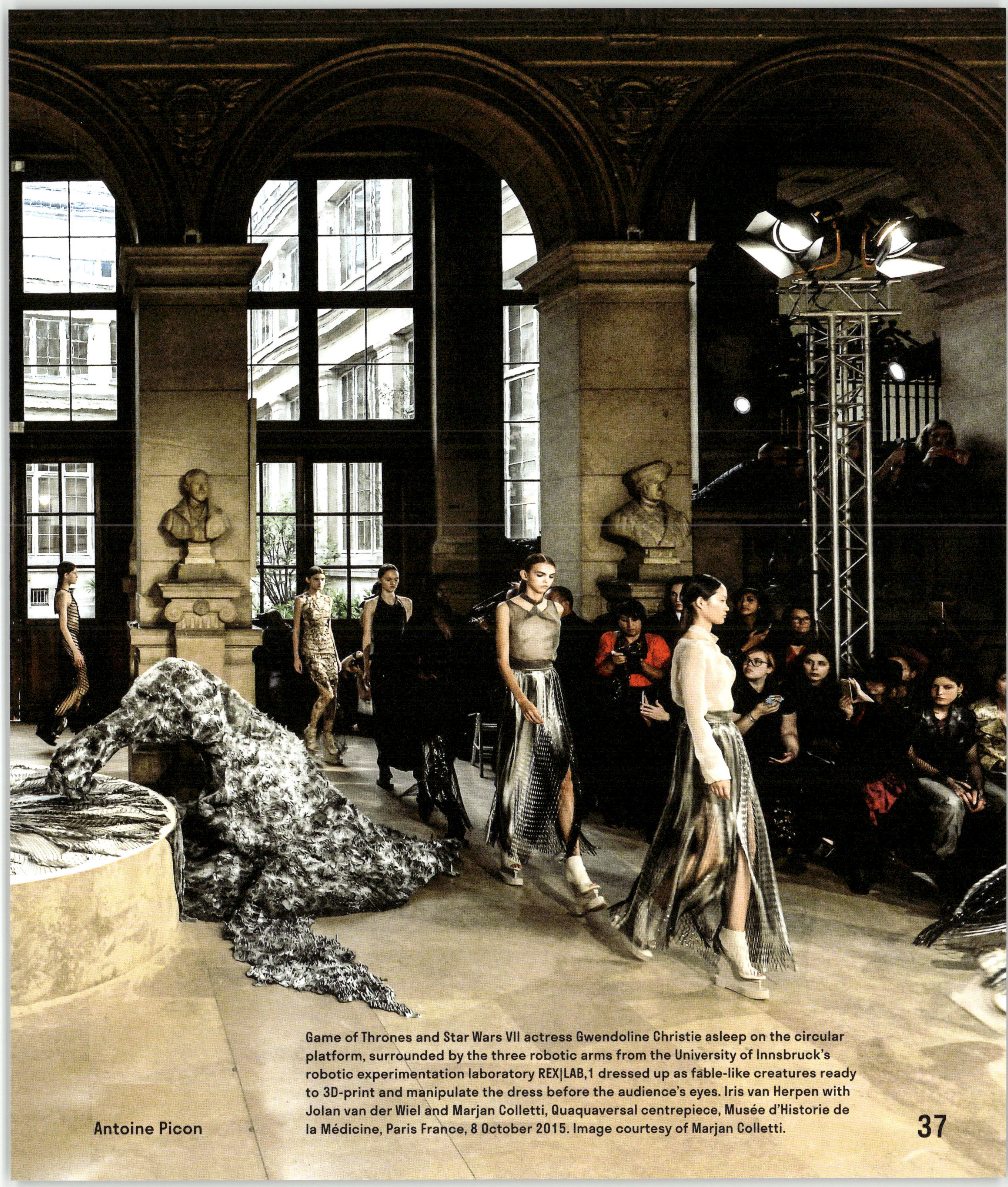

Game of Thrones and Star Wars VII actress Gwendoline Christie asleep on the circular platform, surrounded by the three robotic arms from the University of Innsbruck's robotic experimentation laboratory REX|LAB,1 dressed up as fable-like creatures ready to 3D-print and manipulate the dress before the audience's eyes. Iris van Herpen with Jolan van der Wiel and Marjan Colletti, Quaquaversal centrepiece, Musée d'Historie de la Médicine, Paris France, 8 October 2015. Image courtesy of Marjan Colletti.

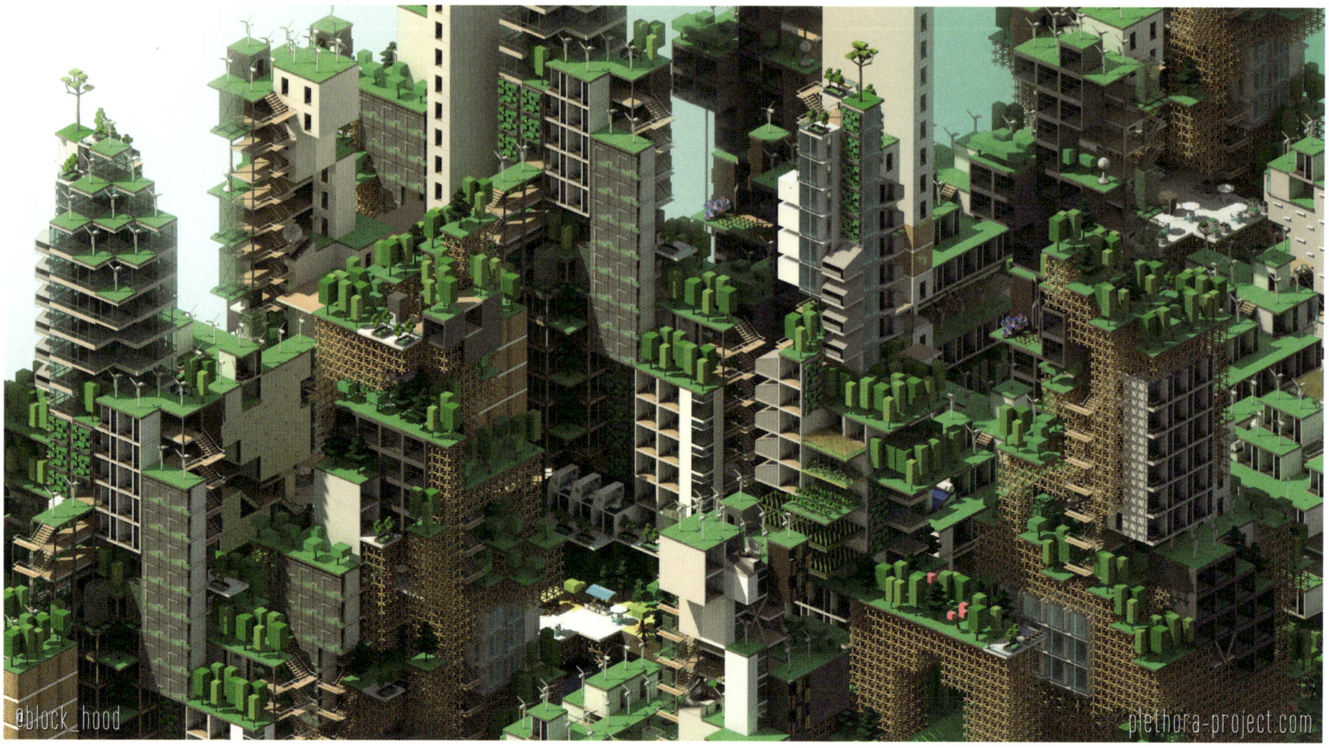

Screenshot of video game Block'hood developed by Jose Sanchez, 2016. © Plethora Project LLC.

The way in which tools are haunted by invisible authors, however, is definitely new. The circulation of models has been present in the architectural world for a very long time.

Some models presented generic features, making them almost comparable to the role played by software today, such was the case with the five orders. My colleague, Mario Carpo, has repeatedly made this point in his various books and articles. At times, some theorists and practitioners ambitioned to be meta-authors in very similar ways to someone who conceives a kind of meta-digital template today. Claude Perrault's ambition was very similar and had his enterprise succeeded, a trace of Perrault would have been detectable in multiple projects using his system. One finds a similar ambition in Le Corbusier's Modulor system much later in history. The circulation of models is something fundamental in architecture and imitation can be more or less literal. Given what is happening in the digital age, we may want to revisit the various situations that have occurred in the past. For instance, Charles Atwood and the Chicago World Fair Beaux-Arts building was almost directly inspired by the Paris Ecole des Beaux-Arts Grand Prize of Rome by Emile Bénard in 1867. And then there's McKim, Mead and White's Boston library influenced by Labrouste's Sainte-Geneviève library, or the Busaras bus station in Dublin by Michael Scott, which is a blend of two Le Corbusier projects, the Maison Suisse and Cité de Refuge.

It would be interesting to revisit these building cases using analogies with software or (why not) DNA. We actually need to reinterpret the history of architecture by giving a more material base to questions of influence, not only as an inspiration but as a tool-based question. As previously menitoned, the compositional analogy of the Dublin bus station to the work of Le Corbusier is partly based on the use of the Modulor and the system of surface divisions involved. What is new? Again, the very tools that we use are haunted by the presence of others more so than by their user. It's somewhat a fractal diffusion of authorship and its various forms, both in the sense of multiple scenarios—

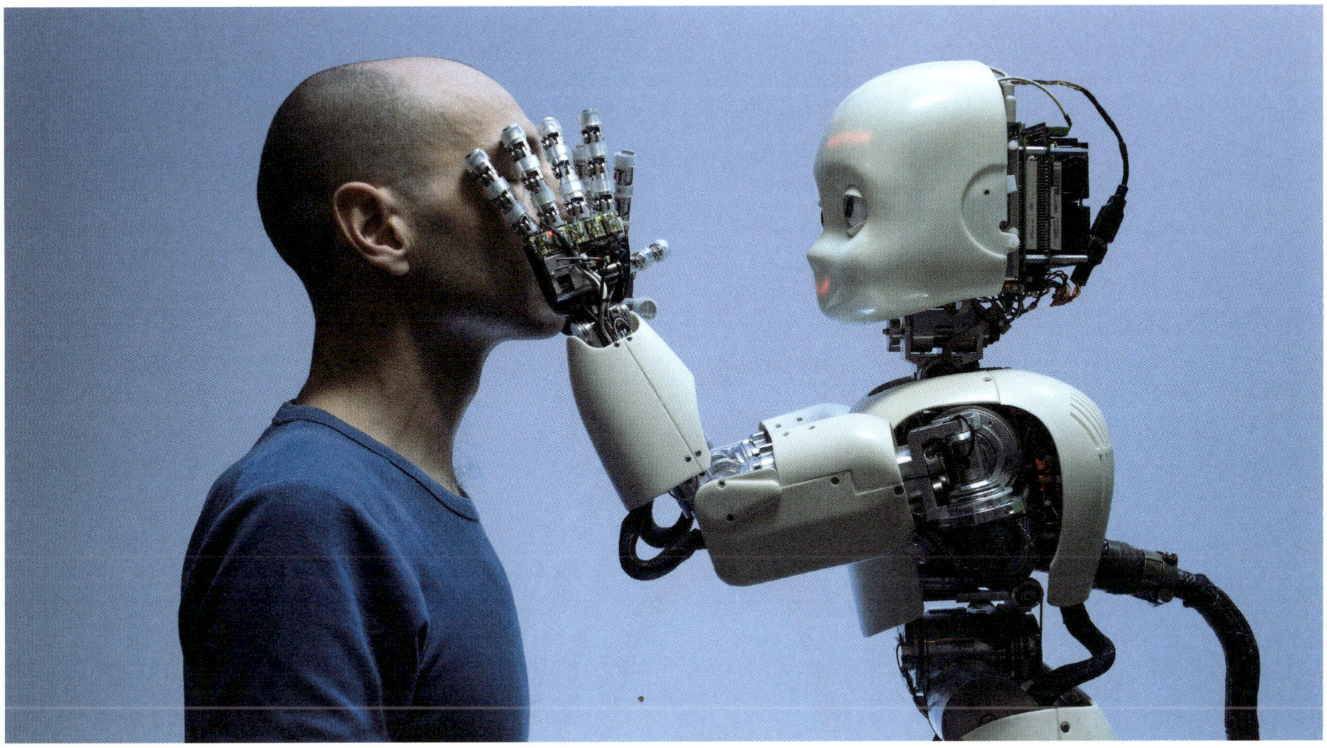

iCub robot at the Robotics and Intelligent Systems Institute (ISIR), Paris-VI University, 2016.
© Emile Loreaux/Picturetank.

of possible ways to be an author—and a complex layering. Authorship is ostensibly an ocean or a seamless fabric that possesses a fractal complexity.

The Open Source Perspective

Open source developed as a possible path for enabling architecture to profoundly change its mode of production. Various authors have evoked the perspective that may stem from it, such as Carlo Ratti from the MIT SENSEable Lab. In many respects, open source is something that aims to be an alternative to the ongoing process of consolidation: not vertical integration, but rather a multiplication of agents functioning as a network. This would enable us to mobilize the creative potential of larger constituencies than designers proper—it is the so-called "citizen-centered design." Jose Sanchez and the Plethora Project is one such example, including Block'Hood, a game in which gaming itself becomes a way to touch a larger public.

The idea of open source is the ability to circulate all kinds of tools and models, in addition to sharing resources. This is what Philip Yuan is attempting in Shanghai through the creation of an open fablab, available to an entire network of designers and potentially beyond to promote an open design world. WikiHouse, an open-source project for designing and constructing houses, enables users to download Creative Commons-licensed building plans from its website, customize them in SketchUp, and then use them for buildout. Resilient Modular Systems is a relatively similar open source attempt geared at developing countries. These initiatives are still marginal endeavors, but they are change-provoking.

The Rise of Artificial Intelligence

Let's go a bit further and evoke what might happen with the development of artificial intelligence. During the first exploration phase, in terms of what the computer would mean for architecture, a lot of researchers were persuaded that the machine would become a true partner of the designer. This was the conviction of Nicholas Negroponte, founder of the MIT Architecture

Machine Group (which eventually became the Media Lab) with the idea to create a relatively intelligent computer environment.

In the mid-1990s, when the computer really arrived in architecture, it had already been reduced to a drawing machine. This is certainly not going to last forever. As artificial intelligence is gaining momentum, new questions of imbricated authorship emerge. We may imagine a dystopian scenario in which all human designers are replaced by machines, but this is not what I have in mind. Rather, we have to consider more intricate scenarios of collaboration. We have to depart dramatically from the tendency of viewing the digital as a means of restoring full authorship in the most nostalgic way.

I recently wrote a piece for *Log* on robotization, which insists on the necessity of understanding that robots will inevitably become intelligent in the near future. We should abandon all these ideas of reinventing the craftsman and the past in dialogue with matter. The hand is no longer alone with matter and an instrument. We have to imagine ourselves working in a network of diverse agencies—some that are humans, and others not.

A Question of Just Compensation

Given all these premises, my claim is that the traditional notion of authorship is challenged. Of course, we have always known that architecture was rarely the work of a single designer. The evolving structures of the profession, the rise of digital collaboration and control, along with the multiplication of possible claims for authorship have radically altered the landscape. Parallel to many other domains impacted by the digital, questions related to how we recognize and adequately compensate the input of all the design collaborators are emerging. As we know, salary is only part of the problem. Despite all the claims for the abandonment of licensing, patents, and copyrights, we are facing an extended copyright issue.

If we really want the system to stay alive we must enable all the actors involved to make a living. This is a general problem right now in the digital. In a stimulating book, *Who Owns the Future?*, computer scientist and philosopher Jaron Lannier made the case that the digital revolution could abort if we do not find a way to compensate all its actors, including those of us who often "work" for free for Google, Amazon or Facebook. This is also true of architecture: if we want the structure of the profession to remain open to new talents, and if we want open source to become a true alternative, we must compensate designers accordingly. In the interest of big firms, like the giants of the new economy, they need novelty to be produced outside in order to capture it.

Rem Koolhaas was quite prescient when he played with the copyrighting of certain concepts introduced in his own writings. In his 2001 *Great Leap Forward*, part of the Harvard Project on the City, he copyrighted one development as Architecture©. Often with Koolhaas, what appears at first as a cynical elaboration on the current contradictions of the discipline, ultimately provides keys to understanding the future. Who owns what and who is compensated for what is quite crucial, yet this is not the most fundamental issue. What takes place may have more to do with a strange conflation of authorship than with ownership.

Past Ambiguities and Possible Futures

We may believe things are new again, however, new contexts often evoke older ones. In this case, the role of history is not to suggest that situations return, but rather to say one may use the past to prepare for drastic changes. Historian Marc Bloch, a founder of the French historical school *Les Annales,* once declared that history is about giving a true sense of the imperious nature of change. Let us use Roger Chartier, another historian and an inheritors of the *Annales* school, as a guide to unpack some similarities between present and past; moreover, not to suggest a return or repetition, but rather to open up the field for new possibilities.

Roger Chartier studied the history of the book industry extensively and the cultural practices attached to it, beginning with reading itself. His studies reveal a number of interesting, yet disconcerting facts. First, authorship—as we know it—is a relatively recent phenomenon. Few authors were considered as completely distinct voices. Italian poet Petrarch was among the few authors that benefited from such a

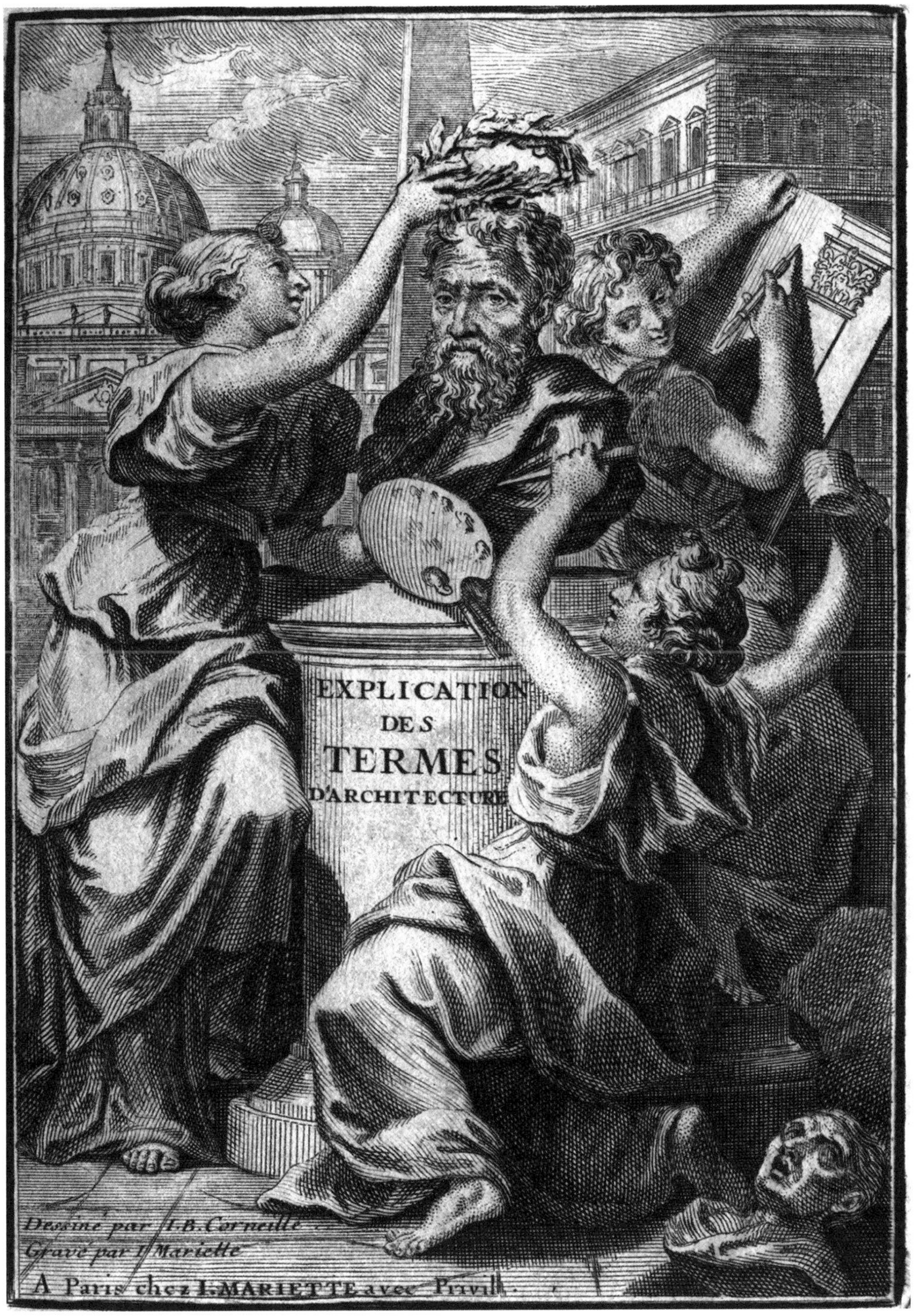

Frontispiece for Charles d'Aviler's 1691
Cours d'Architecture by Jean Mariette, 1720.

distinction at the end of the Middle Ages. For a very long time, the habit of binding together texts from different authors was related to this practice. Copyrights did not exist and neither did the idea that the integrity of an intellectual contribution should be preserved. This led to multiple new editions of architectural treatises bearing the same title, but with quite different content, such as the *Course on Architecture* published under Charles D'Aviler's name in France. The ambiguity increases with the realization that D'Aviler himself presented his work as a commentary on Vignola.

The internet practices we associate with today—like cutting, pasting, sampling, editing, and customizing—were quite common in early-modern library practices, which are rooted in a different relation with the text and are not based on the ideal of a private intercourse. Concurrently, reading was not the solitary activity it gradually became during the 18th century, as epitomized by Fragonard's famous painting of a young lady reading alone. In actuality, reading was often a collective activity, something linked to the scarcity of light resources at night. In two pieces from 17th-century engraver Abraham Bosse, based on the parable of the foolish and wise virgins, two figures are seen reading together. In painting and sculpture, we find the same ambiguities with one painter completing the work of another, or the structural intricacies of workshops, as in Rembrandt, Ruben or Bernini. In contemporary terms, one could say that Rembrandt, Rubens or Bernini were as much brands as individuals.

It is towards the middle of the eighteenth century that things begin to change. Philosopher Denis Diderot, again after Fragonard, plays a role in this evolution. His critiques of the Salon, the annual exhibition of painting in Paris, are permeated by a new vision of the author as an isolated individual. What emerges is the modern figure of the artist. In architecture, the same phenomenon happens and it presents a series of consequences, giving a new importance to projects versus buildings. Architecture was very much about buildings and buildings only. Principles were at the core of the architectural discipline, and buildings like Bramante's Tempietto were such illustrations. This extended disciplinary core begins to include unbuilt projects as the expression of an individual capacity for invention or genius that is interpreted in a new fashion. Boullée's enormous and unbuildable projects are typical of this turning point, and this is also the context that sees the development of Piranesi's works.

The Romantic period adds new layers to this vision of authorship-as-fundamentally-individual, despite a growing nostalgia for more collective forms of authorship. Such nostalgia is extremely present in John Ruskin's interpretation of the Gothic, in which he seeks to reconcile collective inspiration and authorship with individualized contributions to the work. His theory of ornament is permeated by this question. It is interesting to observe how the question of the collective has not been recaptured by those various contemporary digital theorists and practitioners who claim inspiration from Ruskin, such as Lars Spuybroek's *The Sympathy of Things: Ruskin and the Ecology of Design*.

In many ways, we have remained faithful to the regime of authorship that emerged at the dawn of the modern age until recently. Yet in other ways, we are in both a climactic moment of the author and on the verge of something else, like a new regime of authorship. We have never wanted to believe so much in individuals and their shaping power. Beyond her radiant personality and the importance of her work, part of the shock created by Zaha Hadid's premature death may be linked to the fact that we are afraid she might be one of the last success stories. At the same time, we have doubt and are playing on the very ambiguity between individual and brand with lines of products. We have no choice but to go beyond the Romantic vision of authorship in order to make our understanding of architecture more compatible with the reality of its professional structures. History may help by reminding us that a large number of what we call architects today were not actually sole designers for a very long time. Instead, architects were found in various guises—as entrepreneurs, or as real estate developers.

For instance, Brongniart was active as a real estate investor, the Woods who built Bath, and the Circus by John Wood the elder. For all these people, making money was central. Ownership was a determining feature of the architectural scene as authorship. The liberal figure of the architect who advises his client and designs for him only is relatively recent, appearing in the 18th century. This figure was always contradictory because it retained an entrepreneurial dimension in many cases. Consider Auguste Perret's architecture or what Le Corbusier had attempted with the DOM-INO. Additionly, there was always a possible conflict present between the architect as a professional and the architect as an artist. What exactly does an architect produce? Services or work? We have never clearly answered this question, hence the difficulty of professionalization. Let's use history to open up the future.

If we succeed in going beyond the simplified vision playing an ideological role in the architectural field, which does not mean abandoning any claim to creativity, we may begin to discover other ways to be an author. The point is not to say that individual creativity is dead, but rather that we have to invent alternative ways to recognize creativity in a society where it is more pervasive. This is accompanied by a shift in creative practice with the rise of sampling, assembling and customization. These specific activities go with a long tradition: the author as a strategist. This is a very essential point, especially if we consider the strategy of Zaha Hadid Architects, for example, and the articulation of a hypertrophied formalism.

The "why" before the "how" has become a fundamental question. Why design? Should we even design? This explains why mapping and diagramming has taken such an importance in the field. Although diagrams failed, we should not forget what they were about; the "how" is an organizational and political process as much as it is a technical and artistic one. BIM architecture will require organizational and political skills. Architecture is a form of action. We have thought too much of architecture as a work, and it can be in a number of instances, but it is more akin to making a move in the world. Form happens, form performs. This is strangely what starchitecture introduced, beginning with Gehry's celebrated Guggenheim in Bilbao. This notion is also something that Eisenman had foreseen at the time of his archeological projects like Romeo and Juliet—architecture as a series of operations.

There is the possibility of conciliation between artistic ambition and the "saving the world" syndrome. Architecture does not only produce objects, it creates situations. Rahul Mehrotra and his Hyderabad building are an example of such an architecture. Of course, this is not completely new if you consider the architecture by Karl Friedrich Schinckel. An architecture that creates meaning that can be shared. These are probably essential conditions to imagine that designers will not be, to a large extent, replaced by artificial intelligence. Architecture is literally about what matters. We have to finally come to terms with the fact that architectural creativity is not only about inspired and inspiring individuals. Instead, we have to acknowledge the existence of a collective and make the collective more sustainable. The author is a network, just like the individual of the digital age. Branding is a collective identity instead of the glorification of a single hero. Zaha Hadid is a hive.

Going back to Ruskin, if the author is a network, how is the individual creative impulse articulated to the whole? Not the isolated individual, as many discourses on the digital craftsman would have it today, but the individual as part of a collective. Instead of the collective spiritual inspiration, rather in addition to it or even serving it, ownership is a shared system. This is where Chartier probably had it wrong. He was led to believe that the age of copyright could be brought to an end. In actuality, this seems less and less plausible as information sharing and profit sharing are two sides of the same coin. This is a revolution in architecture especially, a profession that has accepted a strange mix of despotism and capitalism as ruling features. Patrik Schumacher may be a caricature of it, however, he is actually quite typical. The future might be a style of collaboration and shared ownership, but otherwise, the risk is the disappearance of individual creativity.

The idea is not that individual creativity should be abolished and this is not all about the collective, swarm or hive design. On the contrary, ownership is actually a way to regulate a more and more complex professional structure. To summarize, let's imagine blending two versions of Laugier's *Essay on Architecture*, the French and the English.

Discourse on the Ownership Revolution: Lucia Allias with Antoine Picon and Julian Rose, Sylvia Lavin, Ayala Levin, Annie Barrett, Sean Rucewicz, and Axel Kilian

Discourse on the Ownership Revolution: Lucia Allias with Antoine Picon and Julian Rose, Sylvia Lavin, Ayala Levin, Annie Barrett, Sean Rucewicz, and Axel Kilian

Lucia Allais Antoine Picon has just delivered—with signature good humor—a radical indictment on the ideology of the author. Make no mistake: what Picon asks is no less than a revision to the history of the computational paradigm in architecture, as seen through the professionalization and the industrialization of knowledge. I want to highlight some of the ways in which this critique stands apart from others who have historicized the computer in architecture.

Generally speaking, Picon acknowledges that numbers (or calculus) are the basis of the so-called digital revolution, however, he does not offer a new numbers-based ontology. Unlike theorists who see computation as a sudden replacement of previous design modalities, Antoine doesn't see a world transfused with 1s and 0s, or an architecture transfused with code. As a historian of technology, he instead looks for the frictions that this code encounters as it travels along and he does this through the lens of authorship, killing two birds with one stone. First, he refutes digital prophets who proffer an ideology of smoothness, and predicts a smooth transition to a new world: numbers will bring forth a multitude of authors, or smoothly-curved buildings will bring about a liberated society, and so forth. Second, Antoine thereby brings to bear on architecture the challenge against the very idea of historical agency posed by structuralist and post-structuralist theorists in the 1960s. "The coming into being of the notion of author constitutes the privileged moment of individuation in the history of ideas, knowledge, literature, philosophy and the sciences," Michel Foucault writes in 1969. Despite the fact that "the author" had been consistently challenged in art and literature since early 20th century, finally being declared dead in 1967 by Roland Barthes, Foucault warned us to pay attention to the institutions in which "the author function" has survived. It is in "coding" that Picon sees this ghost-like author function operating in architecture today. Coding is a pervasive operation that seems to have transformed architecture into a ghostly apparatus without a master puppeteer.

Three of Picon's themes help us think of the digital paradigm historically.

The first is that digital design allows a continuation of the Beaux-Arts model in the profession, only scaled up and transformed. Against predictions that computers will democratize authorship, Picon describes how architecture has consolidated authorship around architectural "stars." He also references the recent humanitarian wave in architecture, which apparently has consolidated itself around the starchitect. I am also interested in the idea that a generational gap is necessary for the starchitect to operate. Perhaps we could say that the curatorial model taking over architecture follows this generational valley, with various biennials led by a distinguished curator and a series of younger participants. I am curious whether Picon would say this generational dynamic is a legacy of modernism or of academicism—did Le Corbusier's studio depend on it too? Did the ateliers?

Secondly, Picon spoke of the robot's prevalence in architectural culture, an instance where the author function is being performed by a machine. Picon made a distinction here between the first phrase—where the computer was imagined as a true partner—and the "true arrival," when the computer arrived and it was actually a robot. Here, my question is about the choice of the robot. Picon specifies that architecture schools today want a robot as a sign of distinction—like an ornament, worn as a medal, a sign of the prestige. But isn't the robot also a nostalgic choice for a showpiece in a digital age? The robot in the Iris van Herpen

fashion show is very much performing "robot"-ness, rather than doing anything particularly algorithmic. There is so much anthropomorphism in that performance. What's more, the image caption says the robots had to be borrowed from the nearby Fiat factory, as though the digital age had to borrow from the industrial age. In the first wave, the computer was a drawing machine. In the second, computers are actors or performers. The robot is a good choice to perform the loss of authorship because it looks like a massive hand, performing a script in the sense of a play, movie, or performance.

Finally, I want to turn to the book as a medium and an analogy. One argument, for the paradoxically continued relevance of the book in digital culture, is that the book was the original site of code: the codex was the birthplace of text. For example, we are told books are easily digitized because text is linear. Antoine refers to Mario Carpo's argument that the orders were a "black box" in that they could be modified by each architect. But Picon's reference to Roger Chartier reminds us to instead look at book culture and reading culture as a whole. As Friedrich Kittler has argued, books were never linear, the page was always an image. In fact, he argues that before text was on the page, it was already in a grid because the typesetter had to keep characters in a grid, as if they were a kind of pixel. Picon gives us an architectural version of that argument when he mentions architectural institutions, such as the salon, which extend to the city itself. After all, Chartier was the historian who talked about Paris as an "early information society." As Picon's narrative on this time period suggests, information begins to circulate throughout the city in smaller and smaller units; the architectural project is simultaneously untethered from the building and it becomes a massive project—à la Boullée.

All of this commentary on the book is a preamble to a question about scale. Paying attention to only Picon's images and no attention to his words—or maybe if I understood no English or French—I would have spotted a clear pattern in the images. Many of them feature a double-gesture: first a reduction of the architectural unit to something small, at an almost ornamental scale, and second, this detail is scaled up to the size of the building. So what of scalability? For example, Sylvia Lavin's article on Jürgen Mayer H's pavilion in Sevilla argues that architects have taken laser cutting—a model-making procedure—and scaled it up to building-scale. Which raises another question about the effect that the scaling of architectural offices has on the profession: does digital architecture, and the numeric gesturing it implies, offer a new idea of scale?

Antoine Picon I will give a messy answer. For me, the end of the tectonic is linked to a massive crisis of scale—there is no longer an evident referential scale—and this is one theme on the digital I have pursued for a very long time. It is a real problem and we have to reconstruct scale. In some ways, authorship functioned at a certain scale, this is not a coincidence. I was fascinated by this sheer scale of the practices all of a sudden, because we still have a vision of authorship as operating at certain scales and not others; if it changes scale it is something else. Architecture was something that produced relatively big objects in relatively small firms. Architecture now produces super big objects, or (sometimes) very small objects. I am really fascinated by the fact that for the past 20 years we have made a lot of pavilions, gigantic buildings and very large structures—again a disruption of scale. Epistemologically, it is no mystery: information has no scale. That is a big difference between

the information world and the mechanical world. As Galileo noted, the mechanical world is not scalable at will, however, the information world is and that makes a huge difference. I have a student who is completing his PhD with me at the École Nationale des Ponts et Chaussées, he is an artist and you can imagine the rest of the engineering crowd when he speaks. He is doing something quite interesting around dust and the idea that the digital world is a world in which things are pulverized. The pulverization and reconstruction is actually a pretty smart idea and has to do with these questions of scale. By the way, Chartier was a disciple of Foucault, interestingly enough.

Julian Rose Somewhere between Antoine's emphasis on the robot and Lucia's discussion of choice, there is a lot stressed on collectivity and less on the nature of the tools themselves. In a few cases, Antoine suggests authorship is getting more and more confused, but didn't really indicate the transfer of agency. For example, software has agency because someone wrote it, right? I understand that authorship is changing and becoming attenuated, yet the question is whether there is a fixed amount of authorship—there is not less authorship out there, or less human authorship specifically. It is just getting distributed more widely and I wonder how some of these digital tools are actually foreclosing authorship. The idea that architectural authorship has always been very mediated by tools, famously akin to Robin Evans' thought by drawing. In some sense, the computational tools are more mediated and just decrease the amount of authorship that is available to grab, the number of choices humans can make. I am thinking specifically about the "Archaeology of the Digital" conference at Yale a few years ago, where there was a terrifying comment by someone who worked for Autodesk. He described how he can drive through a downtown anywhere in America and tell you which version of Autodesk was used for the buildings. And I believe it because he's not talking about starchitects, he's talking about middle-of-the-road practices that are using digital tools and, in some cases, are not aware of the foreclosure of authorship. They would tell you they designed those buildings, but did they? I am not convinced that the Autodesk programmers did either, so I am curious about this problem.

AP First, I believe that the form of authorship imbedded in software constrains the people who use it. There is more authorship today than less, and that is part of the problem; there is authorship nested within authorship. And if you consider complex software, it is very often the fruit of the history. They have an evolution and it's not always completely rational. I am not sure that Darwinian evolution applies to software, rather it seems to be more of a baroque mode of evolution. The thickness of the tool is compared to Evans, but I think there were limits to what you could visualize before that. Today, there are new possibilities, but there is a thickness and it is an inhabited thickness. What I have found to be one of the strange things with the computer is that the digital is haunted from the start. It is haunted by all traces today—sometimes just traces of authorship, of former authorship, but it is haunted. I am not sure whether the Autodesk guy was not bragging. Is that so terrifying? Take a Hausmannian building, it looks damningly like another Hausmannian building and there was no Autodesk. The reason the information world and the mechanical world. As Galileo noted, the mechanical world is not scalable at will, however, the information world is and that makes a huge difference. I have a student who is completing his PhD with me at the École Nationale des Ponts et Chaussées, he is an artist and you can imagine the rest of the engineering crowd when he speaks. He is doing something quite interesting around dust and the idea that the digital world is a world in which things are pulverized. The pulverization and reconstruction is actually a pretty smart idea and has to do with these questions of scale. By the way, Chartier was a disciple of Foucault, interestingly enough.

Julian Rose Somewhere between Antoine's emphasis on the robot and Lucia's discussion of choice, there is a lot stressed on collectivity and less on the nature of the tools themselves. In a few cases, Antoine suggests authorship is getting more and more confused, but didn't really indicate the transfer of agency. For example, software has agency because someone wrote it, right? I understand that authorship is changing and becoming attenuated, yet the question is whether there is a fixed amount of authorship—there is not less authorship out there, or less human authorship specifically. It is just getting distributed more widely and I wonder how some of these digital tools are actually foreclosing authorship. The idea that architectural authorship has always been very mediated by tools, famously akin to Robin Evans' thought by drawing. In some sense, the computational tools are more mediated and just decrease the amount of authorship that is available to grab, the number of choices humans can make. I am thinking specifically about the "Archaeology of the Digital" conference at Yale a few years ago, where there was a terrifying comment by someone who worked for Autodesk. He described how he can drive through a downtown anywhere in America and tell you which version of Autodesk was used for the buildings. And I believe it because he's not talking about starchitects, he's talking about middle-of-the-road practices that are using digital tools and, in some cases, are not aware of the foreclosure of authorship. They would tell you they designed those buildings, but did they? I am not convinced that the Autodesk programmers did either, so I am curious about this problem.

AP First, I believe that the form of authorship imbedded in software constrains the people who use it. There is more authorship today than less, and that is part of the problem; there is authorship nested within authorship. And if you consider complex software, it is very often the fruit of the history. They have an evolution and it's not always completely rational. I am not sure that Darwinian evolution applies to software, rather it seems to be more of a baroque mode of evolution. The thickness of the tool is compared to Evans, but I think there were limits to what you could visualize before that. Today, there are new possibilities, but there is a thickness and it is an inhabited thickness. What I have found to be one of the strange things with the computer is that the digital is haunted from the start. It is haunted by all traces today—sometimes just traces of authorship, of former authorship, but it is haunted. I am not sure whether the Autodesk guy was not bragging. Is that so terrifying? Take a Hausmannian building, it looks damningly like another Hausmannian building and there was no Autodesk. The reason

I insisted so much on patterns and models, among others, is that one fundamental activity in architecture is copying each other. But it is true that there is something still happening; that is to say we have tools which are now more mediated, complex, and layered.

JR What is potentially insidious is that these tools pretend to be not mediated. For example, scale is another point of mediation or abstraction in a traditional physical model, yet the dream of BIM is to do away with scale entirely. With BIM, the whole thing is built one-to-one in the computer to work out all of the bugs—there is nothing hidden. There is this pretense of unmediated reality, that is where the disjunction gets concerned.

AP I became interested in these things because the digital generates so much ideology, it is disconnected from what actually happens. It is not to say this is definitive knowledge in the profession, but I do believe it is. Also fascinating is the development of inter-continental practice; it has become completely common to see people with an office on every continent, yet it was relatively rare before the internet. For example, if you look at how Le Corbusier built Chandigarh, it was quite a messy process. It is a very different world today.

Sylvia Lavin What is an author in all of this? Alive and dead is one thing, but I am still trying to make sure I understand what constitutes authorship here, because in this conversation it sounds similar to the mark of individuation and the kind of singularity we know. Whether or not we preserve or replace singularity could we not also ask if that, in fact, is the only version of authorship available?

AP No; that is the romantic vision, which is precisely what we need, in some ways.

SL Would the term decoder be a useful way to talk about these nested authors? This would add to the vocabulary of the 1960s that differentiated a writer or a scriptor from an author on the basis of different models of production.

AP With the pervasiveness of the code, what happens now is that the code generates more and more without falling into the realm of Autodesk. When the writing has so much effect on production, however, it is no longer strictly code writing. It is actually a defining perspective on the world, which is one of the things that has changed. I am strangely attached to a certain role of the individual. The only way to save it is to accept that this is no longer the romantic vision, but that this is a far more complex individual and the individual can be a network. We also need to deconstruct two centuries of discourse on creativity. Strangely, the early modern period is an interesting period because they were individuals. Bernini is definitely larger than life; it would have been interesting to imagine Bernini talking to Zaha and see who would have made the last point. They were super individual and yet a lot of questions we now ask ourselves about individuality and creation were not relevant.

SL I recently learned that Bernini never signed anything, which is to say, the signature was already such a problem that it was not automatic but a self-conscious decision. Do we even know who signed what in our field? It is such a sophisticated subculture in art history, but I don't think we know very well in architecture exactly who used a signature.

LA In literature, when Barthes declared the "Death of the Author," it was to announce the rise of the reader. There is a desire to have differentiation without having to trace it to an individual.

AP Something like the signature is especially tricky in architecture. François d'Orbay was pretty unknown, but signed the plan for Jules Hardouin-Mansart; therefore, the only documents we have of Hardouin-Mansart are actually signed by d'Orbay. Does it mean that d'Orbay is the author? In architecture, you see the conundrum because what you sign is not completely clear. This is also why my interpretations on the rise of Boullée-like drawings, which were not drawn by Boullée as many of them were drawn by his chief draftsmen, Durand, who is not so well known. You begin to see how complicated all of these things become.

SL The architectural field has a habit of celebrating and claiming this complexity; I wonder how much of architecture's unique complexity is a myth that we need and why we need it. For example, art historians are now looking at the material production of modern sculpture and discovering incredible complexity. Perhaps, what is unique is less architecture's particularly complex modes of production but that the discipline claims it as a matter of pride and, more importantly, of self-definition.

AP What we do is actually more complex: we claim that it is complicated, that it is actually a collective thing, and then we reinvent what we do. One of the reasons Foucault and Chartier always interested me was because they endlessly announce the end of the author, and the author was continuously resurrected. This is the movement in architecture—we perpetually announce the end of the author, but it is not going to be an end of the author, it is simply that the author will evolve dramatically. And we better be prepared because, in certain ways, we function a lot like the movie industry and it is a very complex thing. There is a team that does the sound, while another team does the lighting and, in the end, there is this isolated figure who subsumes everything. It may no longer be the problem, yet at the same time, we do have the "star" system.

Ayala Levin To Antoine's point about architecture being active, the object is an action and it is a performance. Going back to the Barthes notion, architecture would be the text that is being recreated and re-performed, acting in various ways. Here, authorship can relate to different kinds of agencies but doesn't necessarily stop when the object is created. I wonder whether the question of agency—historical agency or responsibility—comes into play in Antoine's examination of this category.

AP It does. I actually just finished a book manuscript on materiality, which I define through this question of agency and ideas of constructing situation. By the end, it is a very abridged version of that, but I had something much simpler in mind. We would like to believe in objects because they are reassuring, they are static. It is probably because of my background in the history of engineering and rationalization, but one of my big obsessions is how we move from objects to function, from function to field, to things which are more and more unstable. At a certain point, it is the old Eisenman question: how can we think of architecture, which is often seen today as the

very act of stability? It is still very difficult for an architect to build in time and not build in space, to not build forever, theoretically at least. The *Smart City* books revolve almost entirely around the idea that we substitute thinking of cities in terms of objects and in terms of flows; instead, we think in terms of scenarios. The digital controlled us to a kind of hypertrophied regime, which is hard to consider because we tend to think about the reassuring stability of objects. This is very perturbating for a discipline like architecture. The question of action is not a small question, and I do think it is one of the ways to overcome the "saving the world" syndrome.

Annie Barrett **I want to revisit Antoine's notion that there can be an individual author if that individual author is a network. In the discussion of scale, I am curious if the individual could not be a network. Considering Boullée, those ideas were so big and we think the big ideas that come out of architecture today indemnify the network. They are very contingent and reliant on the software, technologies and sciences, and I wonder—not thinking about scale as an object, but more as an idea—is it feasible of architecture to come up with big ideas decoupled from that network?**

AP That's a good question. I do believe in architecture, but what strikes me is the power of the primitive. Very frankly—and it may seem paradoxical given what I have just said—as a form of action, architecture ultimately needs objects. You need tangibility. Boullée did all of these drawings, but he also built. Strangely, in the age of the digital, you realize that the most expensive thing is the physical.

LA **What if architects were not contributing to tangibility itself but to a sensibility of tangibility?**

AP Tangibility is present, definitely. I am often struck by the fact that people have little interest in technology within the departments of history and science; you have to go to an architecture school to see a real interest in technology. Let me be clear when I say "object," architecture is a specific mode of approaching the question of material culture, or how materiality constructs culture. I do believe that there are various ways. I don't claim to be an architect, but I claim to be part of the architectural world and architectural culture. In the end, I discuss with a cultural geographer, or whomever, that architects were strangely interested in things.

SL **Some art historians, at least ones that I find interesting, are working more along the model of originators of discourse, rather than authors. They are looking for things that trigger the production of other things, and I think this would then move to Antoine's question, what is a big idea and what form does it take? What is interesting, despite the irony in the use of the word "original," is that originators of discourse are not entangled in the control mechanisms of authorship and don't rely on a heroic notion of originality. Instead, the concept embraces multiples, collectivities and even anonymity within an overall system of production.**

AP I don't think originality is a good category for architecture. If you are too original, then you are no longer an architect in some ways. Architecture is also very much about twisting the codes while not going completely outside the prevailing code, which is partly why

invention was always a problematic notion for a very long time in architectural theory. Originality is actually a complicated term in a discipline that relies so much on rules.

Sean Rucewicz Expanding more on Antoine's ideas of action and the example of the two castes being juxtaposed through the Mehrotra garden project, I am curious what an architect can do. A couple of years ago, I spoke with an artist who said it was a lot easier to "function" or to do social projects as an artist than as an architect, because you are not necessarily subject to the same codes or the same rigmarole to execute the project.

AP That's true, but when you succeed in architecture, it goes deeper in some ways than a work of art. To be honest, I have a series of thoughts behind this: one is the idea an architectural intervention that creates a bifurcation, the possibility of a choice in the world. The other idea is situation. The thing I was interested in with Mehrotra's Hyderabad project is the question of visibility as I was thinking very much about Rancière and the idea of aesthetic regime. Architecture is a very powerful way to prescribe what is visible and invisible, and yet it may also make things visible that are usually invisible. For me, making things visible is a form of action, which again creates a kind of bifurcation.

Axel Kilian Models and the process of production weren't highlighted much, yet it seems there is a reason why the digital has led to such an explosion of objects. There is a distinction between the invention of a model of operation, which we operate on many considered more original than they are new, when in actuality, have formed over the decades. They have a bigger impact because they are implemented—it's an interpretation rather than implementation, partially used in the moment. Whereas the models that are capable of being numerically implemented, meaning the code and programming, become uncritically replicable by anyone who has access to the computation. Suddenly, there is production in areas that are much more implementable, so theoretical models have a huge impact on those areas of numeric-geometric equivalence. In this sense, authorship is also layered: there is the theoretical inventor of the model, then there is an implementer, and maybe another user of that model claiming authorship through the model itself without acknowledging the two-to-three layer depth.

AP Agreed. this is what I call "nested forms of authorship." One of the reasons it raises all of these questions about authorship, is because we have the idea that the digital leads to writing, such as code writing, so it clearly involves certain kinds of authors. Even still, the digital also triggers a very old and almost archaic vision of automatism. There is no author with automatism, rather the only author is nature. In the digital we constantly have both aspects. Is it written? Is it automatic? Is it us? Is it nature? In architecture, we are completely in the middle. The same questions will arise with artificial intelligence: is artificial intelligence something we designed, or is it something that harnesses the automaticity of nature? It is strikingly parallel with the new materialists and all of the current discourse on emergence. It is very much the old question of automatism, the people who are more interested in the writing and the code—yet it is both.

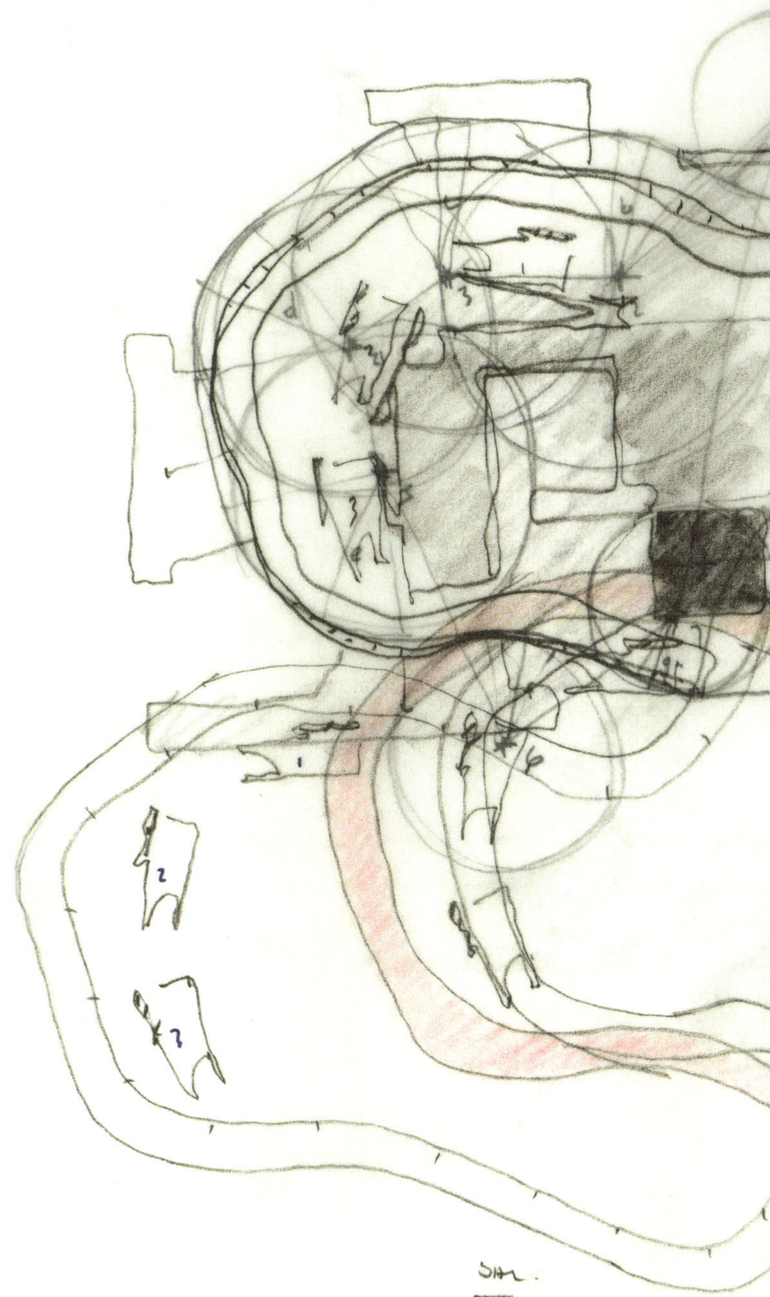

Thom Mayne

Thom Mayne, On Architecture & Other Selfless Subjects

Jesse Reiser

Thom Mayne has claimed that architecture is completely impersonal and yet highly authored. This provocative way of thinking about authorship opens up possibilities for re-thinking the relationship between the work of architecture and those who produce it. His provocation asks that since we no longer know what the author is, part of the project of architecture is at least to find out what the *authored work* is.

Mayne's claim begins to make sense when we consider that his work is not the product of an isolated genius, but that his genius is lodged in a larger project coming out of the 1970s and 1980s and up to the present that used drawing as a vehicle for exploration. The panoply of radical architectural techniques (at least for architects), including superposition and collage, did not belong to him *only*, but in the '80s was part of a wider set of speculations through drawing, and only secondarily through built projects. It was sustained by an academic network of architects and their students working on these problems, stretching from the Architectural Association in London, to Cooper Union, to SCI-Arc on the West Coast, and Cranbrook later on. In this context, instead of being used as a conventional or technical instrument, drawing actually became a vehicle for architectural speculation. Bound up with the promise of drawing's capacity to generate the new and the unforeseen is the notion that design is not simply a rendering of a pre-given idea or concept, that the very act of drawing would release the new. So in some sense, Mayne is as much a witness to his work as its author.

The delirium of his process then and now allows him to lose and displace his ego, and fuse object and subject. He even admitted to being high some of the time (a cultural technique already commonplace by the '60s, but certainly new to architecture). I don't know if one would call this subjective or trans-subjective work, but that is probably the point. Technique and process, however, are never the goal—it is the succession of individual artifacts and their achievement, as well as the failures (and failures are important) which comprise his overall project in architecture. "If you are not surprised by what you do, why do it?" Peter Cook has said. This involves not setting up a project, or a drawing, a priori. The project is always different from what you thought it was. Much of the problem is wrestling with and overcoming preconceptions, and allowing the project to change. And then the project takes over. It is the opposite of a conceptual project.

There are also objective forces at work on his authorship. Since Mayne is an architect as opposed to an artist, his expression is necessarily mediated through objective systems of translation and construction. The drawings for some time have ceased to be an end in themselves, and they certainly aren't attempts to deliver a pure essence of the soul. Rather, like any contemporary practitioner, his design work is already enmeshed in a complex of technologies, which extend from the design studio to the construction site. Even though the projects emerge from his obsessive interests, the way projects are delivered are always mediated by construction technologies, codes that have their own inertia, algorithms, and programs invented by others. And then there is the whole office. There is a technical apparatus and a set of disciplinary problems that are being worked through, that remove it from being merely a personal project or problem.

Part of the fundamental strangeness of Mayne's oeuvre derives not from novel techniques, but from the culture of that moment in the discipline, when drawings became an end in themselves. When the chance to build became possible, the intense focus of drawn space carried over into actual building, reversing the conventional relationship between drawing and building, such that the physical building is rendered a strange, secondary representation of the drawing.

Mayne is also speaking from the peculiar culture and context of schools on the West Coast, particularly SCI-Arc and UCLA, that are involved in a range of what might be termed evolutionary projects for architecture. Studios are set up to explore a certain focused set of directions, which relate to the larger body of drawn and built work of the faculty. The design process is more about how such projects evolve and devolve in the schools across many years and generations of students than in any particular project or student work. This is very different from a conceptual *program-based* approach. In fact, there is a huge divide between the evolutionary project and conceptual projects in architecture. Evolutionary projects unashamedly embrace formal concerns. Thus, when Mayne disparages formal agility, he speaks from within a context where formal agility is the norm. Within his own practice he has that facility himself. In the LA scene, formal projects are dispensed by every student and every architect. It is only in this context of assuming that others have the same skill that Mayne claims to dismiss formal projects out of hand.

Mayne's adeptness allows him to engage with considerations outside of form, from within his formal project. He is very consciously trying to engage social, political, and environmental realities, which in architecture means information. That is, more information informs form than simply form. In an account of the genesis of Frank Lloyd Wright's Larkin Building in Reyner Banham's *Architecture of the Well-Tempered Environment,* Banham discusses how the HVAC system enabled Wright's flash of insight that transformed his crude sketch into the building's final form. Once Wright started to work with the environmental system, Larkin's towers became more discreet, more refined. The final formal and organizational expression for the Larkin Building was necessitated by the logic of an outside technology. Mayne does a very similar thing. There is a lateral crossover from architectural superimposition, bricolage, and collage, which Mayne has been using for thirty years, to the systematic layering of environmental systems, which characterizes his current work. Formalism is typically seen as being in complete opposition to sustainability, but in Mayne's case, the two are inseparable.

Beyond information would be rhetoric. When Mayne lectures in architecture schools, he alternates between speaking *en famille* to other designers and architects, and speaking with a more popular or accessible rhetoric to people outside of the discipline. In Mayne's discussion of responsibility, he was speaking to what architects can draw from within the discipline to realistically contribute to social, political, and environmental concerns, rather than from without as amateur social scientists, politicians, environmentalists, etc. He celebrated Steve Jobs for his refusal to have focus groups—which I think is actually very correct. He cleaves to the now unfashionable idea that enlightened authorship might be more universal and objective than harnessing the soft sciences. This is a dilemma in the discipline—the assumption that in order to move outside of subjectivity you look at presumably "objective" material through data mining, surveys, focus groups, and the like, that are a compilation of opinions that at best will produce an average, but will never produce anything new.

Koolhaas does with Manhattan what Mayne does with drawings. That is, the drawing is a process tool as much as it is a product. Mayne will do a drawing and then look at it retrospectively to mine certain features he wants to develop in the same way that Koolhaas interrogates Manhattan. The drawing enables Mayne to work retrospectively and project forward. Rather than preconceiving an idea, the design process is about projecting ideas into the drawing, thus using drawing as a medium, an enabler.

A final note. Thom described an early fascination with the work of Aldo Rossi—a fascination which turned to frustration when he attempted to extend Rossi's project into his own. Two or three projects in, Thom realized that whatever he did—whatever he attempted to add—ultimately did not add more to the project, but in effect, created less. I heard the same frustration over taking on Rossi's work from Steve Holl, whose attempt occurred at the same historical moment—the late '80s. Two contemporaries, the same dilemma. Their impasse not only hinges on the merciless contingency of time and place, but whether Rossi's project was continuable at all. Or whether it was a project already foreclosed, and in its tragic perfection an epic enactment of memory and loss that was inherently undevelopable. Rossi's project was a summation, the ending of a larger enterprise perhaps, not a beginning. Rossi himself, much like late DeChirico, could only make pale copies of his definitive projects by that time. I reflect on this now as we witness renewed attention to architectural post-modernism. Less risky perhaps for the historians among us but for the architects, this return of interest seems to be a warning that Thom and Steve's dilemma may still be ours. Thom's subsequent work, while it may have appeared a fool's leap at the time, retrospectively yielded a thirty year body of work arguably still pregnant with possibility. Then, as now, the Americans add and the Europeans subtract. Foreclosure in the '80s was for Rossi modernism, for Thom, Rossi. Modernism or modernisms offered Mayne greater possibility, and certainly more hope. Let's hope that the now universal inclination to add, collect, and repeat (among progressive practices at least) keeps pace with the capacity to forget.

Discourse

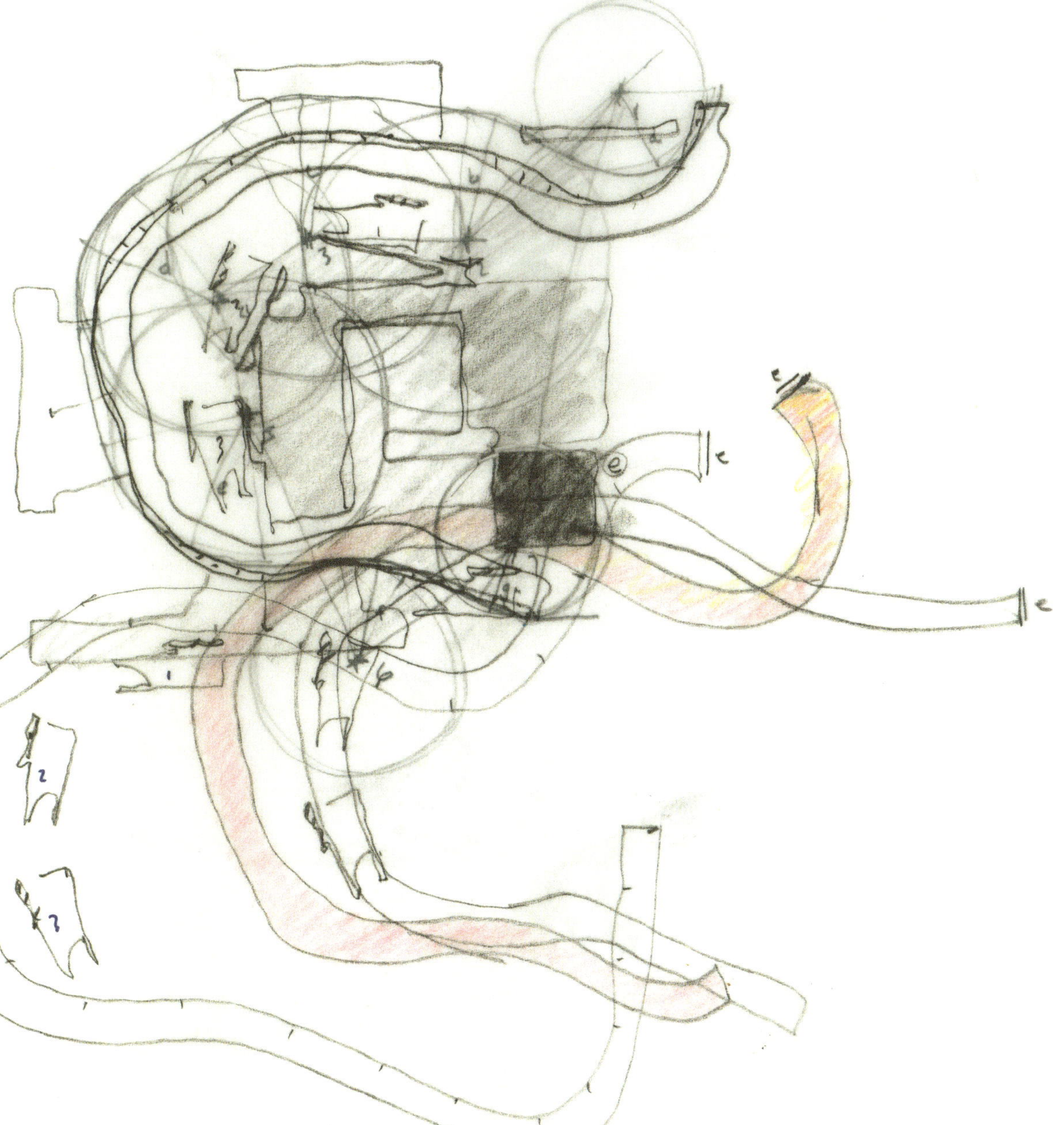

Hypo Alpe-Aldria Center Sketch 2, 2000. Courtesy of Morphosis Architects.

CENTERFOLD

W.I.P. #183 Thom Mayne

Selections by Eda Yetim

From his early days as student of Ralph Knowles, to Design Director of Morphosis, Thom Mayne chronicles his ontogenesis through selected architectural work. Contrary to the precision of a refined android—as often suggested by Morphosis' work or Mayne himself—each project reveals a humanist aspect to the architecture, one that is fraught with fear and doubt, yet simultaneously exudes a spirit of exploration and optimism.

This photo essay highlights five key motivations from five specific projects that capture the rigorous ethos of Mayne's practice. Rather than a close reading, this graphic narrative is comprised of snapshots accompanied by quotes as a thematic way to visualize the process of Mayne's personal and collaborative work.

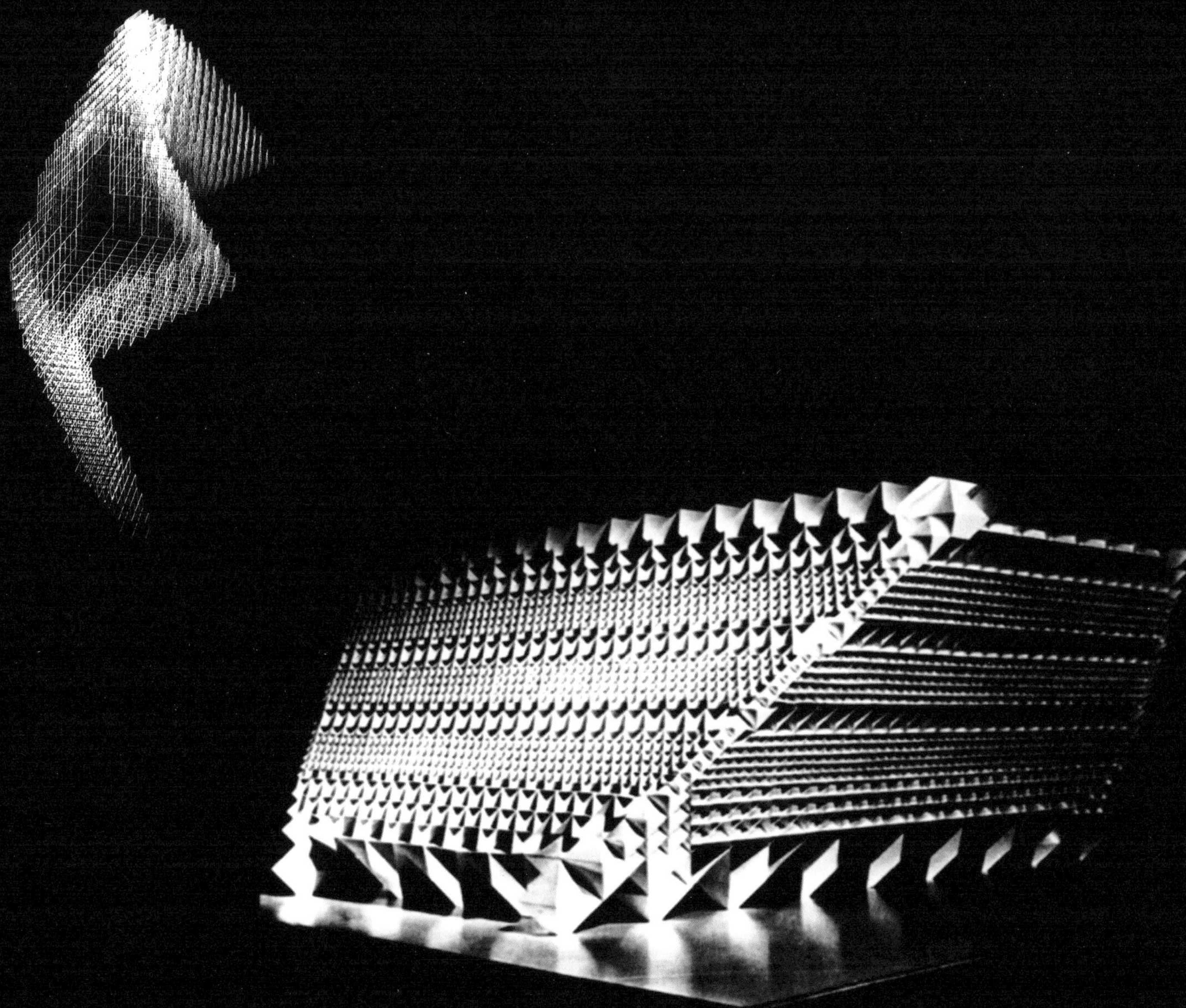

Model and drawing from Ralph Knowles' Second-year Studio at the University of Southern California. Courtesy of Ralph Knowles.

1—
Control

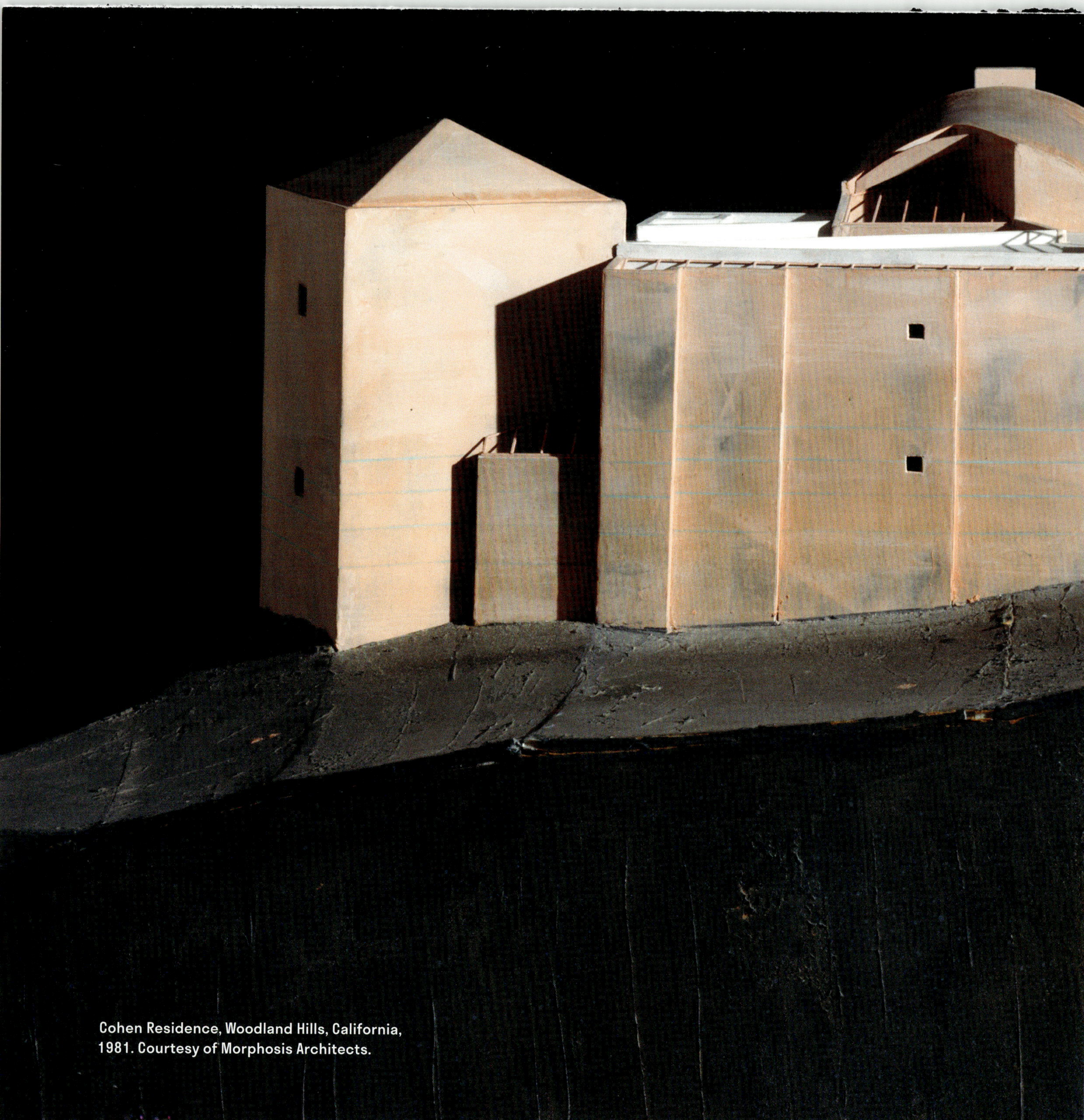

Cohen Residence, Woodland Hills, California, 1981. Courtesy of Morphosis Architects.

Cohen Residence (1981)

"I met Lebbeus Woods and Raimund Abraham in New York with Leo Pistelli; they were diggers and I became interested in this primitive idea of inhabiting earth and digging. Soon, this interest manifested in all of my work and its relationship to site.

Architecture is connected to a happenstantial nature that you have no control over, and if you are into control, like me, it's deadly. You are going to invent and produce, but ultimately architecture will occur in two parts: in your internal world—an artistic world of innovation, invention and interpretation—and in the *ring*, where you move back and forth continuously.

Shortly after these realizations, we received our first project ... and I had no idea how to proceed. I was probably closer to the Archigram boys, but I also looked at materiality, context, and learned how to make stuff. In West Coast culture, which was a very unsophisticated culture, I realized that I had to take more responsibility for the process of making and protect my own creative capital." T.M.

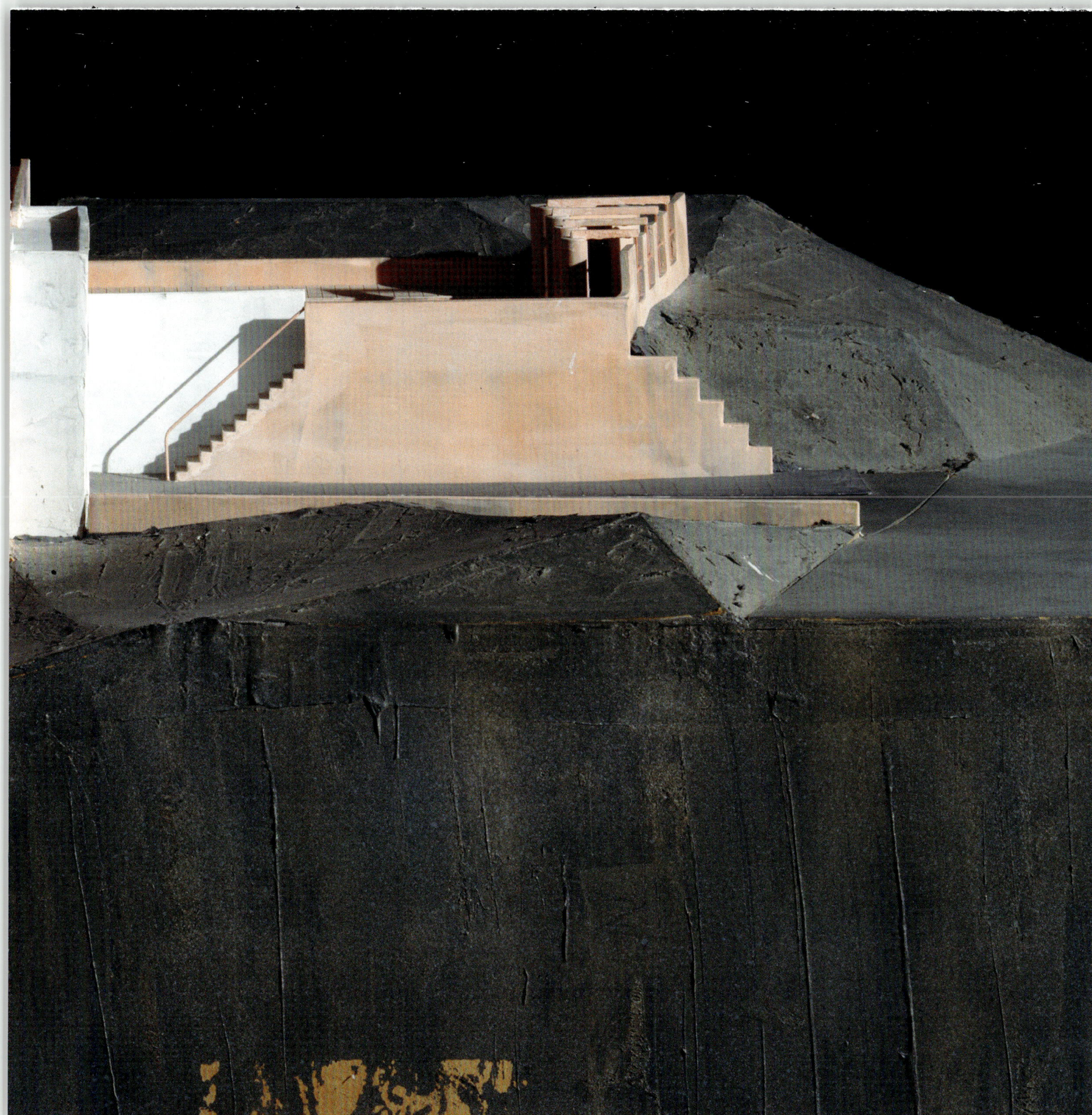

2—
Catharsis

Lawrence House (1984)

"At the end of this first large project, I was totally uncomfortable and absolutely aware that I was completely lost with this thing we just built. I did these drawings after the building was completed. They are cathartic drawings—I worked on them again and again. As I was drawing them, it became clear to me: what's most interesting is the differentiation of the rooms, every room has its own elevation." T.M.

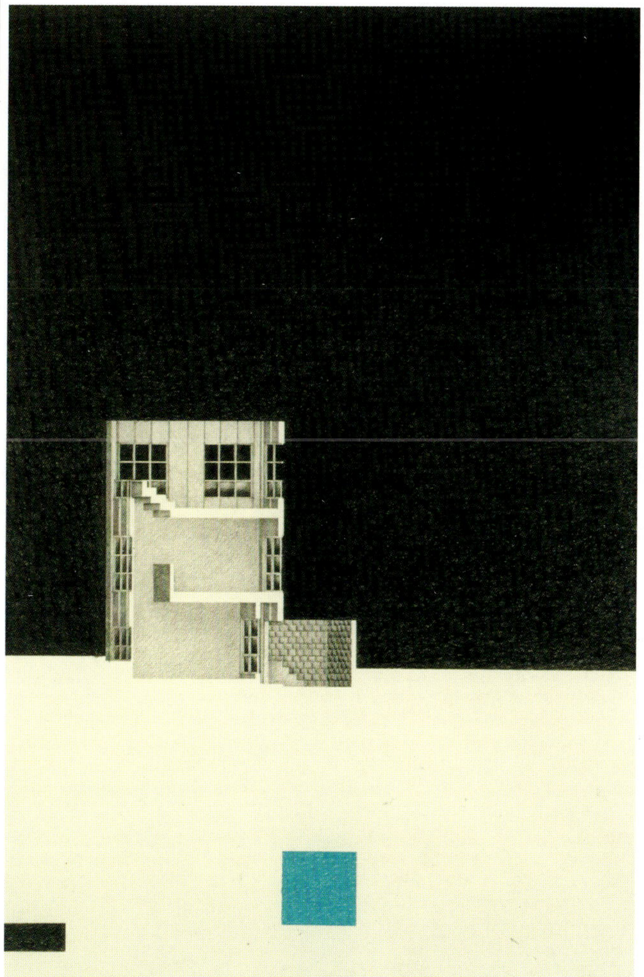

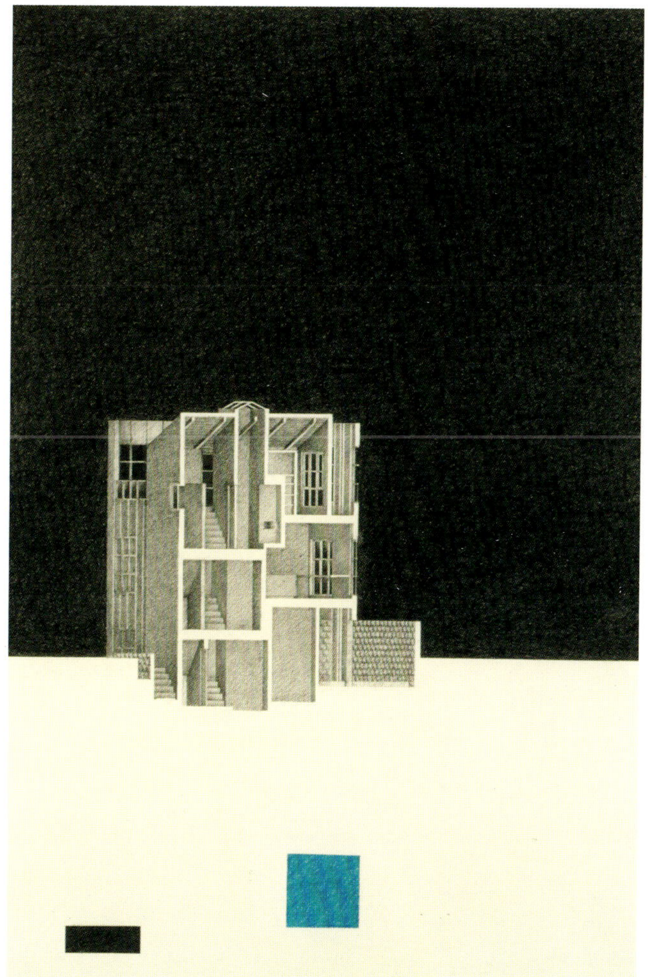

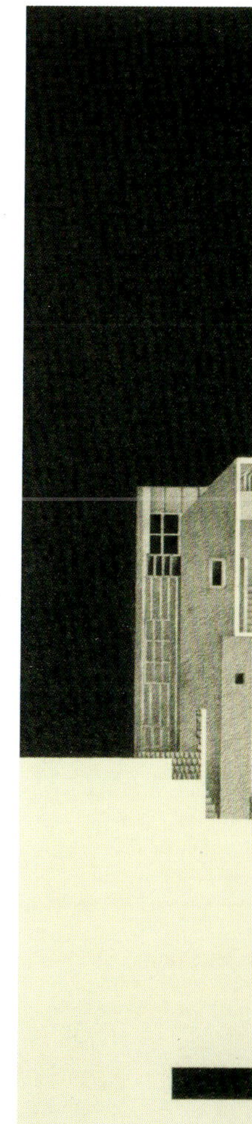

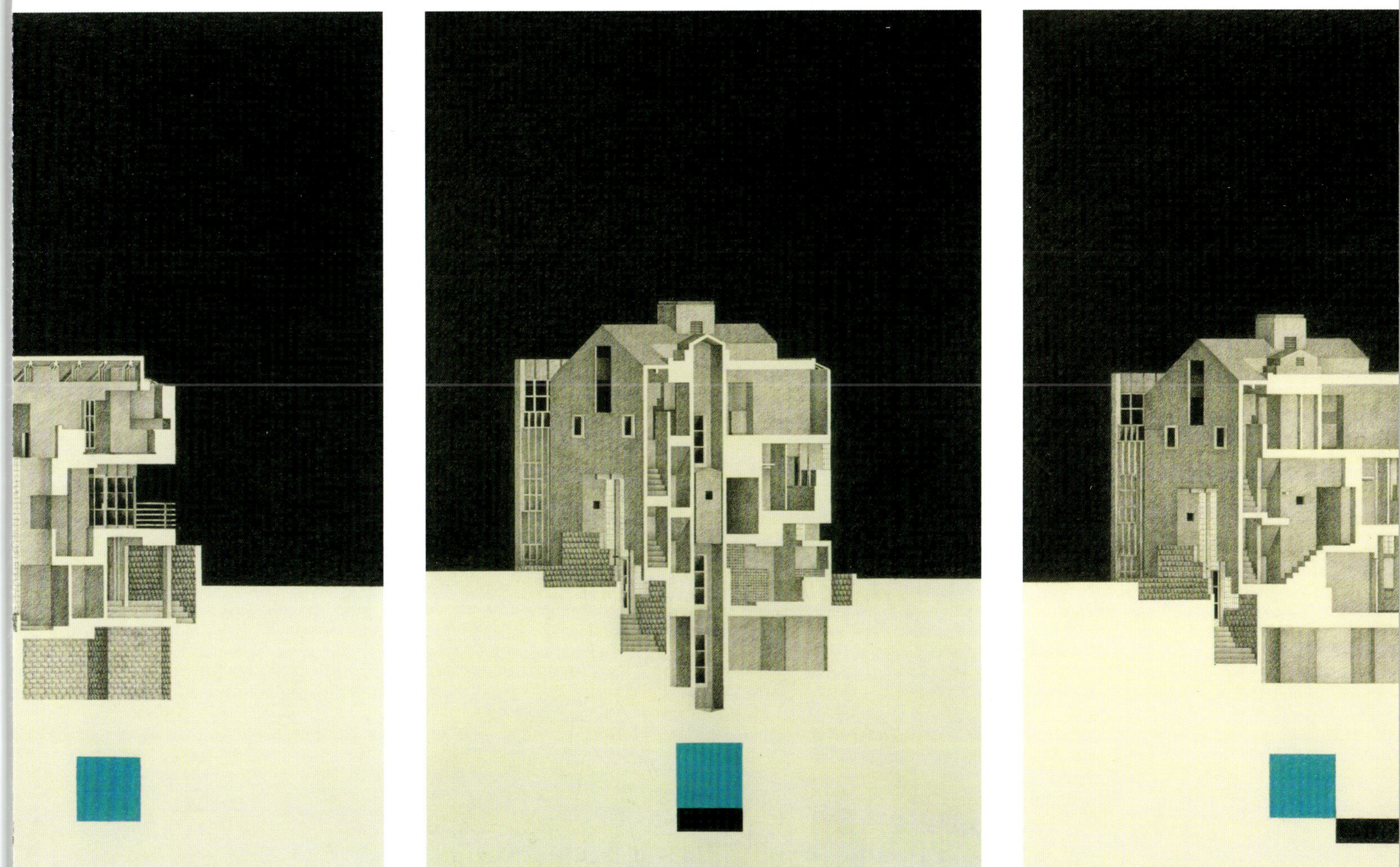

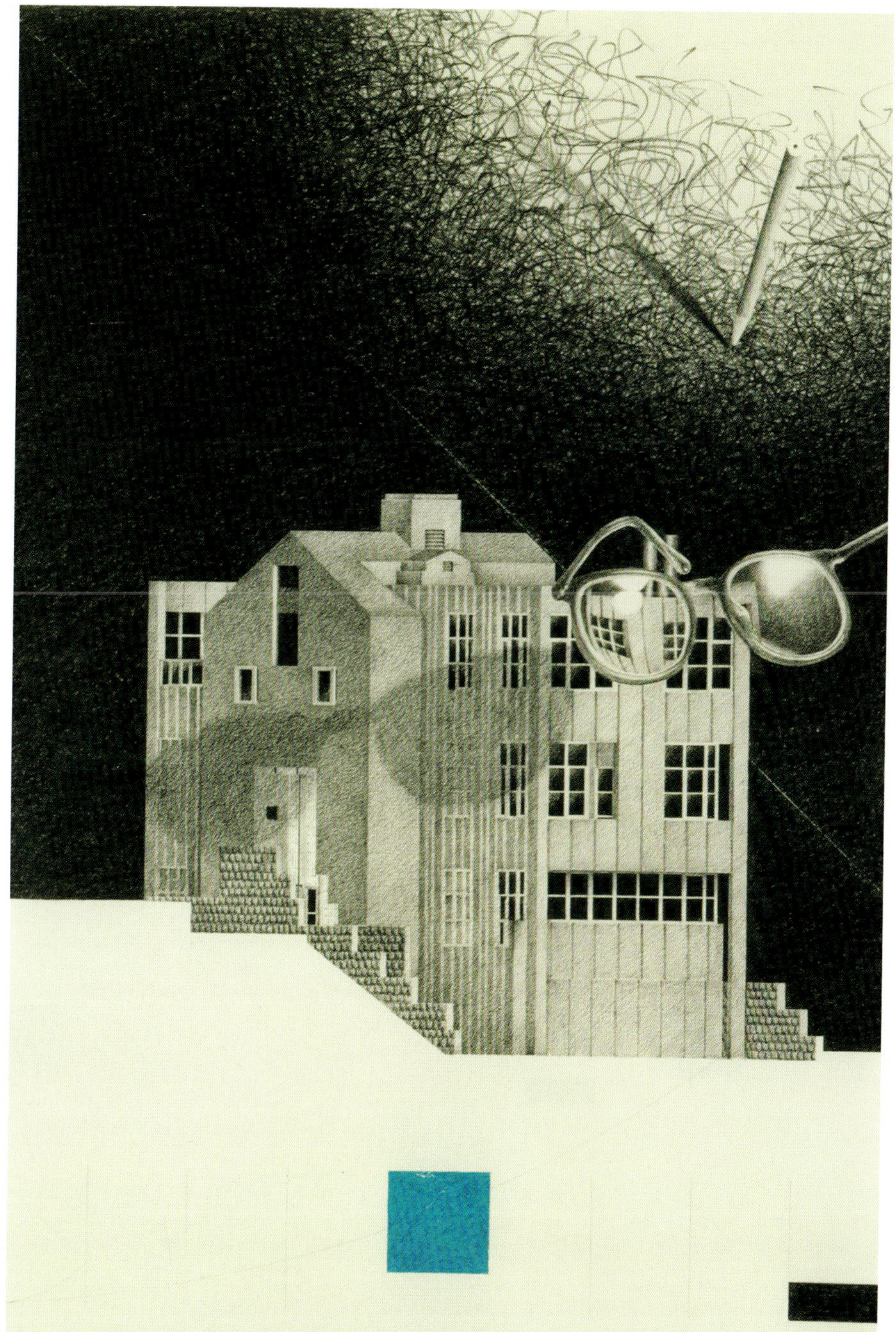

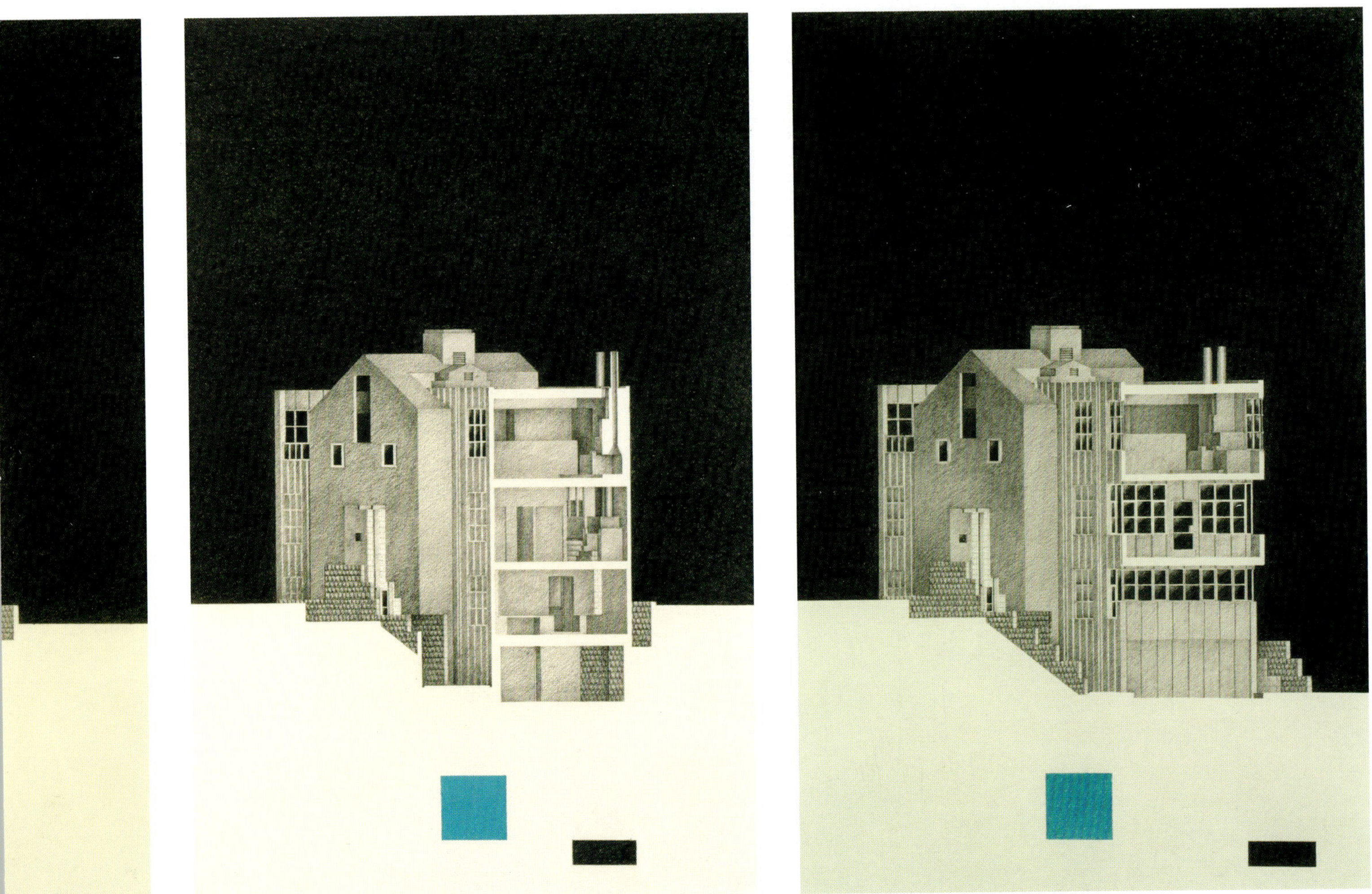

Lawrence Residence, Hermosa Beach, California, 1980. Courtesy of Morphosis Architects.

3—
Let Loose

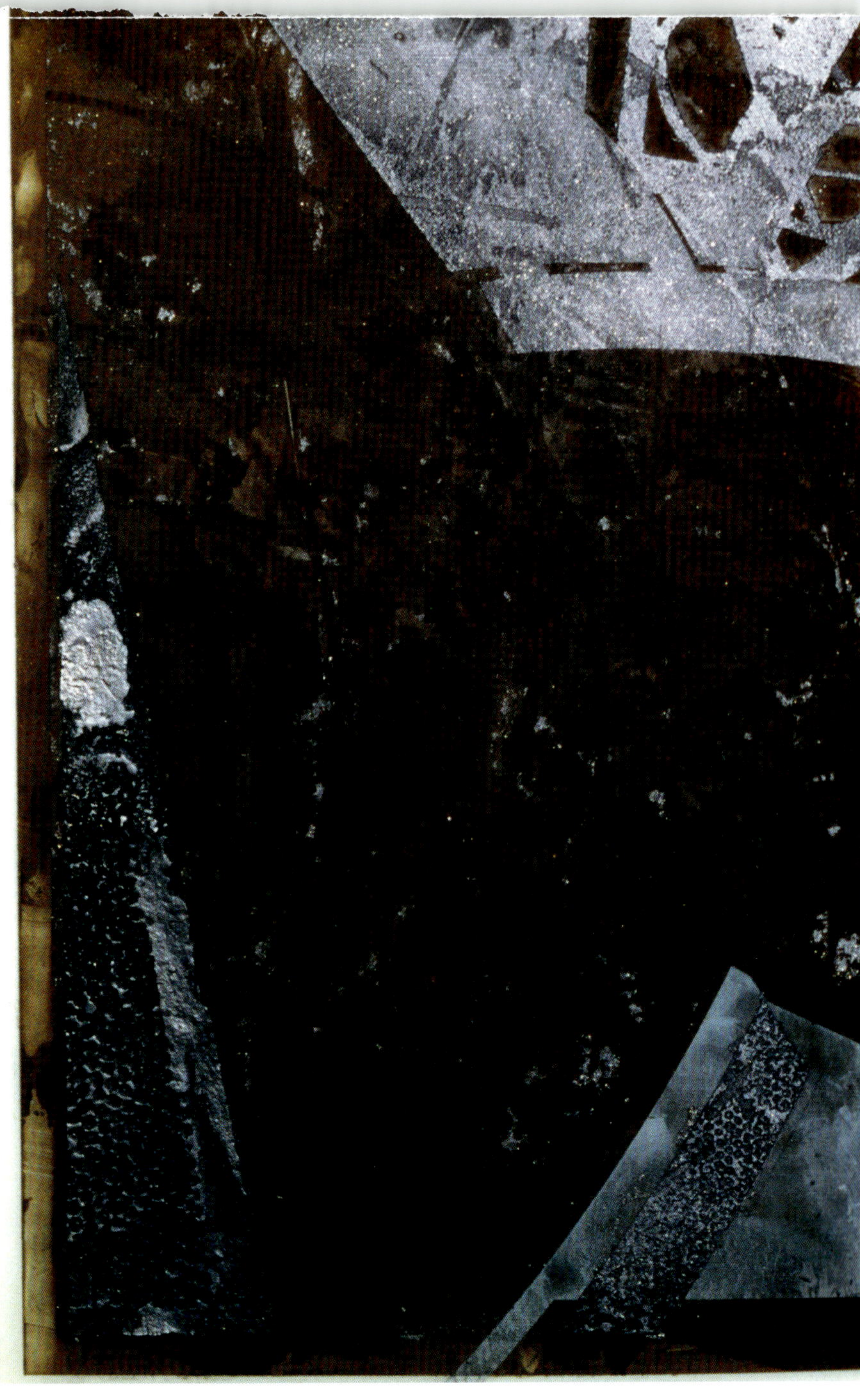

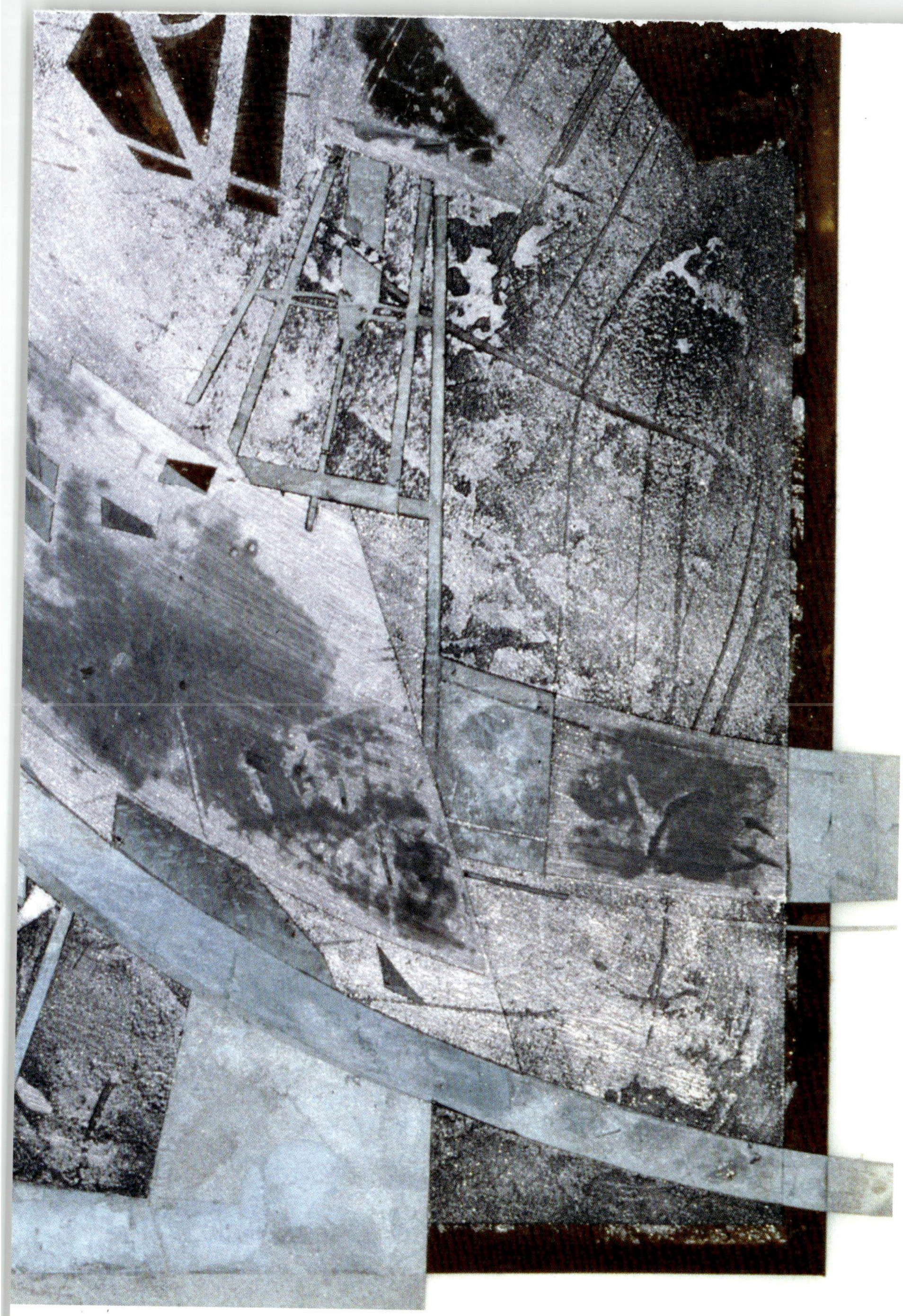

MTV Studios (1990)

"At some point, I worked by myself from noon to five o'clock and would draw for drawing's sake. I listened to Thelonious Monk and John Coltrane ... I was emotionally in the spirit of the moment. Drawing became a preoccupation. I would constantly draw things that I didn't even understand; they were more or less free associations and became more specific with use of materiality in parallel with the work. The beginning of a language emerged—which I didn't comprehend quite yet—of associations and connections between things that remained unresolved. The drawings were more conceptual and they allowed the architectural work to be even more literal than before.

Eventually, we wanted to locate ourselves in the culture of architecture and architecture itself. We saw ourselves in very autonomous terms: we were not connected to the world we lived in and had our own set of interests—we fought it out for our interests. We had no concern with selling things, we were just engaged in architecture as an autonomous act and somehow found a way to negotiate with clients. We had no interest in selling things, we were just interested in architecture as an autonomous act and somehow found a way to negotiate with clients. We constantly looked for mechanisms; the drawings were both a combination of the mechanical and a continuous loosening of part and whole." T.M.

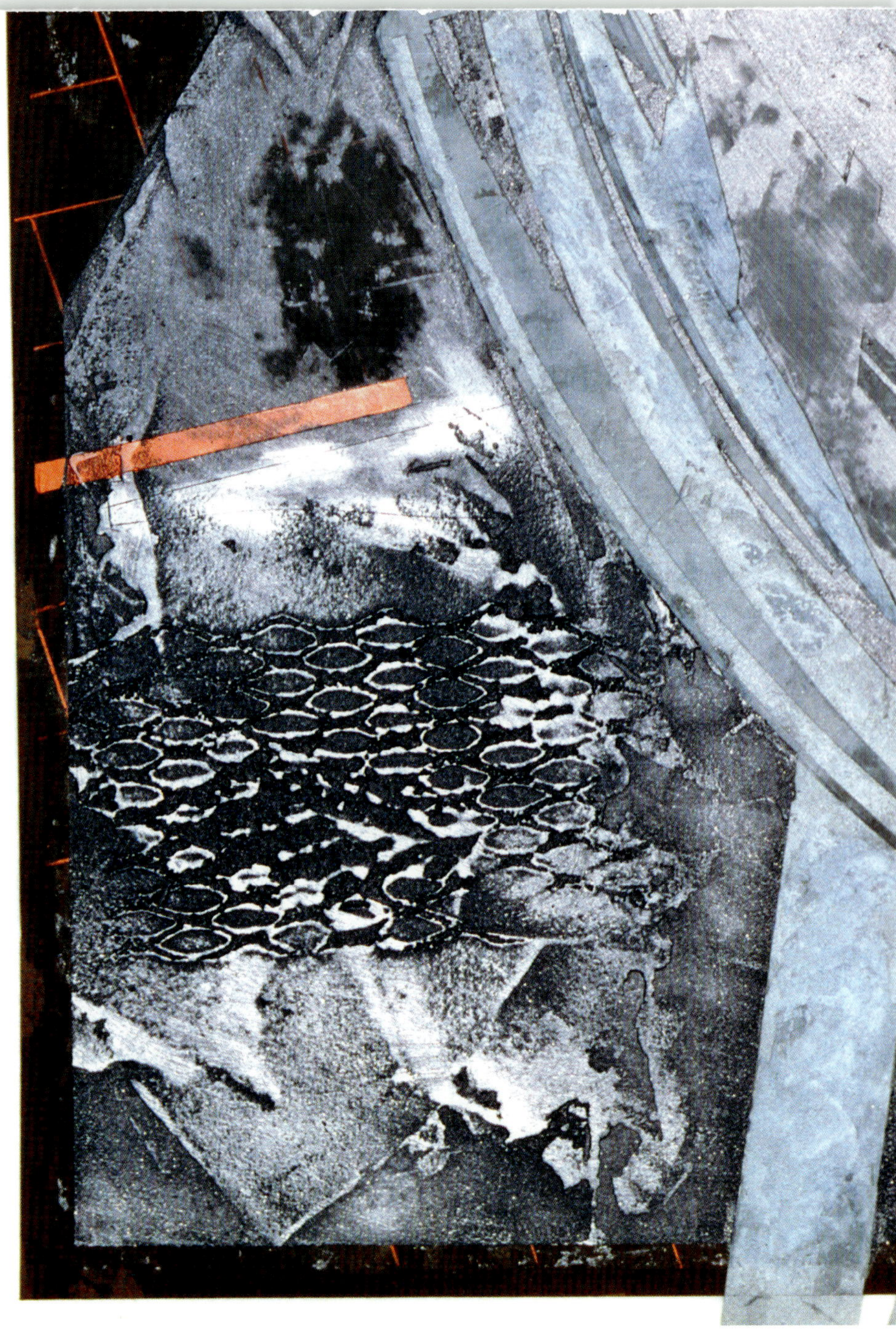

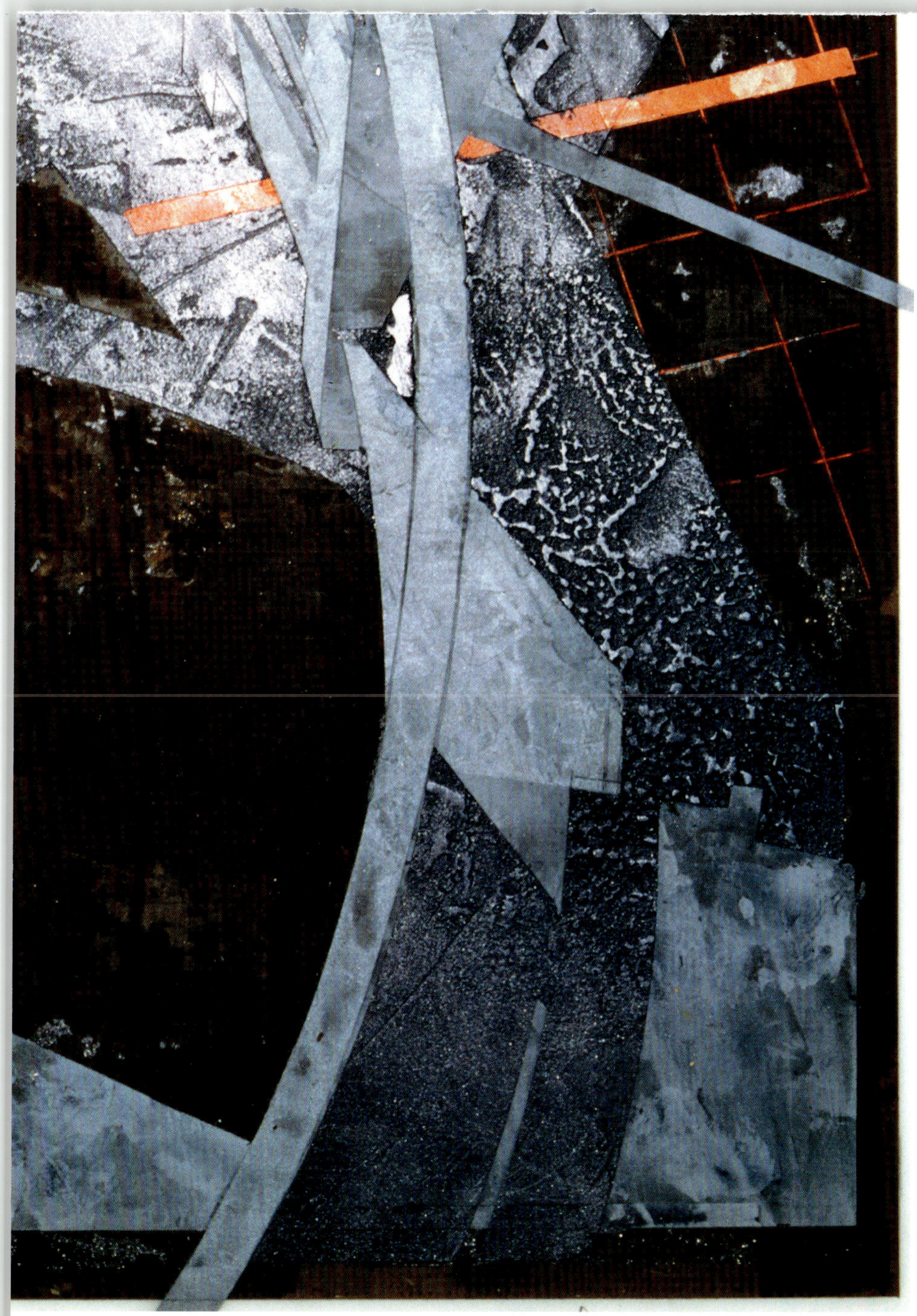

MTV Studios, Los Angeles, California, 1990.
Courtesy of Morphosis Architects.

4—
Control Over Language

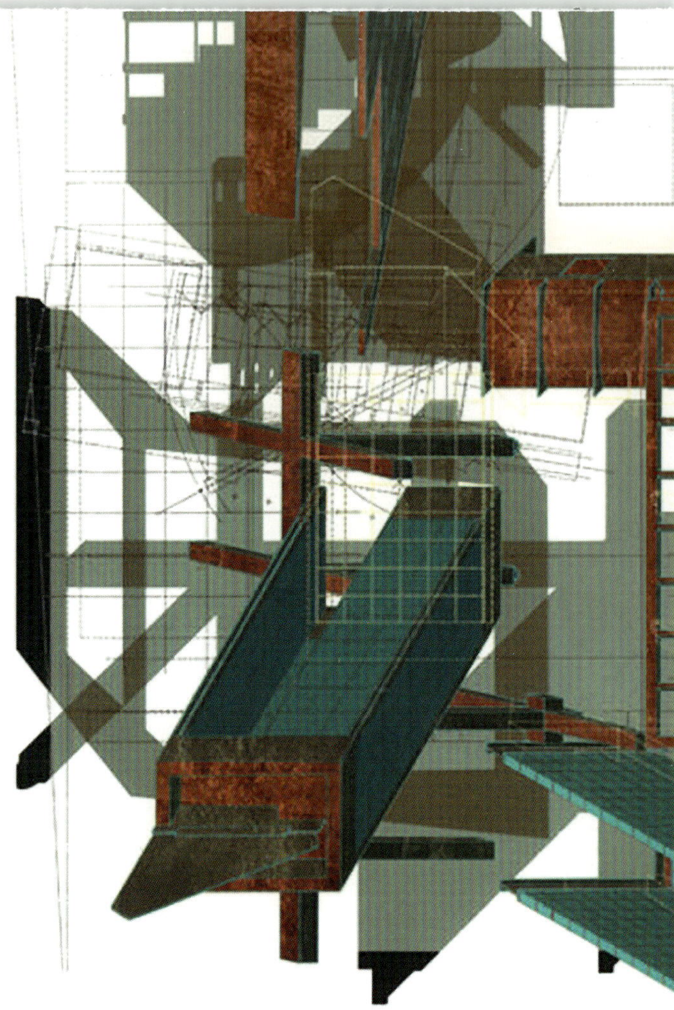

45/50

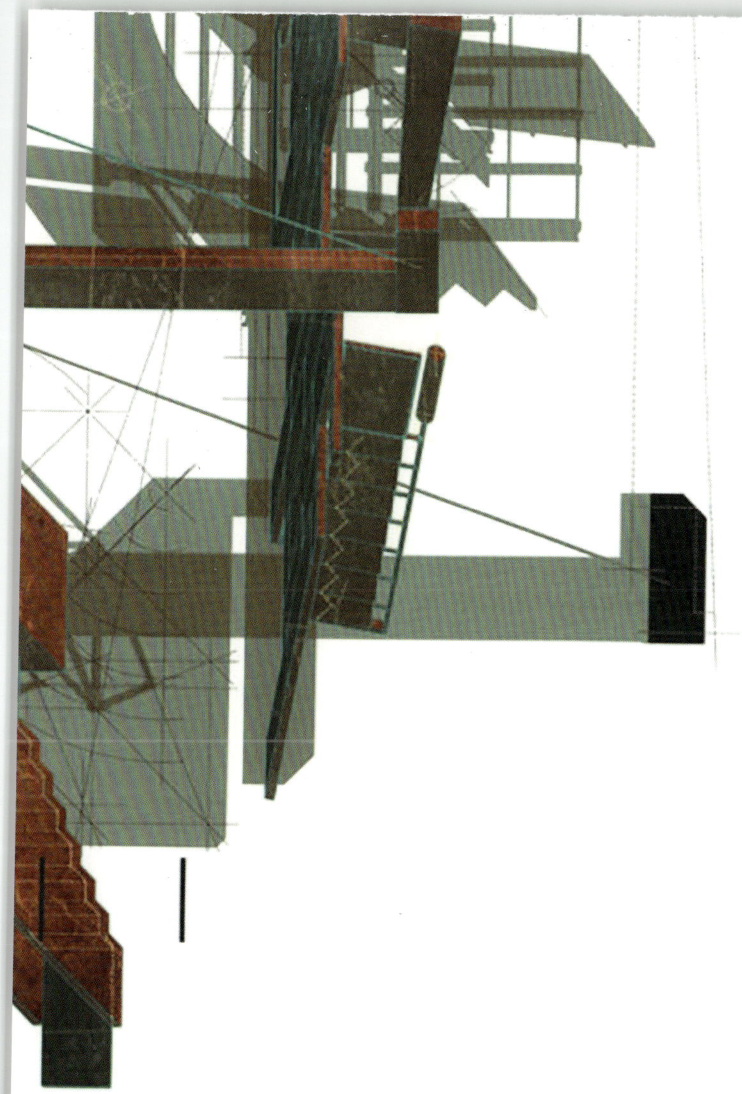

Sixth Street Residence (1987–92)

"There is a piece of work, and then there are the intensified events that give energy to our work. Mistakes were made as the materiality, the construction, and the organization of a project came from different forces to find coherence. We were really interested in the unfinished and the fragment. In the past, we understood this interest in the open-ended as implied by the unfinished and its energy, which speaks more to construction and the activity of making. This interest also directly led to the Sixth Street House. At this point, we were no longer interested in conventional elevations, proportions, or the relationship between part-to-whole in a literal sense, but rather through associations." T.M.

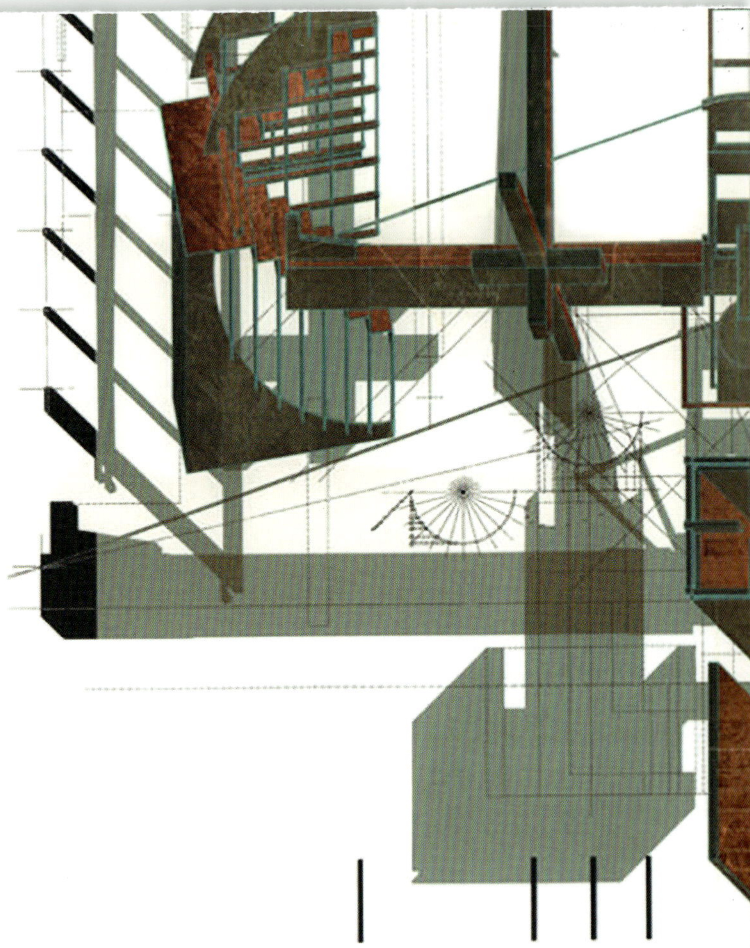

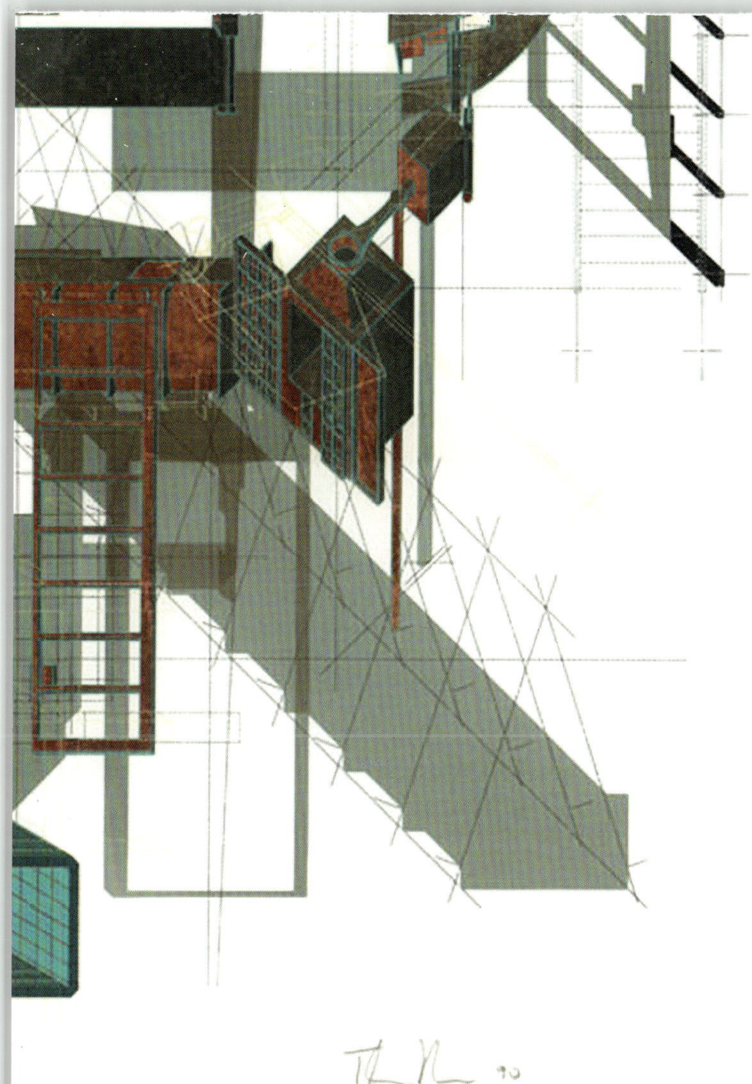

Sixth Street Residence, Santa Monica, California, 1987–92. Courtesy of Morphosis Architects.

5—
Performance and Prototyping

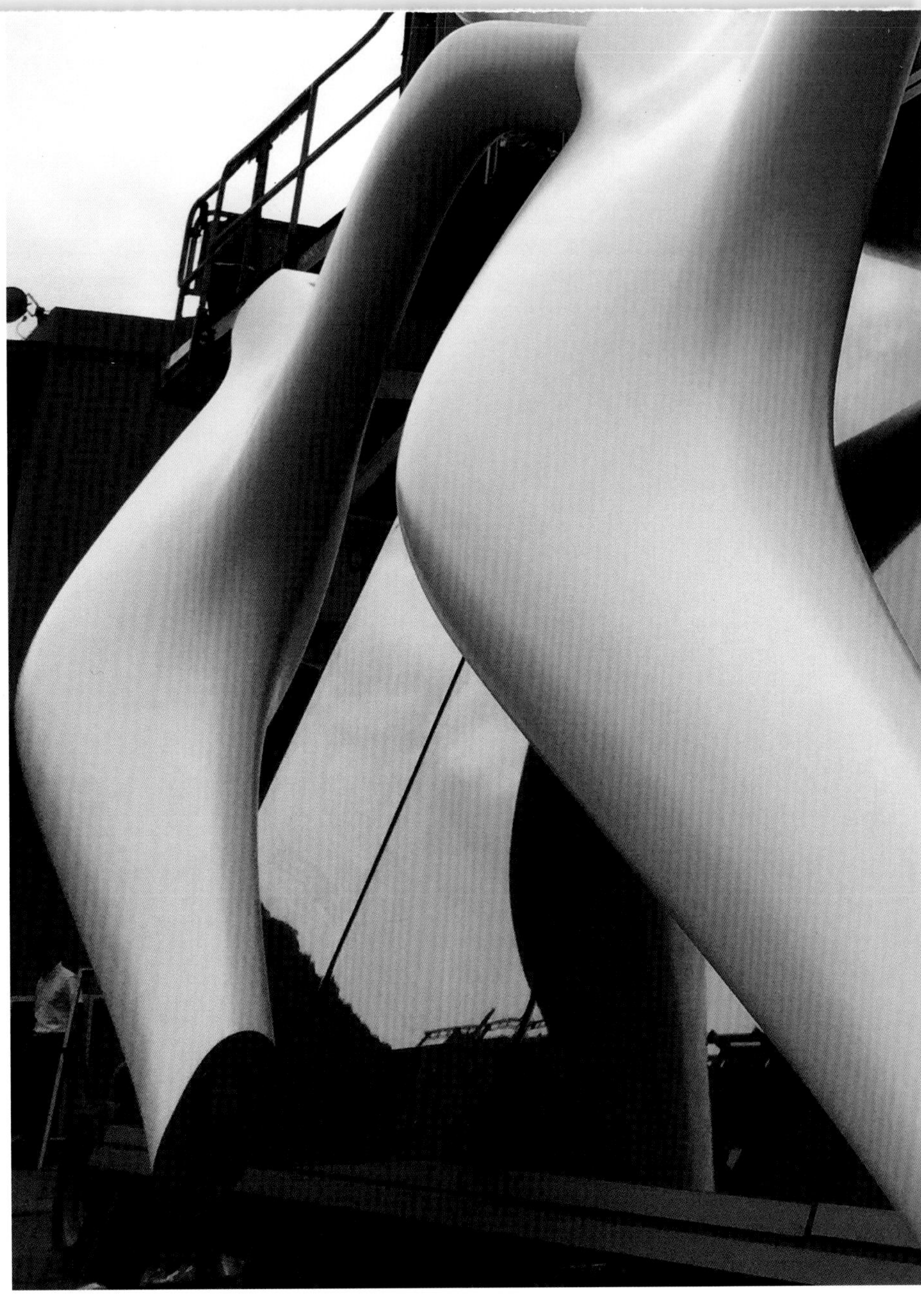

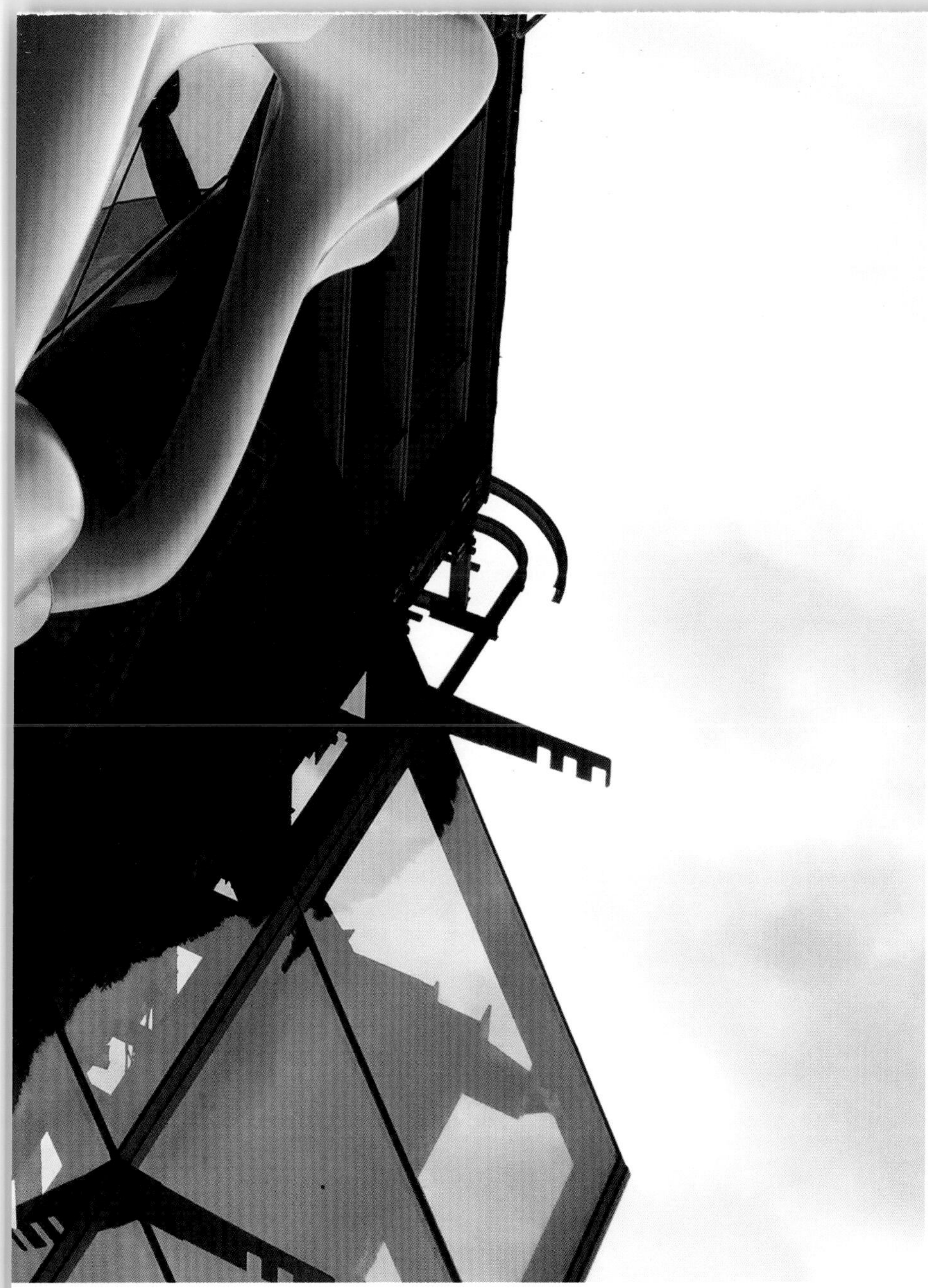

Kolon Future Research Park (2018)

"As the tools developed, I realized that there is no return to old classical drawings and architecture has to be three dimensional—it operates beyond an a priori capacity. In this sense, we no longer begin with formal language and see ourselves autonomous. Our projects are deeply embedded in political, social, and economic issues, which refer back to the initial, early projects.

As the buildings get larger, they also become more strategic. We brought in Paul Nakazawa to strategize the office and develop tactics on how to approach design, especially if you want it built. We are comfortable working as autonomous characters with an artistic sensibility and, by essence, it is more and more performative. With the proper tools, we are now able to simultaneously operate at an urban level and architectural level. We produce urban complexity and diversity, though the complexity in our work is the result of dealing with problems that stem from multiple sources.

Everyone in the office has a specialization and we develop both the project and the prototype. We are aware that the tool simultaneously works for the generative effects of materials and enhances the number of performances." T.M.

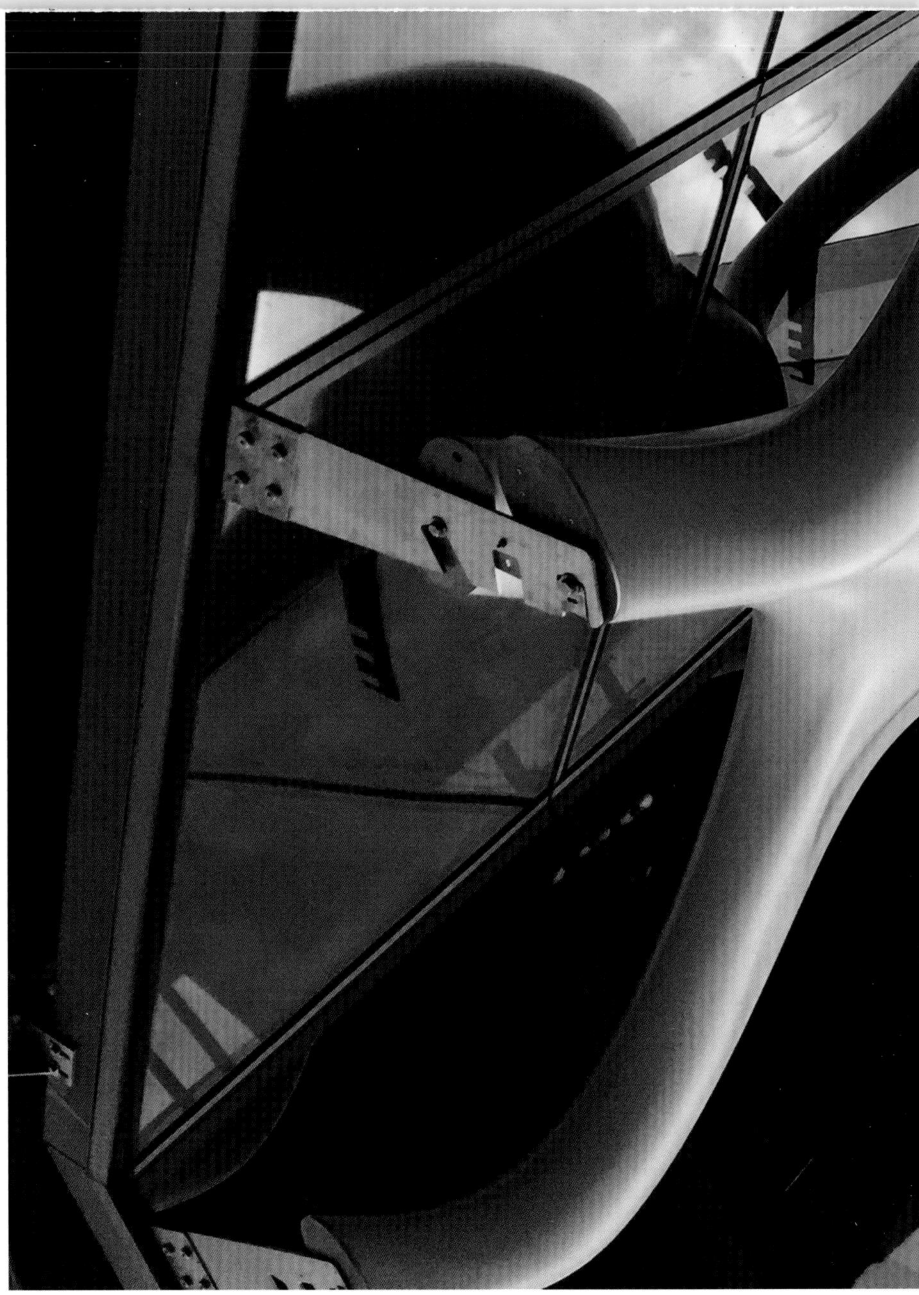

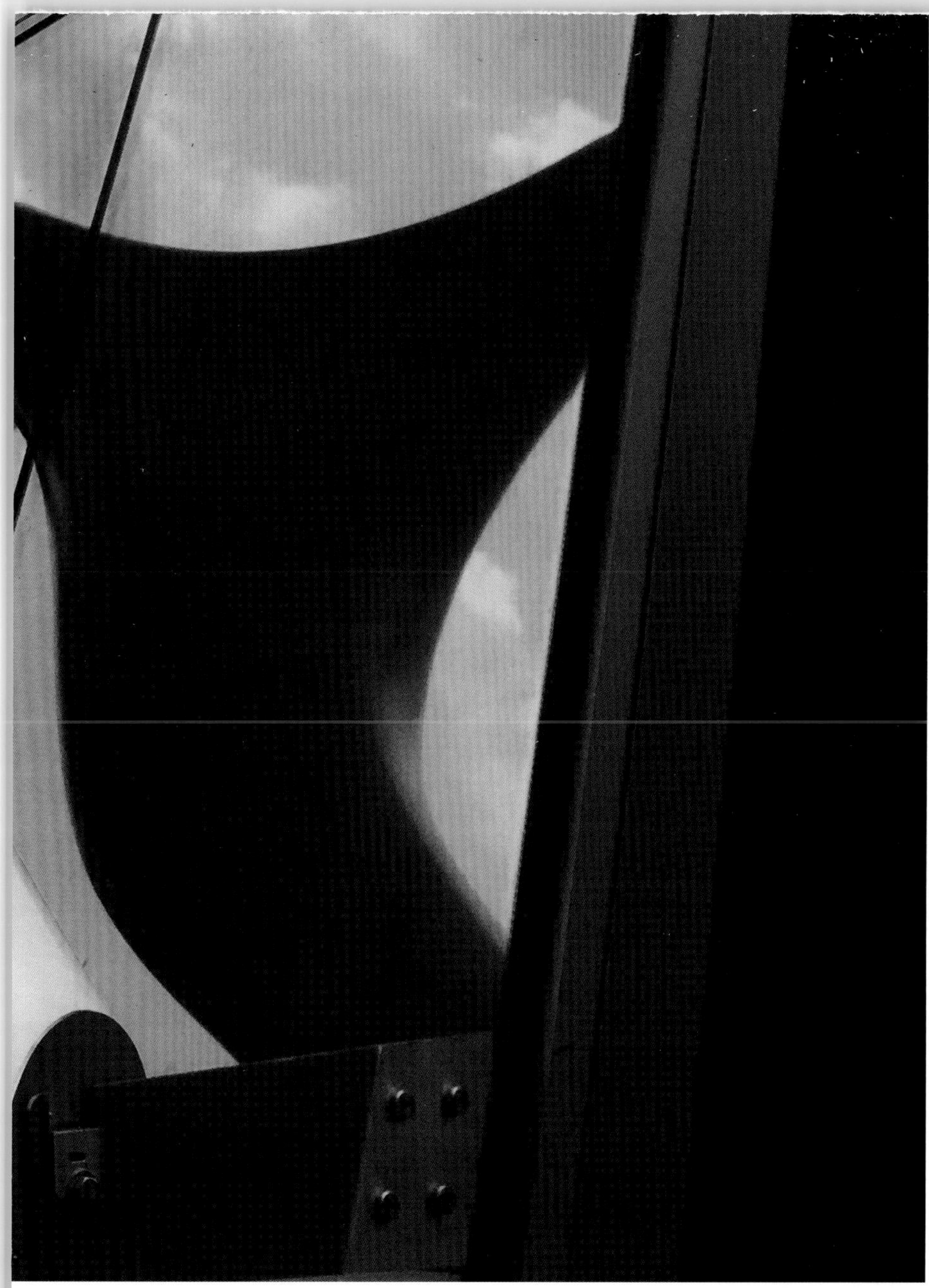

Kolon Future Research Park, Seoul, South Korea, 2018. Courtesy of Morphosis Architects.

The End of Authority:

Peter Eisenman in conversation with Julian Rose

The End of Authority:

Peter Eisenman in conversation with Julian Rose

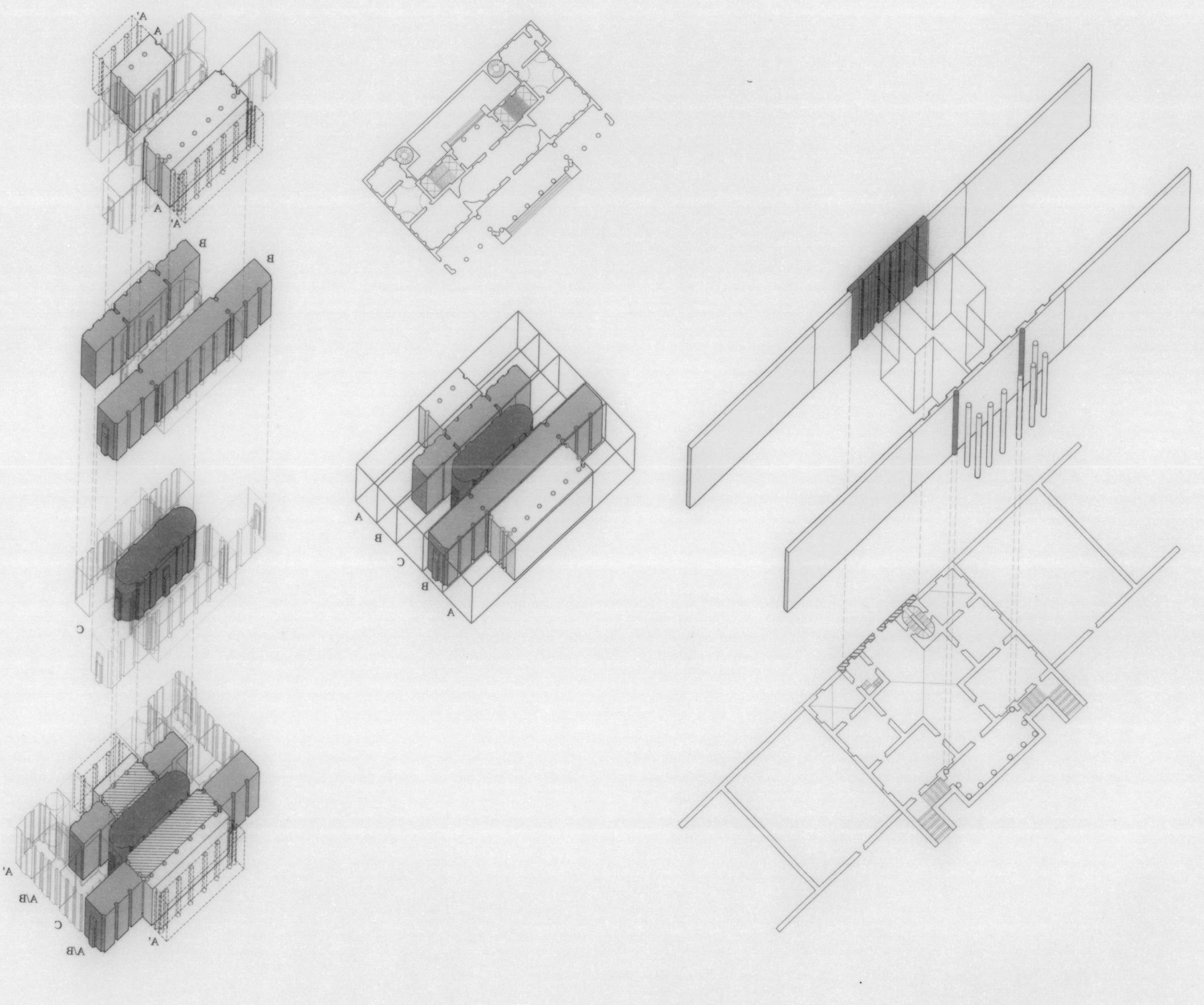

There was to have been a series of garden walls at the Villa Foscari—proto-barchesse—on which the main body of the villa sat. Diagram of Villa Foscari from *Palladio Virtuel*, 2015. © Peter Eisenman with Matt Roman.

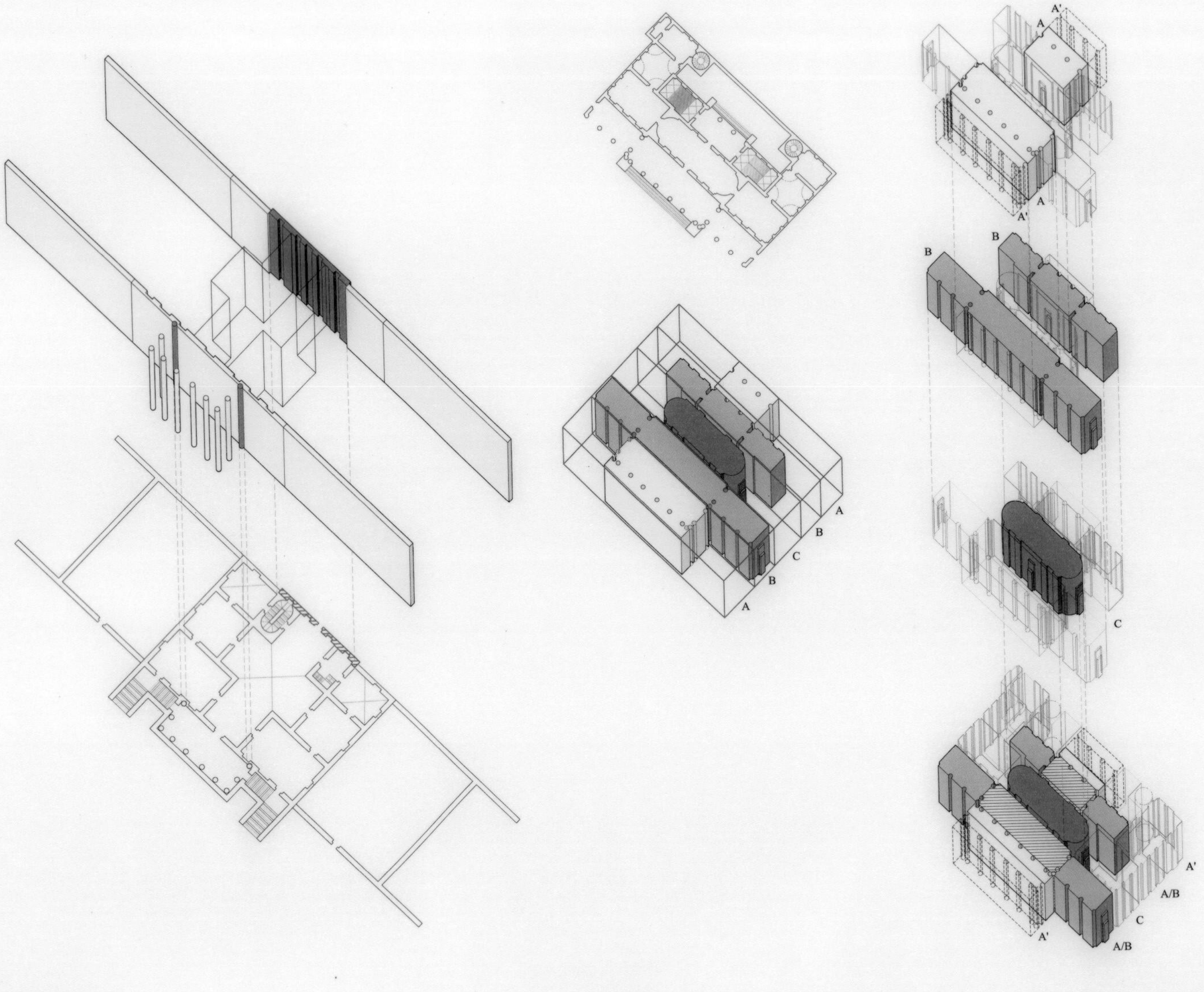

There was to have been a series of garden walls at the Villa Foscari—proto-barchesse—on which the main body of the villa sat. Diagram of Villa Foscari from *Palladio Virtuel*, 2015. © Peter Eisenman with Matt Roman.

Julian Rose The theme of our lecture series this past fall was authorship, but you spoke about authority. While I can see how the two might be related, I think there are important distinctions between them as well. One can certainly imagine modes of architectural authorship that don't appeal to authority—collective authorship or different kinds of mediated authorship in which the author is perhaps even trying to undermine his or her own authority. I would like to begin our conversation by asking what you see as the relationship between these two terms.

Peter Eisenman We need to re-establish the idea of authority in architecture. When Michael Graves and I taught at Princeton from 1963 to 1967, for example, Le Corbusier was an authority. And we didn't have to have any pedagogic position other than the fact that we referred to Le Corbusier. We referred to the five points, the four compositions. Every student had the *Oeuvre Complete* on his desk. (*His* desk. There were no hers.) And the people that we invited to the juries understood all the same references. There was an authority, but there was no authorship.

JR It's impossible to imagine a similar situation today.

PE The modern is no longer an authority. But I still believe that a student needs a starting point for every project. You give them an empty site, you tell them to do a housing project or a museum. What does the student do? How can they proceed? They must have some kind of precedent. And that precedent, in a sense, is the authority. It changes from time to time. The precedent could be renaissance, baroque, classical, modern, post-modern, digital, whatever, but we still need a pedagogy to establish what the nature of authority is. And it is always a disciplinary authority—which has nothing to do with authorship. It has to do with some external condition that animates one's own work. Whether it is Mies, whether it is Corbusier, whether it is Wright.

JR If I'm following you, your point is not that those figures should be celebrated as great authors, per se. You're saying that each of them is addressing certain disciplinary problems in their work and, in a sense, students can use them as a lens to examine those same disciplinary problems.

PE That's exactly right. My book *Palladio Virtuel*, for example, is about a pedagogical theory that I am working on, which says that the way to move against power in architecture is to move against the ideal. This is something that Rosalind Krauss talked about in her article "Death of a Hermeneutic Phantom." She argues that architecture is held back by a certain latent idealism—a way of thinking about technology, material, etc. In the other arts, modernism was about breaking down the idealism. That's what happened in painting, sculpture, film. But Krauss says that modern architecture never realized its full potential because of this latent idealist phantom. And we, as a discipline, need to exorcise this ghost. So I go to Palladio, who is held up by Colin Rowe as a step in the evolution towards an idealist condition of the Villa. *Palladio Virtuel* says this is wrong and that Palladio was actually about the declination of idealism. All of my teaching and my work in the last five or six years—Eisenman's late style, you might say—

is an attempted denial of the ideal. I am not working against authorship, I am against the disciplinary authority of the ideal. In other words, I am attempting to open up architecture to other kinds of disciplinary authority.

JR If there is no central point of reference, with what do you replace the ideal? Is it a pedagogical problem that there is no equivalent to Corbusier today?

PE It might be a good thing. If Corbusier's pedagogy is laced with the ideal then we need to replace it.

JR I don't know whether to believe that this is an entirely new turn for you. Did you ever take Corbusier at face value, even back in the 1960s, when you say you held him up as the ultimate authority? Didn't you already understand yourself as somehow continuing or inflecting the modernist project? I am not necessarily saying that you were already post-modern.

PE I would argue that I have always been a modernist but one that never realized the modernist project. Modernism has been a project of questioning idealism, even if—as Rosalind said—architecture never achieved that in the same way as other disciplines. My dissertation, *The Formal Basis of Modern Architecture*, which is the beginning of my work, is an attempt to replace a late 18th century, early 19th century idea of authority, the whole notion of the ideal that comes through Kant, with something from today—whatever today is. And this "today" has extended for forty or fifty years now. I'm not the only one who tried this. Venturi took a stab at it. Rossi took a stab at it. Stirling, Ungers, Koolhaas—there are any number of them today and there are other examples of questioning the idealism of architecture.

JR It's interesting to me that you just mentioned Venturi, Rossi, and Stirling. One way of trying to undermine the authority of modernism (and here I'm referring to the idealist, Kantian side of modernism that you've identified as a problem in architecture, not the other side of modernism that Krauss was talking about, which we could maybe call the critical project of modernism), is to refer back to history. History is one form of disciplinarity and I would argue that Venturi, Rossi, and Stirling all looked for an alternative there. But how do you position yourself in relation to architectural history? For me, *The Formal Basis of Modern Architecture* is not a historical book—I'm not quite sure what to call it—but maybe it is a methodological book, in a way that *The Architecture of the City* is not.

PE It is a grammatical book.

JR That's a better term.

PE And that is where linguistics comes in. My interest in linguistics has always been as a way to study the internal grammatical structure of architecture. In the '60s, I spent two summers in Italy with Colin Rowe. And what did we look at? Painting. But get this, I wasn't allowed to look at the Sistine Chapel. I was not allowed to see the Laurentian Library. Because that was Michelangelo, and Michelangelo was a problem. His work was pure affect. I was on the track of the grammatical, which stands opposed to

LA SEGVENTE fabrica è del Conte Odoardo, & Conte Theodoro fratelli de' Thieni, in Cigogna ſua Villa, la qual fabrica fu principiata dal Conte Franceſco loro padre. La Sala è nel mezo della caſa, & ha intorno alcune colonne Ioniche, ſopra le quali è vn poggiuolo al pari del piano delle ſtanze di ſopra: Il volto di queſta Sala giugne ſino ſotto il tetto: le ſtanze grandi hanno i uolti à ſchiffo, e le quadrate à mezo cadino, e ſi alzano in modo, che fanno quattro torricelle ne gli angoli della fabrica: i camerini hanno ſopra i loro mezati: le porte de' quali riſpondono al mezo delle ſcale. Sono le ſcale ſenza muro nel mezo, e perche la ſala per riceuere il lume di ſopra è luminoſiſsima, eſſe ancora hanno lume à baſtanza, e tanto più che eſſendo uacue nel mezo; riceuono il lume ancho di ſopra: in vno de' coperti, che ſono per fianco del cortile ui ſono le cantine, e i granari, e nell'altro le ſtalle, e i luoghi per la Villa. Quelle due loggie, che come braccia, eſcono fuor della fabrica; ſono fatte per vnir la caſa del padrone con quella di Villa: ſono appreſſo queſta fabrica due cortili di fabrica vecchia con portici, l'vno per lo trebbiar de' grani, e l'altro per la famiglia più minuta.

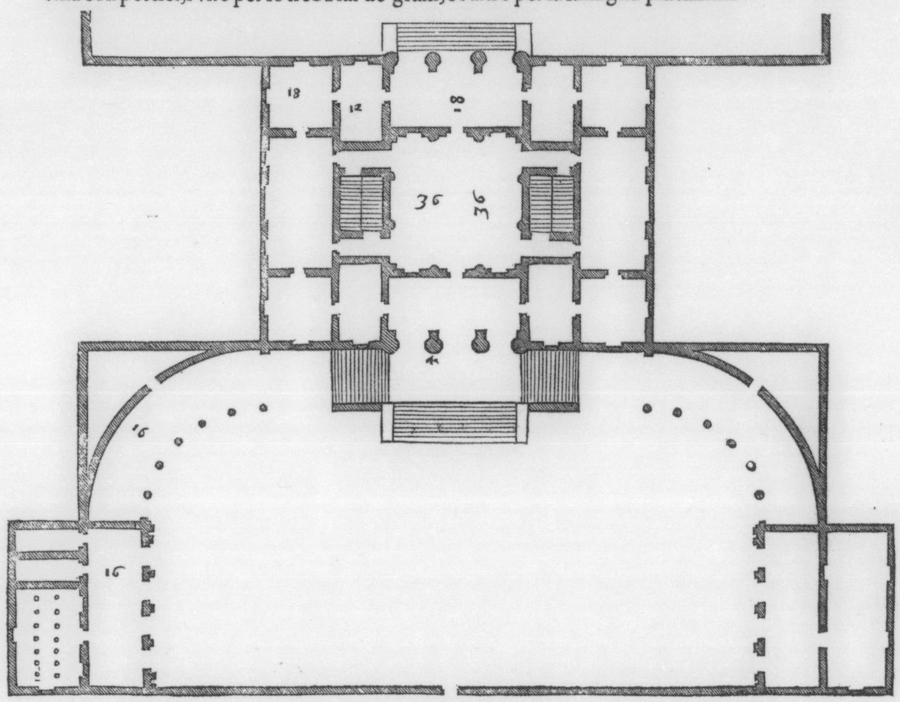

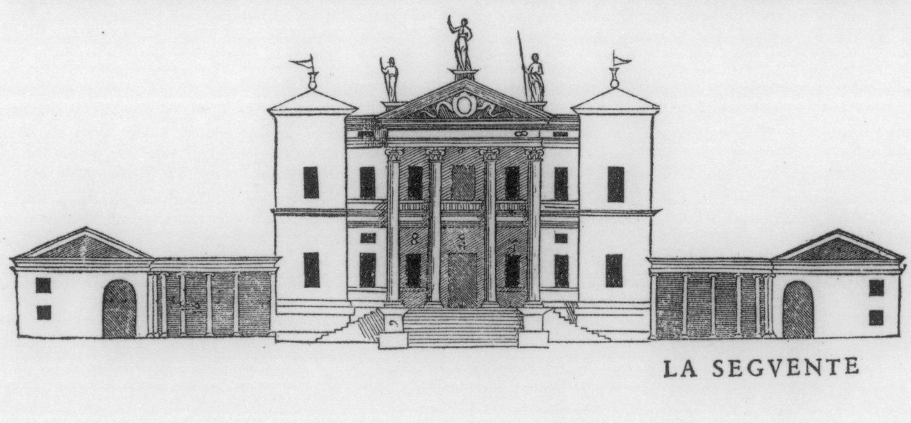

LA SEGVENTE

Andrea Palladio's 1556 plan and elevation drawing of Villa Thiene in the *I Quattro Libri Dell'architecttura*, 1570. Courtesy of Peter Eisenman with Matt Roman.

LA SEGVENTE fabrica è del Conte Odoardo, & Conte Theodoro fratelli de' Thieni, in Cigogna sua Villa, la qual fabrica fu principiata dal Conte Francesco loro padre. La Sala è nel mezo della casa, & ha intorno alcune colonne Ioniche, sopra le quali è vn poggiuolo al pari del piano delle stanze di sopra: Il volto di questa Sala giugne fino sotto il tetto: le stanze grandi hanno i uolti à schifo, e le quadrate à mezo cadino, e si alzano in modo, che fanno quattro torricelle ne gli angoli del la fabrica: i camerini hanno sopra i loro mezati: le porte de' quali rispondono al mezo delle scale. Sono le scale senza muro nel mezo, e perche la sala per riceuere il lume di sopra è luminosissima, esse ancora hanno lume à bastanza, e tanto più che essendo uacue nel mezo; riceuono il lume ancho di sopra: in vno de' coperti, che sono per fianco del cortile ui sono le cantine, e i granari, e nell'altro le stalle, e i luoghi per la Villa. Quelle due loggie, che come braccia, escono fuor della fabrica; sono fatte per vnir la casa del padrone con quella di Villa: sono appresso questa fabrica due cortili di fabrica vecchia con portici, l'vno per lo trebbiar de' grani, e l'altro per la famiglia più minuta.

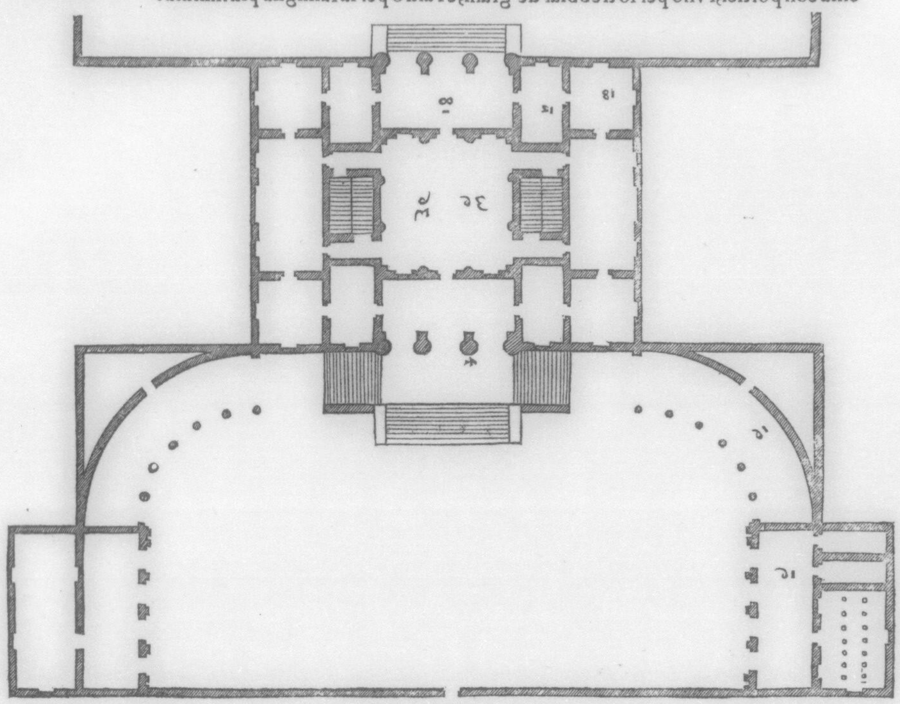

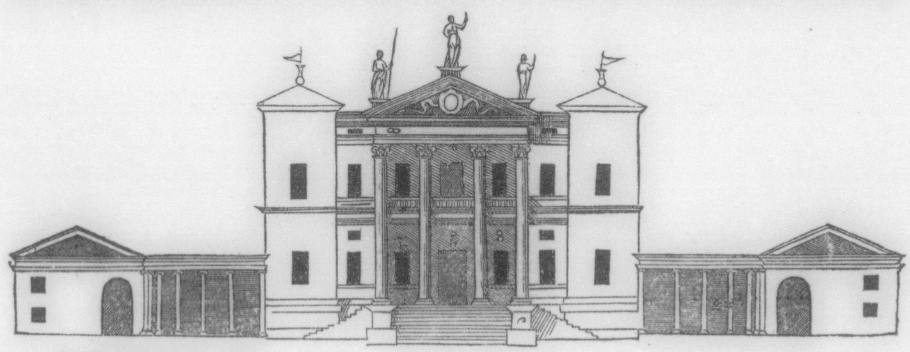

LA SEGVENTE

Andrea Palladio's 1556 plan and elevation drawing of Villa Thiene in the *I Quattro Libri Dell'architecttura*, 1570. Courtesy of Peter Eisenman with Matt Roman.

affect. And I still take my students to Italy, 50 years later.

JR I want to get back to affect, because I think that is something that you and I both have strong feelings about. But first a quick question about the process you're describing, which I think could be defined as teaching the act of looking. Maybe one answer to my earlier question about the pedagogical problem raised by the lack of a single authority figure is simply that the necessity for these methods of looking closely has not changed. So the fundamental pedagogical mission is the same, no matter what precedents you're looking at or who you consider to be the authority.

PE I would argue that, yes.

JR We're talking about looking, we're talking about grammars—all of this seems to presuppose a viewer, a reader, some kind of subject. Does your theory of formal grammar require a corresponding theory of subjectivity? It strikes me that this other side of things, the side of reception, doesn't get talked about as much in relation to your work.

PE I am not convinced that what I do demands a subject. I am talking about an eye—one that is an architect's eye as opposed to a historian's eye or a theoretician's eye. In other words, Tafuri couldn't see at all, in this sense; Colin Rowe could see, but only see in a very limited sense. An architect must see as an architect but they have to be taught. That is not a theory of the subject. That is pedagogical.

JR Ok, so you're more interested in methods of reading than readers themselves.

PE Joyce, for example, had no interest in the reader. He wrote. And I have no interest in the subject.

JR But Joyce takes us back to modernism and to ideas of difficulty, or even illegibility, which I know you've written about. I could argue that that was a political project. The goal was precisely to have a certain effect on the reader or viewer, to heighten their awareness, in a sense. Viktor Shklovsky's theory of defamiliarization might be the best example of this.

PE Shklovksy is part of my idea of ineloquence. He is talking about using art as a device to disrupt the easy flow of information.

JR Exactly. So what I want to propose is a way in which a disciplinary project doesn't necessarily have to be only self-referential or autonomous, as we architects might say. There's a way in which disciplinary technique can itself be a source of agency. To use another example from modernism, consider the development of the housing block in the early twentieth century. You could say that this is a fundamentally architectural move—it's expanding the discipline by inventing a new building type, it's exploiting new construction technologies, experimenting with new theories of spatial organization, and so on. But it's also directly addressing a social problem—the housing of workers—so it is also a form of political action.

It's not what we might call activist architecture today, it's not asking every worker to build his or her own house, but it's still inherently political.

PE Right, the housing block was a political instrument for modernist architecture. But it isn't any longer. Today, we're moving in the opposite direction. Everyone is questioning the idea of expertise, of disciplinary thinking. Why do we need an expert? We want everybody to participate. The activist argument today is that we don't need any authority, in fact we need to get rid of authority to have agency.

JR Certainly that was one of the arguments put forward by the last Venice Biennale.

PE But the problem for me, and this is also what Jeff Kipnis argues in his essay "By Other Means," is that the kind of activism represented by Aravena's Biennale is merely an alternative prescription for power. In other words, it is using power in a sublimated way. It is a form of populism.

JR And is that where affect comes back into the conversation? Because populism, arguably, always trades in affect.

PE That's why I don't do affect, and why I am not interested in the experience of architecture. Experience is easy to coopt.

JR Hence your emphasis on grammar, which offers more resistance?

PE Exactly.

JR That's interesting. I have always understood the focus on grammar as primarily a turn inward. This conversation, however, opens up the possibility for a kind of architectural expertise that could enable a form of authorship, one that is not authoritarian and doesn't need to be opposed to activism, which could maybe even help architects regain some level of political agency—authorship in a positive sense—precisely by leveraging their disciplinary expertise. Which gets back to your emphasis on pedagogy, I suppose.

PE Right. I can't argue against the populist Aravena line, but I don't need to, because you can't escape certain architectural questions. Ultimately, every architect—and every one of our students, yours at Princeton and mine at Yale—has to give form to something.

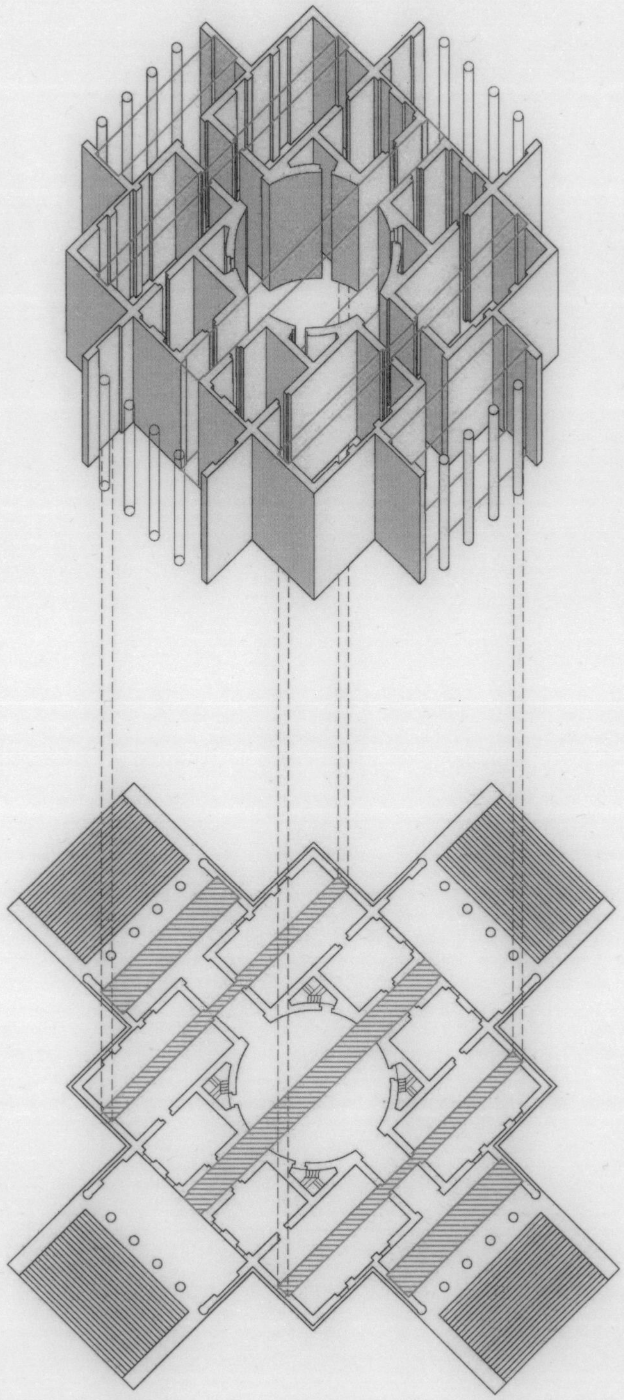

Contiguous lateral layers in the Villa Rotunda. Diagram from *Palladio Virtuel*, 2015. © Peter Eisenman with Matt Roman.

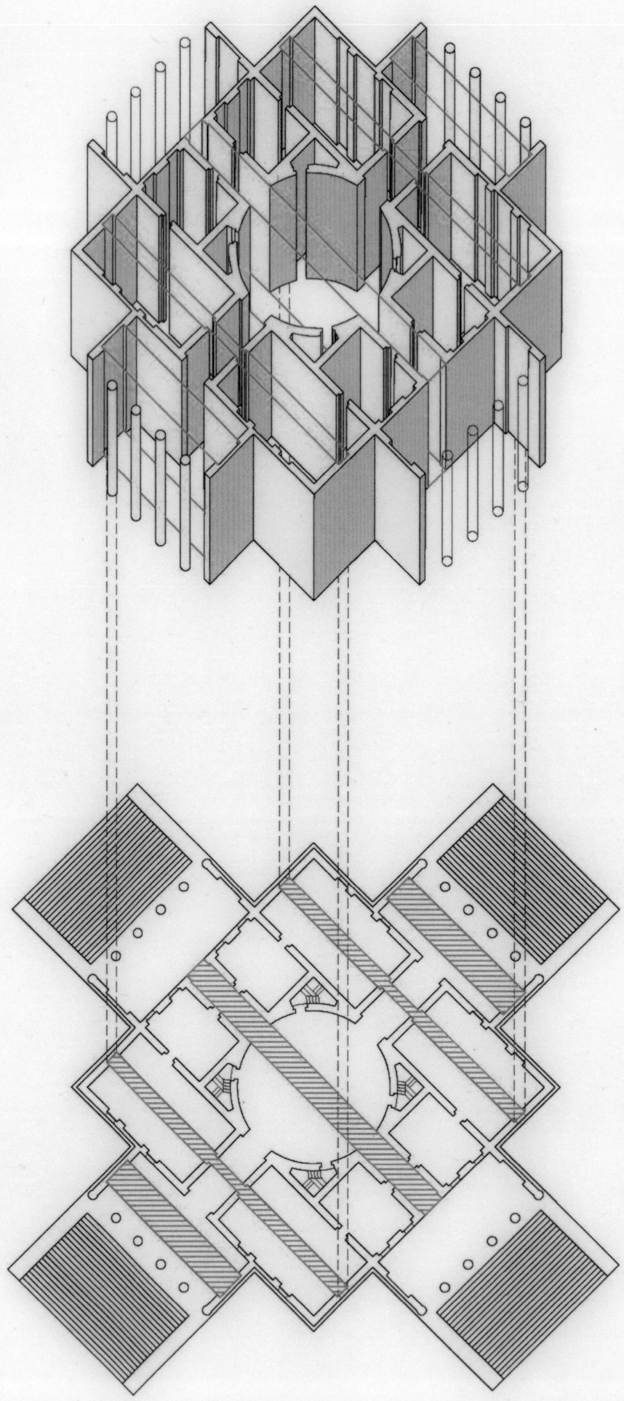

Contiguous lateral layers in the Villa Rotunda. Diagram from *Palladio Virtuel*, 2015. © Peter Eisenman with Matt Roman.

Creative Miscegenation in Architecture, a Theorem

Marshall Brown

Model view from above the Tower with the Temple and Black Box Theater in foreground, Dequindre Civic Academy, 2016. From the collection of the San Francisco Museum of Modern Art. Courtesy of the author.

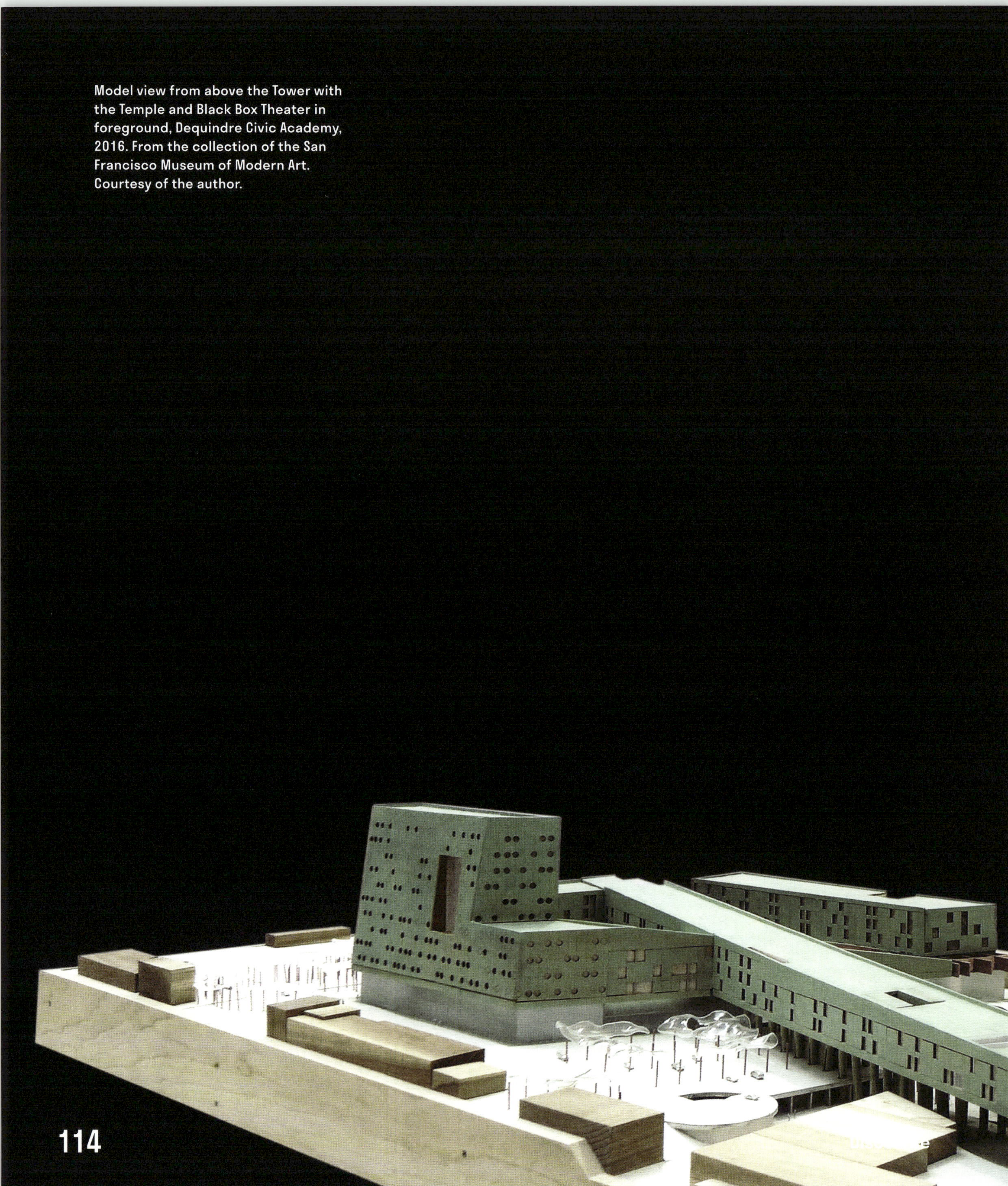

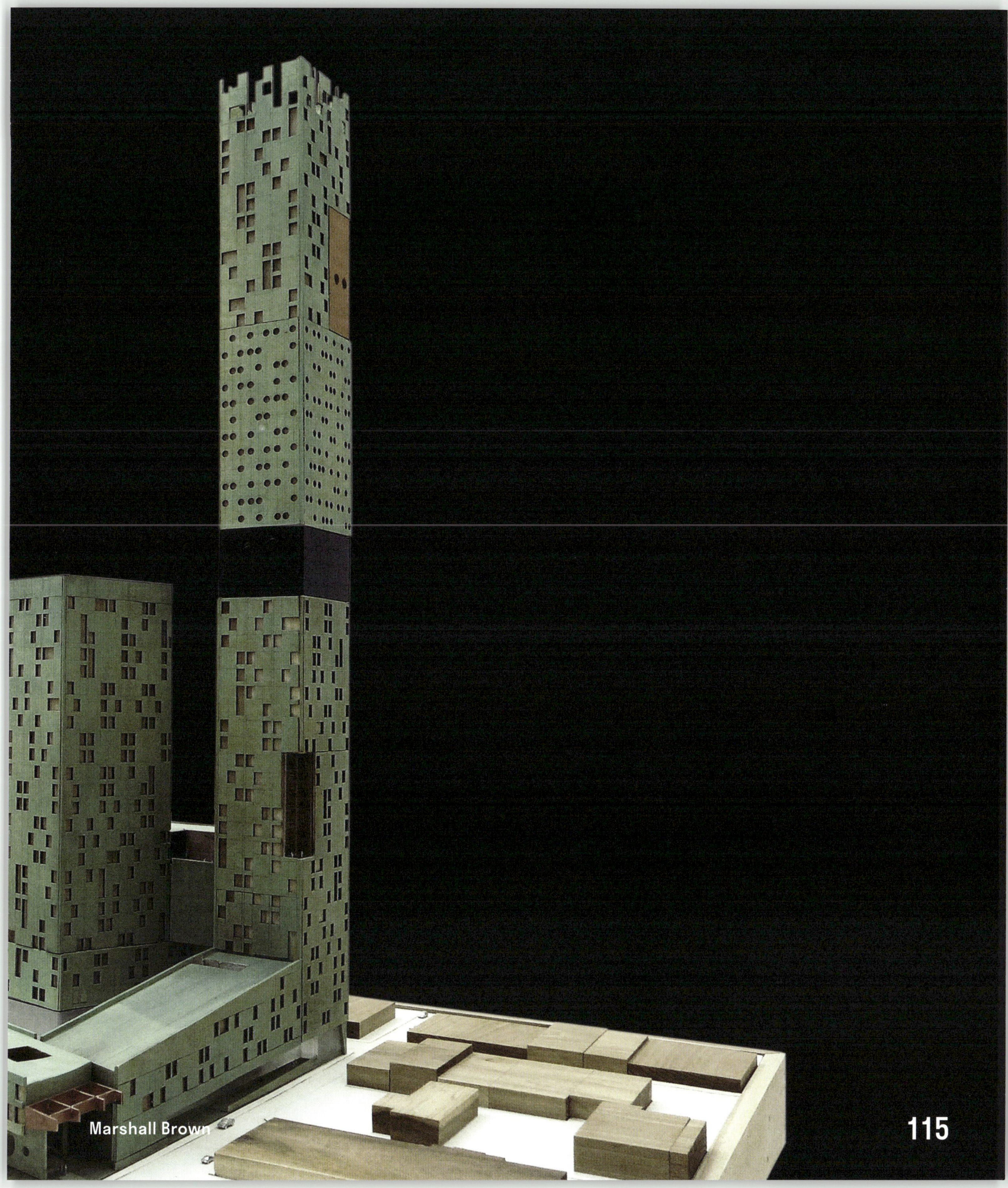

What are the sources of architectural ideas? Every project by any architect is infected with references from across architectural history, regardless of their awareness or recognition of the sources. Yet unlike many other fields today, the culture of architecture still worships lone creative geniuses and traffics in myths of sole authorship. The crisis of copyright has made the notion of authorship both highly unstable and indeterminate, as originality is increasingly difficult to claim and influences are far easier to trace. Authorial control, ownership, and copyright are highly endangered concepts as digital media becomes widespread. The last forty years of technological development radically transformed our entire concept of creation across the creative fields. Sampling, remixing, open source, digital fabrication, and parametric technology have replaced prototypes with *versions*—the limitless production of options without ideal types. We now live in a world of relentless variation, where anything and everything is a readymade subject to sampling and remixing. Open source culture has in many ways contributed to what Peter Eisenman is now calling "the end of authority." However, authority is a matter of overt control. As such, authority may be less important for architecture than the more subtle workings of influence, which is perhaps as strong a force as it's ever been. Authority must be challenged in order for any creative field to progress. In the case of architecture, the historical evidence for this argument is abundant. But the novelist Jonathan Lethem reminds us that influence (not authority) is actually the social intercourse that binds creative work within what he calls a "gift economy."[1] In "The Ecstasy of Influence, a Plagiarism," Lethem writes:

> Finding one's voice isn't just an emptying and purifying oneself of the words of others but an adopting and embracing of filiations, communities, and discourses. Inspiration could be called inhaling the memory of an act never experienced. Invention, it must be humbly admitted, does not consist in creating out of void but out of chaos. Any artist knows these truths, no matter how deeply he or she submerges that knowing.[2]

My own search for an authorship embracing, in Lethem's words, "filiations, communities, and discourses" has led to projects that not only depend upon influence, but also celebrate it as an architectural idea. At the levels of technique, content, and form, the idea of sole authorship is consistently undermined through active and open engagement with architectural references. The work revolves around a theorem. This theorem of creative miscegenation states that *the legibility of architectural configurations is engendered by their promiscuous associations among a generalized discursive field.* Miscegenation is, of course, an archaic term typically associated with racist laws that forbade mixed marriages and racial interbreeding. In this context it serves as an adequately subversive name for the sublime world of architectural half-breeds.

The theorem's first assertion is about legibility, which means a work of architecture cannot be understood outside of the larger field of which it is part. A recent project from my practice is a demonstration of this principle: an expansive series of collages named from the mythical three-bodied monster in classical literature, the Chimera. The images are rapid, individualized, and serial acts of world-making. Architectonic fragments are sampled from journals and books, then hand cut and pasted to create new architecture. Careful attention is paid to the concealment of seams between different sources, resulting in what could also be called stealth collage. The Chimera have neither programs nor sites, rather they have the quality of sketches or ideograms. One collage became the source material for Ziggurat, a garden folly for the Arts Club of Chicago. In the tradition of garden follies, this ten foot structure clad in foamed aluminum has no program. The project is translated from a single collage comprised of Peter Eisenman's Koizumi Sangyo Corporation Headquarters, Frank Gehry's Schnabel House, and Zaha Hadid's Rosenthal Center for Contemporary Art. As in the collage, the articulation of seams is critical to the project's design. One-half inch open reveals run across surfaces and around corners, unifying the volumes and creating the illusion of large masonry-like masses.

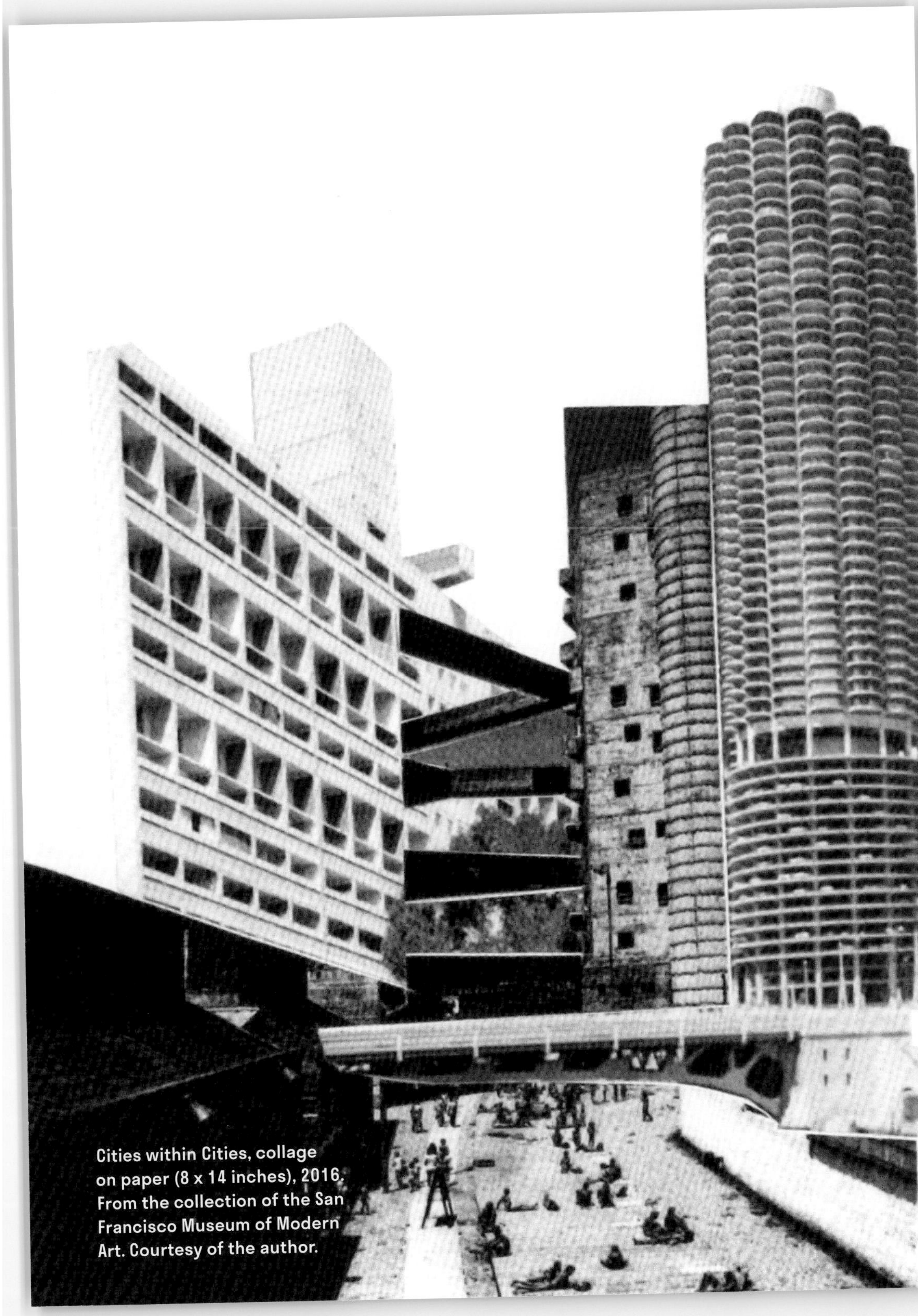

Cities within Cities, collage on paper (8 x 14 inches), 2016. From the collection of the San Francisco Museum of Modern Art. Courtesy of the author.

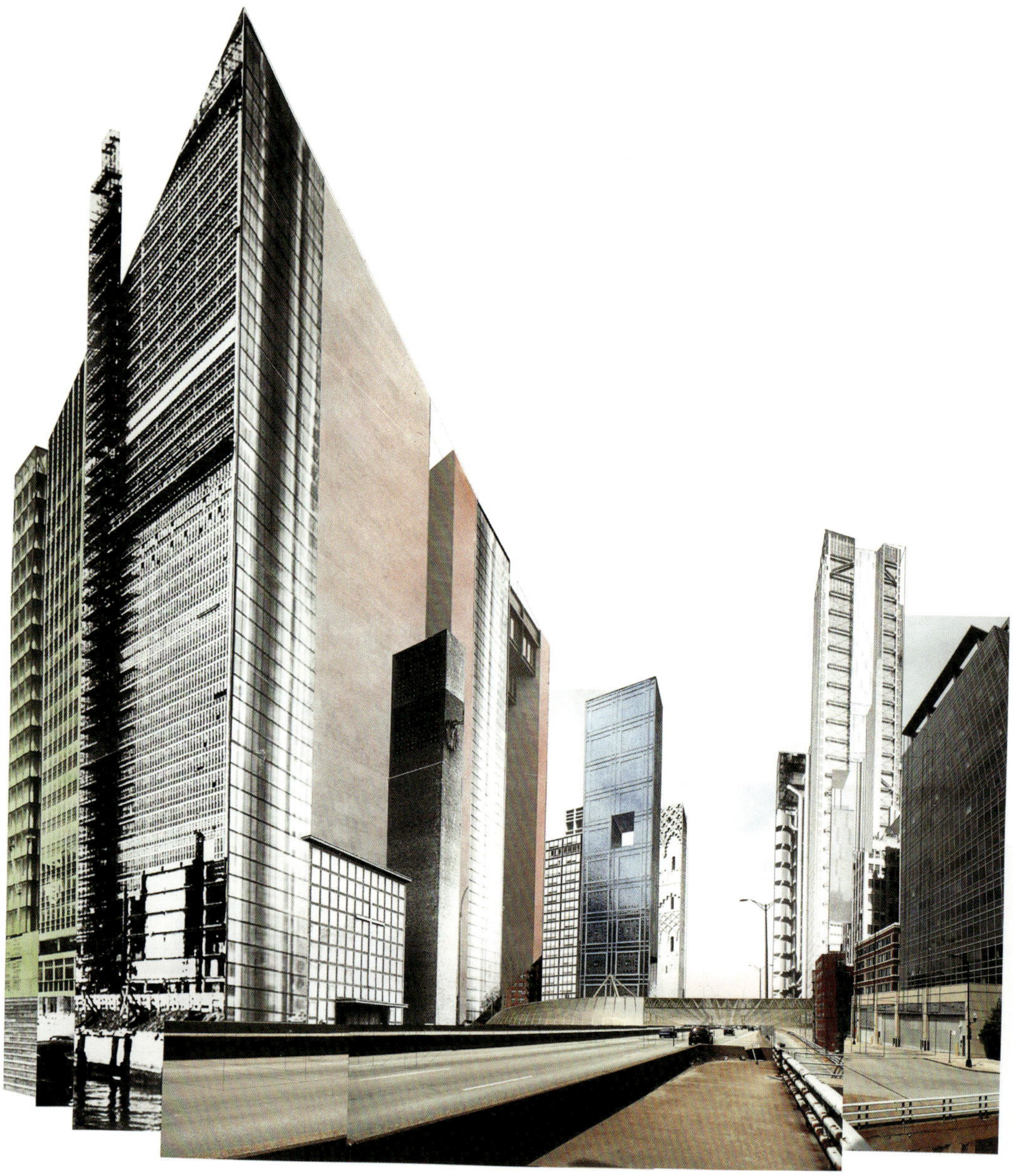

“Holy City #1” from The Chimera Series, photomontage on inkjet print (50 x 36 inches), 2013. Courtesy of the author.

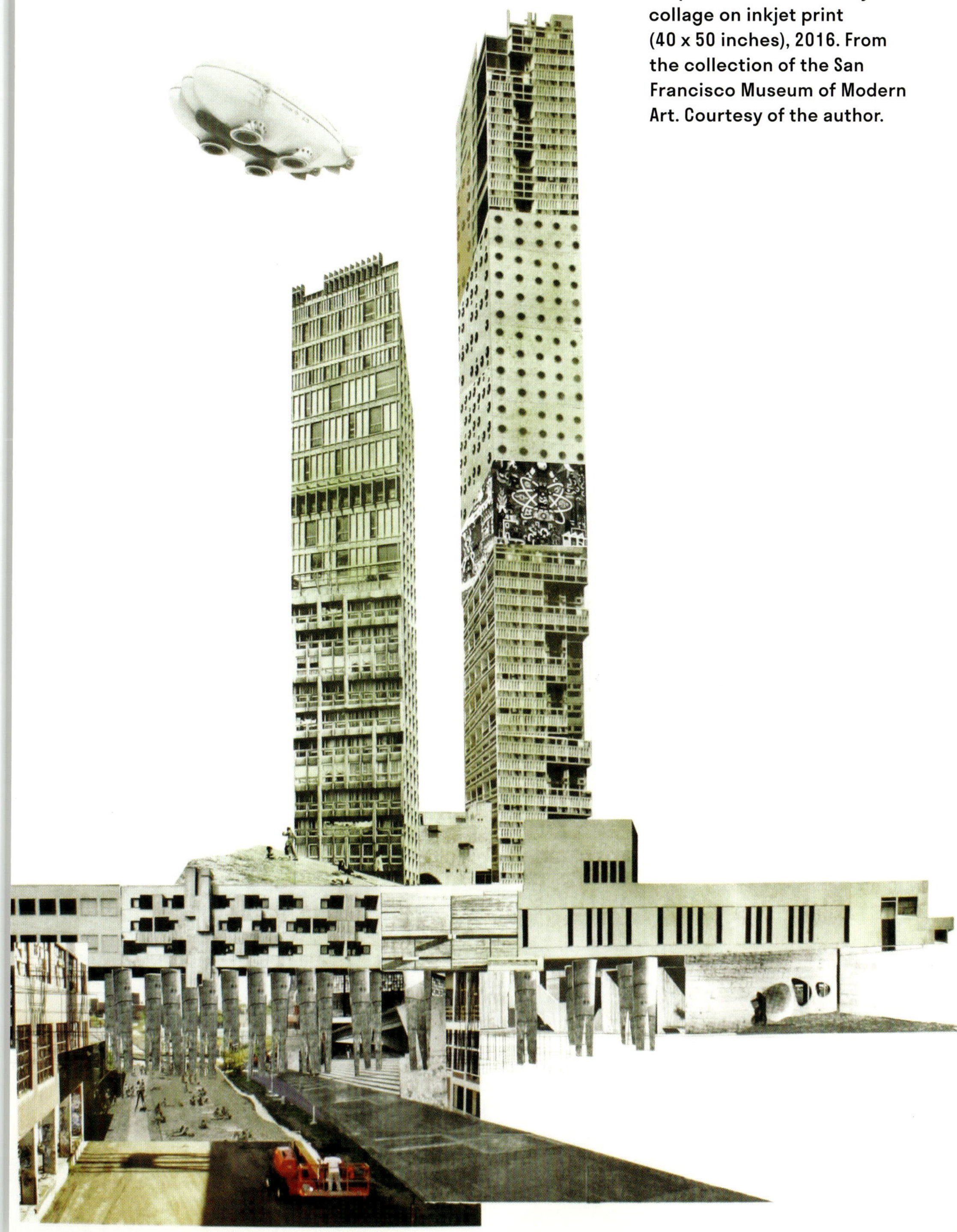

"Towards A Coordinate Unit," Dequindre Civic Academy, collage on inkjet print (40 x 50 inches), 2016. From the collection of the San Francisco Museum of Modern Art. Courtesy of the author.

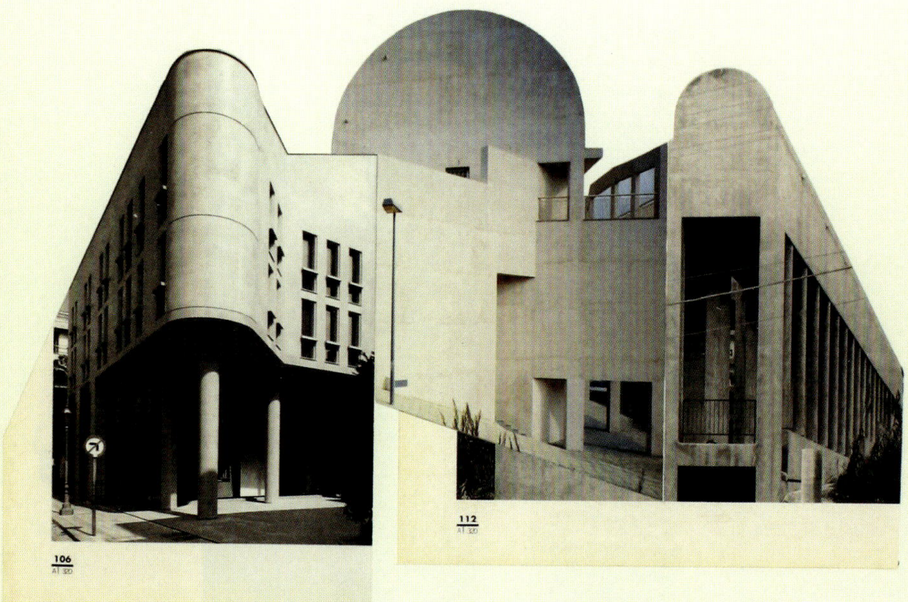

"Chimera 14-03-20" from The Chimera Series, collage on paper (14 x 17 inches), 2014. Courtesy of the author.

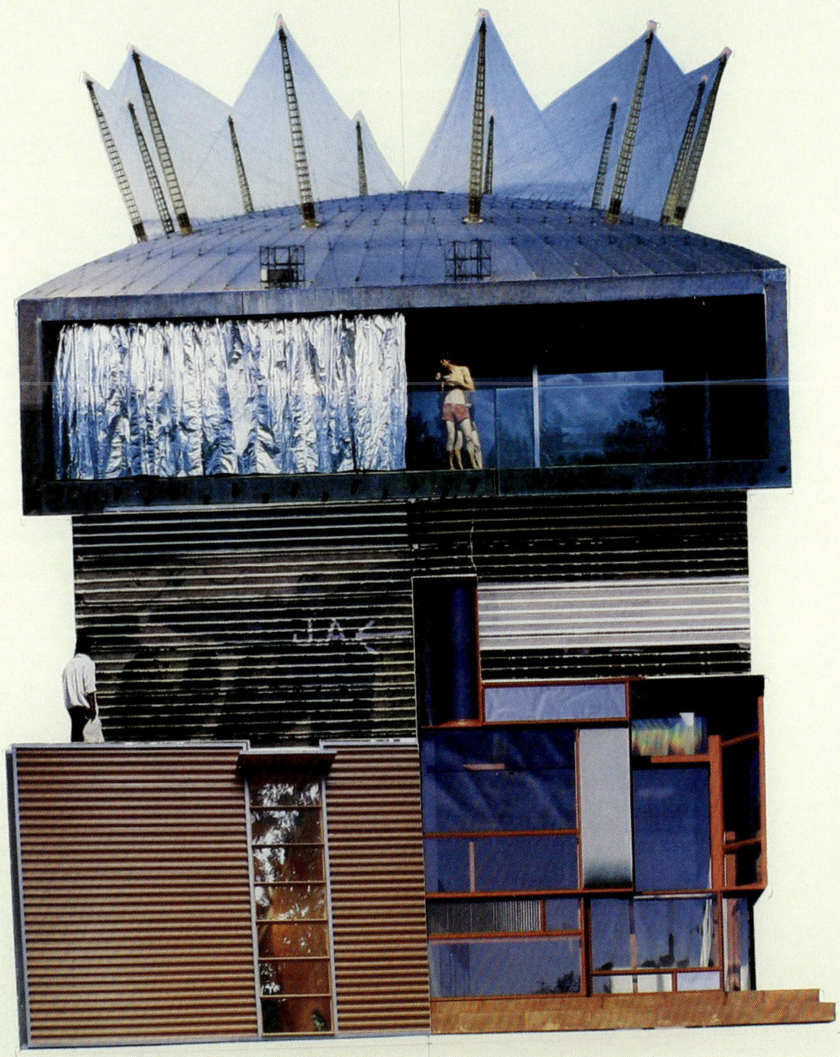

"Chimera 14-12-17(2)" from The Chimera Series, collage on paper (14 x 17 inches), 2014. Courtesy of the author.

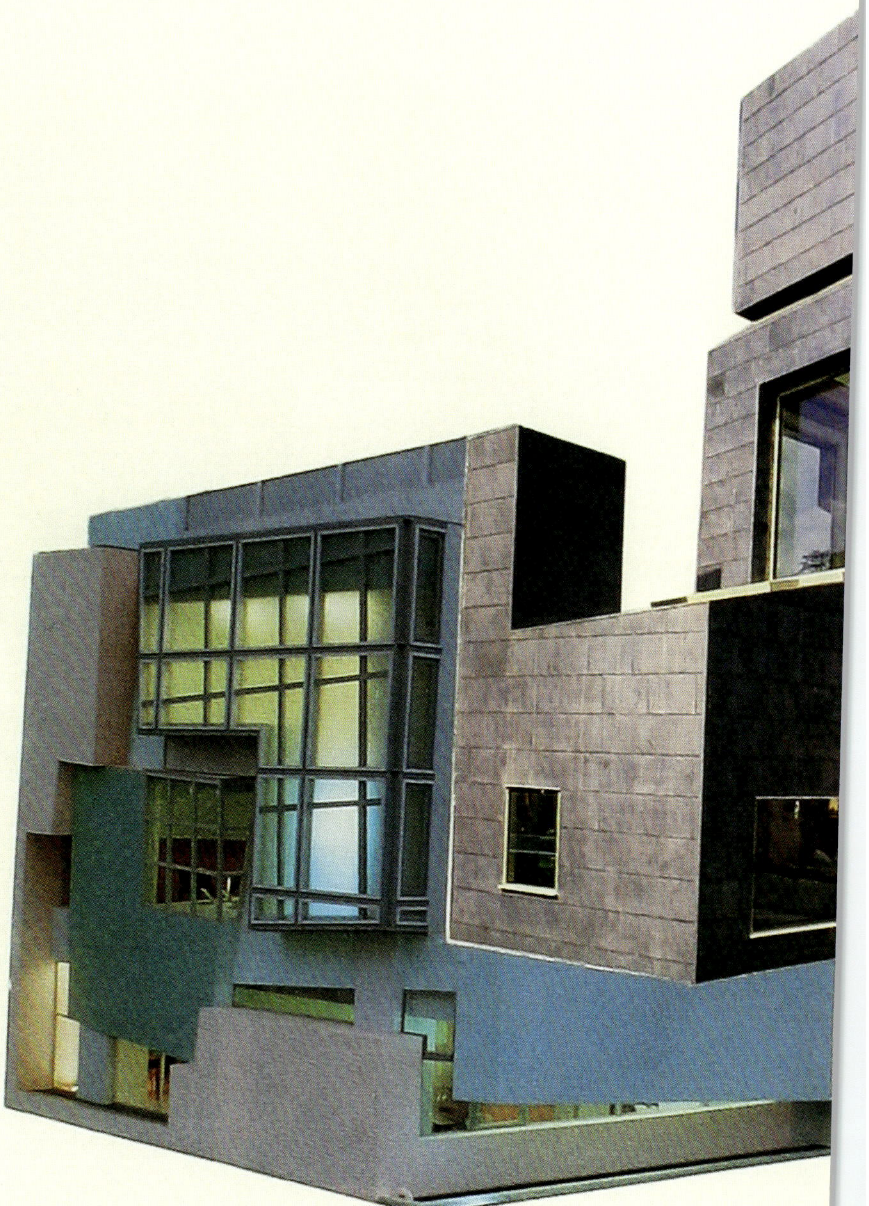

"March 10, 2014" from The Chimera Series, collage on paper (14 x 17 inches), 2014. Courtesy of the author.

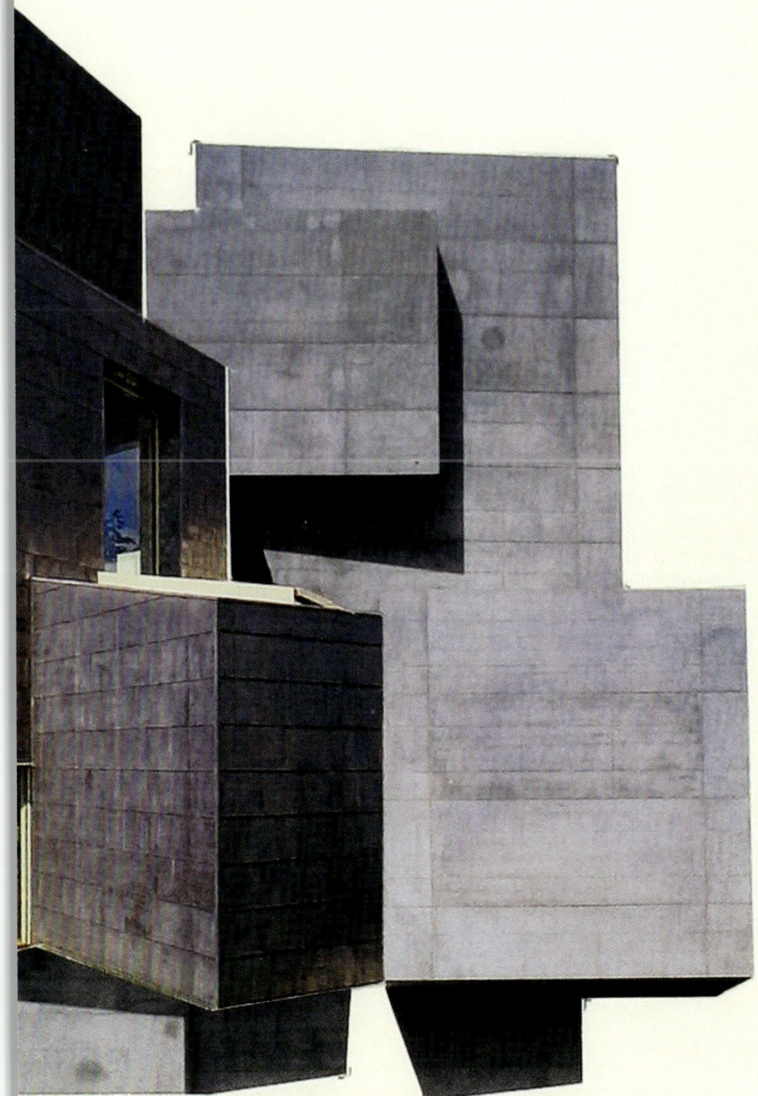

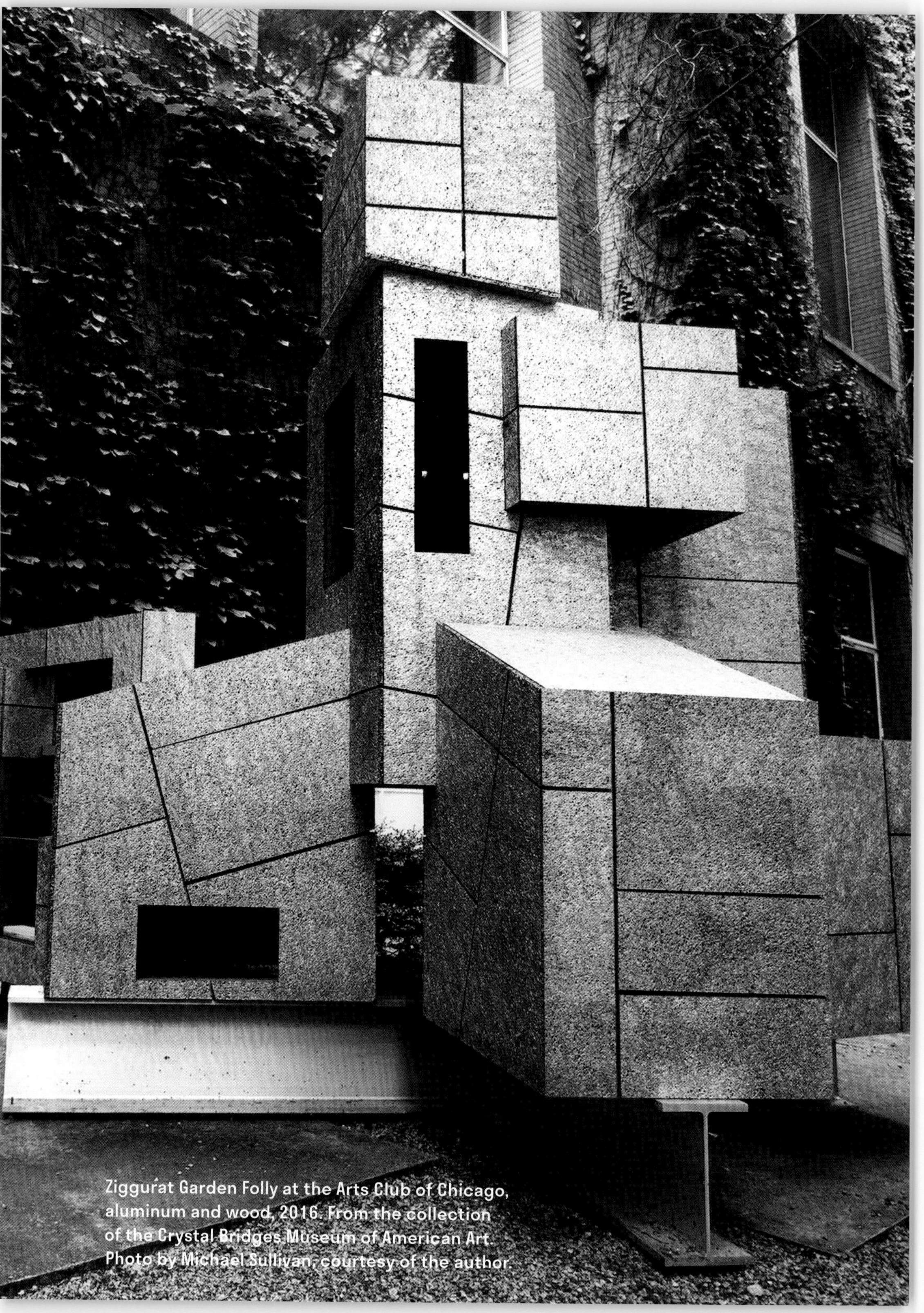

Ziggurat Garden Folly at the Arts Club of Chicago, aluminum and wood, 2016. From the collection of the Crystal Bridges Museum of American Art. Photo by Michael Sullivan, courtesy of the author.

Though the Ziggurat begins with discreet and identifiable sources, the sources are subsumed within the whole, resulting in a new work of architecture. This leads to the second assertion of the theorem—promiscuity—in which a work is not constrained by its precedents, but creates a new set of possible relations between them and itself, a kind of ménage à trois. The Dequindre Civic Academy (DCA) for the U.S. Pavilion at the 2016 Venice Biennale is an extension of the "city within the city" paradigm that has existed for some time in architectural discourses. The smallest collage included in the exhibition is a sketch produced after the initial site visit. It brings Le Corbusier's Unite d'Habitation, Lina Bo Bardi's SESC Pompéia, and Bertrand Goldberg's Marina City together in a single urban complex. In more complex projects like the DCA, the collages work as both sketches and provocations. They ground the project in a particular architectural legacy, instilling it with specific architectonic and formal qualities. Drawings and models then struggle to reconcile the dream of the collage with the demands of site and program. When comparing the collages with more detailed models and drawings that followed, it becomes evident that the project supersedes its sources, while still carrying their influences at various scales. Such intermarrying is a transgression of form making as the imposition of order and identity.

Though the architecture of creative miscegenation begins with the violence of cutting and tearing, it is still a constructive praxis. What begins with intuition and error proceeds with discipline, as the inheritance of history and material culture are dismantled, realigned, and painstakingly reassembled to create new forms and spaces. One hundred years ago, the Dadaists and Constructivists used collage to shock by employing juxtaposition and disjunction. Postmodernist architects used collage toward the end of the twentieth century to recover form as petrified history. The architecture of creative miscegenation has a different agenda. Even if the samples are sometimes identifiable, all parts are synthesized within the whole. Creative miscegenation is architectonic—an art of joining. The collage of disjunction becomes a collage of deception through merging disparate elements. This approach expands the possibilities of authorship in design by positioning architecture as the formation of new alignments and new legibilities that allow us to navigate the increasing complexity of contemporary culture.

1 Lethem argues that creative works exist within a gift economy that establishes a bond between two people, which does not necessarily occur in a market economy, for example. See Jonathan Lethem, "The Ecstasy of Influence, A Plagiarism," *Harpers* (February 2007), 59–71.

2 Ibid.

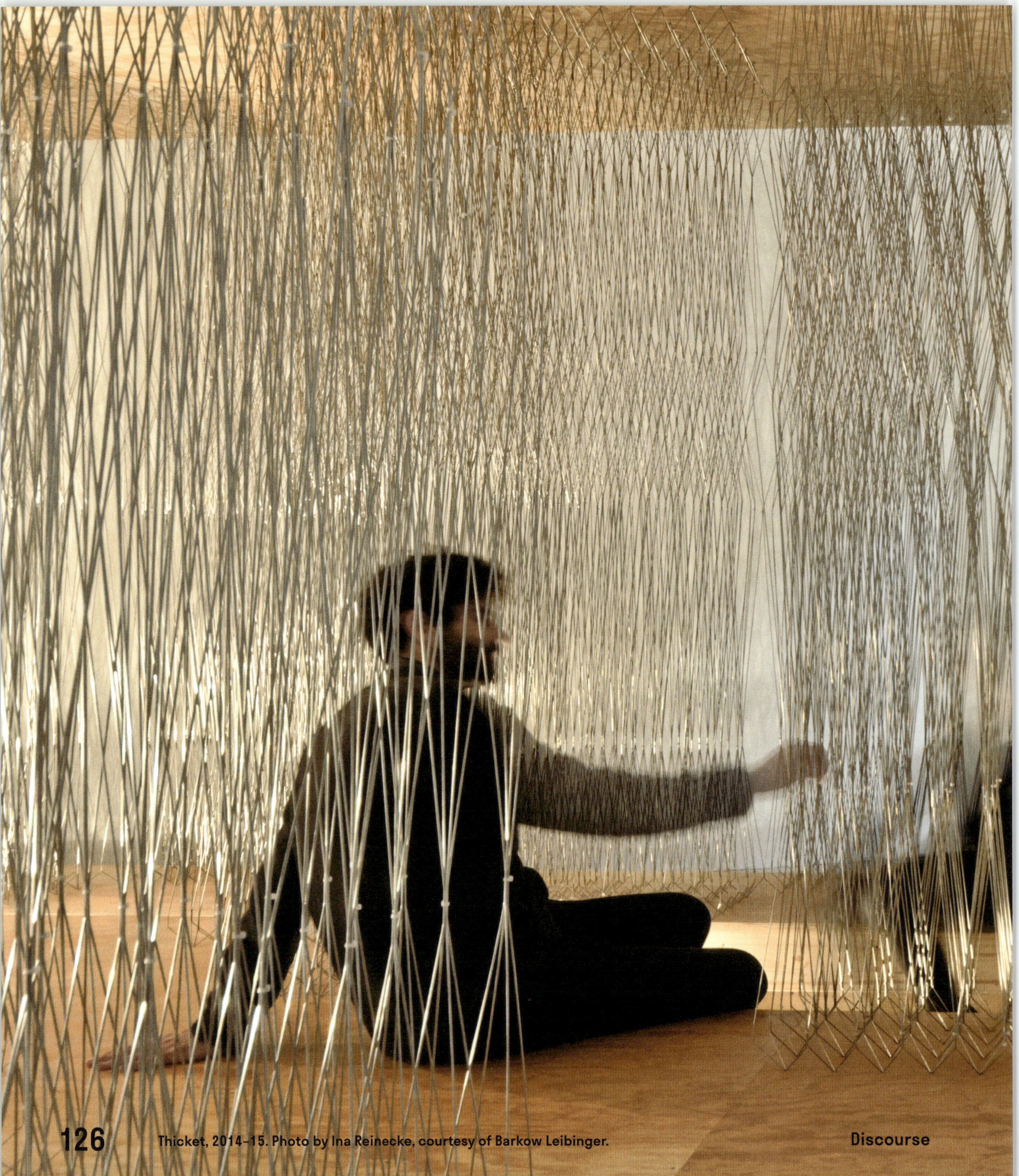

Thicket, 2014–15. Photo by Ina Reinecke, courtesy of Barkow Leibinger.

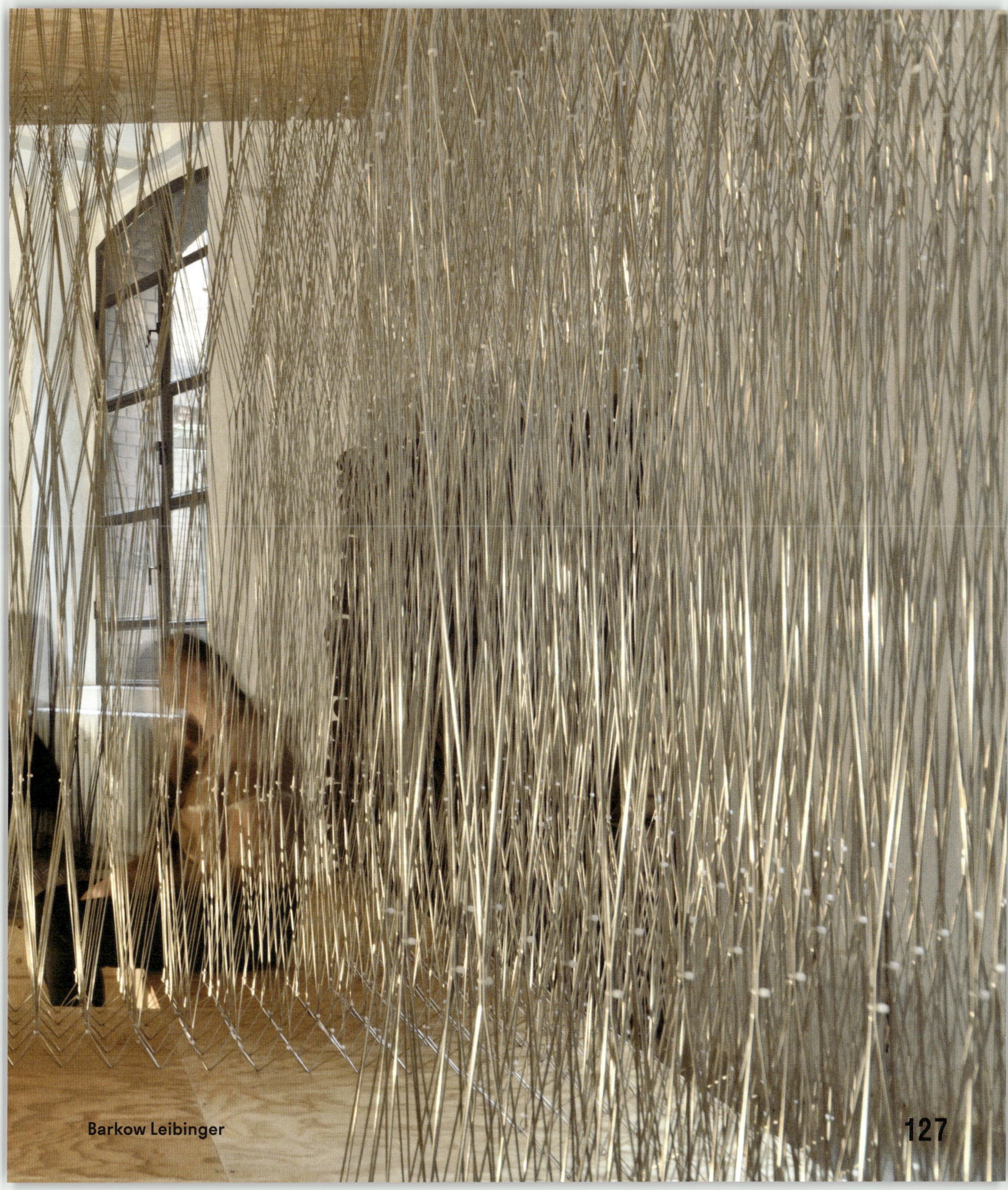

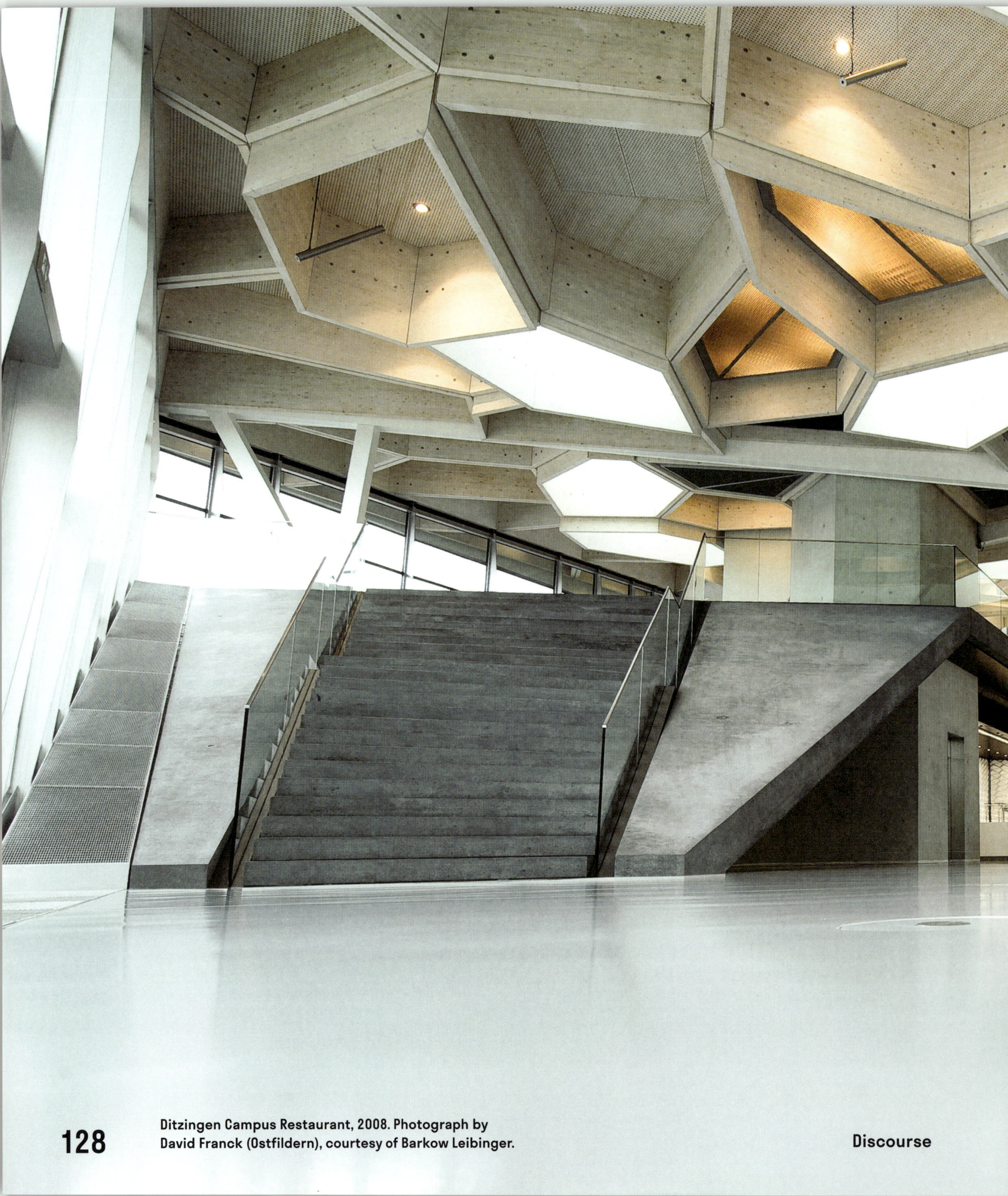

Ditzingen Campus Restaurant, 2008. Photograph by David Franck (Ostfildern), courtesy of Barkow Leibinger.

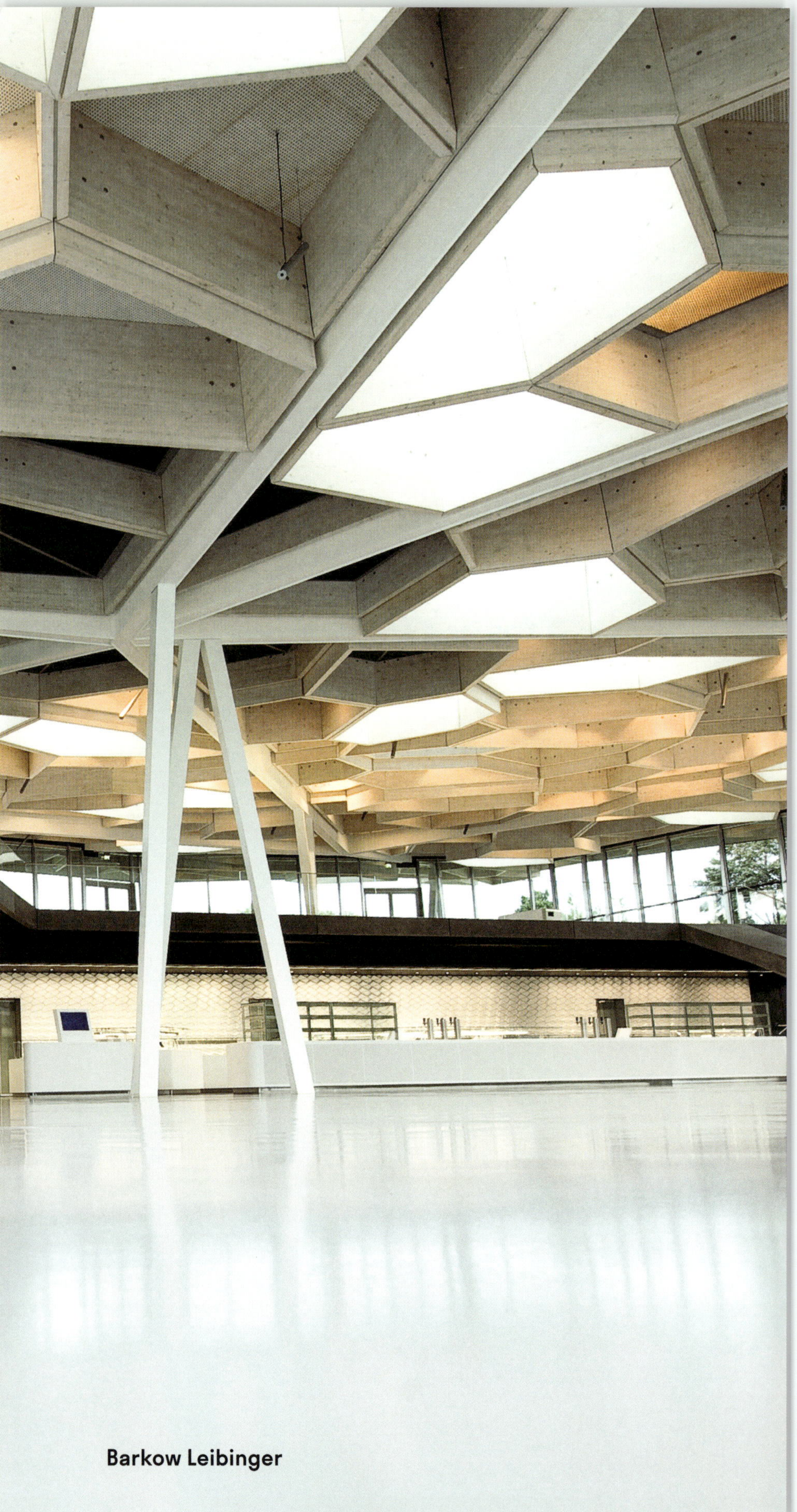

Barkow Leibinger

Architecture as Instrument

Hal Foster

One origin myth of modern architecture involves the voyaging of German designers like Walter Gropius to North American cities such as Buffalo, where they first saw in situ the industrial structures, such as grain elevators, that they had already proposed as models for functionalist buildings in Europe. The partnership of Frank Barkow and Regine Leibinger is a new variation on this old theme of international encounter: in the late 1980s the American Barkow and the German Leibinger met at the Harvard Graduate School of Design (where Gropius had once presided as chair). Already in the literature on the office this encounter is taken as a primal scene: Frank Barkow, the rangy man from Montana, impressed by the huge infrastructural projects and the great land art of the American West (e.g., hydro-electric dams in the first instance, *Spiral Jetty* by Robert Smithson in the second), meets Regine Leibinger, the sophisticated daughter of the innovative director of TRUMPF, the designer-manufacturer of laser-cut tools based near Stuttgart (which is also where a classic of European modernism, the Weissenhof Siedlung, is located). After training at the GSD under the chairmanship of Rafael Moneo, the two young architects set up a practice in Berlin in 1993, at a time when the new Europe came to represent what the old America once did: an expanded horizon for ambitious building.

However devoted to industrial architecture, modern masters often made signature statements with houses; conversely, in our era when art and entertainment are central to the economy at large, contemporary architects have sometimes become household names through museums. Although Barkow Leibinger have produced both domestic and cultural projects, as well as two landmark office towers, the TRUTEC Building in Seoul (2006) and the Tour Total in Berlin (2012), they are best known for industrial architecture. At the same time Barkow Leibinger are fully aware of how such design has shifted in meaning and motive. On the one hand, the factory is no longer separate from other typologies such as the laboratory; on the other hand, work undertaken there is no longer distinct from other activities such as research and experiment, modeling and computing. So even as Barkow Leibinger "recover essential aspects" of industrial

architecture, they have also adapted to its changed parameters, and anticipated still newer ones.[1] If "today technology is representation-less," as Frank Barkow suggests, Barkow Leibinger do not buy into the fantasy of dematerialization that drives the post-Fordist ideology of "light construction."[2] In effect, they see industrial architecture as a set of operations involving materials and techniques both new and old, and they develop these operations in architectural terms, often mimetic of industrial ones, that are "repetitive, serial and additive."[3]

Distinctive though they are as an American-German partnership, trained in the one country and based in the other, Frank Barkow and Regine Leibinger are also representative of a generation that is sometimes called "post-critical." Yet this term is inaccurate, because, although this generation is not reliant on a priori theory, as an architect like Peter Eisenman often was, neither is it dependent on imagistic scenography, as architects like Robert Venturi and Denise Scott Brown, the postmodern opponents of Eisenman, often were. At the GSD under Moneo, Frank Barkow and Regine Leibinger learned to navigate between the Scylla and Charybdis of applied theory and applied images alike.[4] Just as important, as they developed, they steered clear of two younger sirens that might have proved more seductive. In many ways, the theoretical formalism represented by Eisenman morphed into the digital formalism promoted by Greg Lynn, while the scenography represented by Venturi and Scott Brown hardened into the "fetish ornaments" promoted by Zaha Hadid.[5] If the former tendency has largely surrendered the tectonic clarity of much modern architecture, the latter has mostly exacerbated the imagistic superficiality of much postmodern architecture. Barkow Leibinger have resisted both developments: in their view, new materials and techniques hardly nullify considerations of structure—on the contrary—and architecture as a sculptural object is no advance over building as a flimsy sign.

What, then, is the third way that Barkow Leibinger have pursued? Ten years ago, some members of their generation spoke of a "new pragmatism," while others insisted on a "design intelligence" that was "projective" rather than "critical." Both notions pointed to a renewed

commitment to practice, not an aversion to theory or representation per se but, rather, an advocacy of knowledge that is intrinsic to architecture, that emerges from its distinctive protocols of research, experiment, calculation, and execution. Barkow Leibinger favor a slightly different term, "design performance," which can be taken to indicate an architecture that meets the highest standards of industry (or any other client), to be sure, but that is also performative in another sense-inventive, even playful. This is á cohort that, not concerned with a signature style, is responsive to given conditions of client, program, and site, and that is alert to how advances in technology and engineering can be turned to architectural ends.

"For me it always has to be comprehensible and it has to be appropriate," Regine Leibinger remarks. "Those are key terms for [our] architectural approach."[6] That approach is an ethical one too; certainly, it was for the early advocates of modern architecture. The common term for this modern commitment was "transparency," which etymologically means "an appearing through." For the most part, this value operated by analogy: if the materials, structure, and construction of a building were made clear, then, it was thought, other aspects of life often shrouded in secrecy—social relations, economic operations, political decisions—might also be drawn into the open, into the clear light of democratic understanding. That analogy, which was active in modernist art too (where the common phrase was "truth to materials"), was never a strong one, and today it is flouted by many architects whose production of atmospheric and affective effects mostly abets the obfuscation that now dominates these other realms (again, the social, the economic, and the political).[7]

This is why it is so important that Barkow Leibinger insist on "legibility," the term they prefer over "transparency." Again, the legibility they seek is hardly that of a postmodern *architecture parlante*, yet neither is it simply that of a modern structural transparency, the assumed self-evidence of construction in brick, concrete, glass and steel, and so on. If much technology is "representation-less" today, Frank Barkow and Regine Leibinger do not leave it there, in its own black box; they work to put various techniques into action and, in doing so, not only to

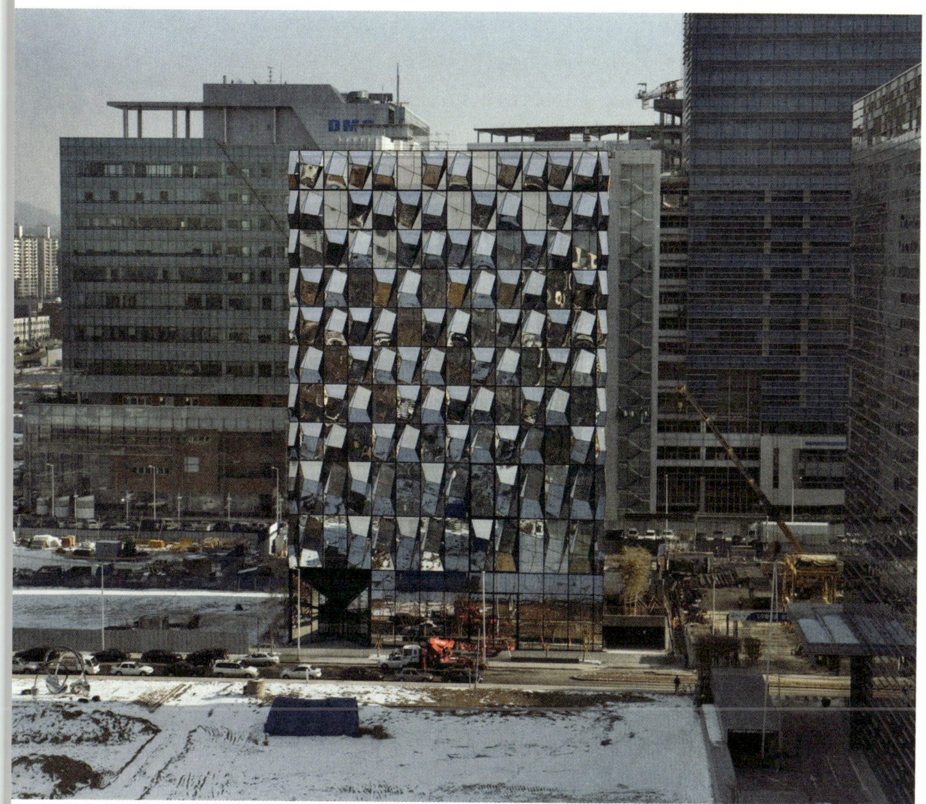

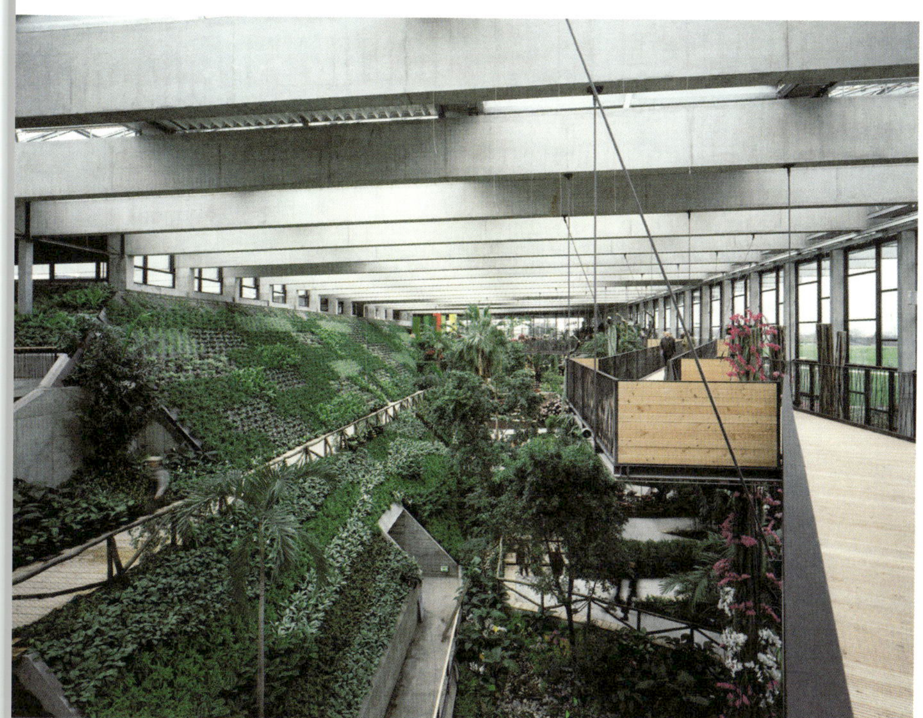

TRUTEC Building, Seoul, 2006. Courtesy of Barkow Leibinger.
The Biosphere and Flower Pavilion, Potsdam, 2001. Photograph by Werner Huthmacher, courtesy of Barkow Leibinger.

demonstrate them but also to transform them in ways that are appropriate to present conditions. A Barkow Leibinger mantra has it that "tools shape materials that make forms, not the other way around," a sequence that reverses the usual order of design.[8] Here they acknowledge the importance of the symbiotic relationship they have enjoyed with TRUMPF, a strong client that led Barkow Leibinger to consider "how digital fabrication technologies can be used to make buildings."[9] Yet they have also worked with other fabricators and engineers to incorporate new materials and techniques into the design process. In this manner, as they look ahead to the advanced world projected by, say, TRUMPF, Barkow Leibinger also look back, beyond modern architecture, to the materialism of manufacture advocated by Gottfried Semper (their interest in "carpeting," for example, recalls his fascination with textiles). The outcome is a distinctive "atlas of fabrication," in which materials and techniques are legible in the structures and spaces that result, in ways that unite design and program as well as construction and site.

Another Barkow Leibinger motto is *Kein Stil, sondern Haltung*, which can be translated roughly as "Position over Style." "Position, in our case," they add, "favors process over preconceived form," and by "process" they mean specific operations performed on specific materials that are deemed appropriate for a given project.[10] Forty-seven years ago, discontent with the pictorial effects of a Minimalist Art that contradicted its own program of literal transparency, Richard Serra also developed a set of specific operations to be performed on specific materials, a protocol laid out in his famous *Verb List* (1967–68): "to roll, to crease, to fold…" These tasks governed his first mature works: sheets of lead rolled, folded, torn, or otherwise manipulated; molten lead splashed along the base of a wall and peeled back in creased rows; slabs of concrete stacked on top of one another or sheets of lead propped up against each other; and so on. In their exhibition catalogue *An Atlas of Fabrication* (2009) Barkow Leibinger present a "list of actions" of their own: "2D-Cutting, Casting, Cutting/Stacking, Bending, Punching, Welding/Inflating, 3D-Cutting (Revolving), Anticipating."[11] Although these operations, sometimes

separate, sometimes combined, are often sophisticated in technical terms, they are usually simple when it comes to legibility. Like Serra, Frank Barkow and Regine Leibinger think of practice as a matter not only of experiment and execution but also of demonstration and disclosure.

Take cutting and rotating, as performed in the façade of the office building in Seoul, for example, or in the roof of the TRUMPF canteen in Ditzingen. In the first instance, Barkow Leibinger had glass panels cut at irregular angles and fitted into two- and three-dimensional steel frames in a way that produced standard types; they then rotated these extrusions through 180 degrees in such a way as to create "a huge amount of variation and nuance within the façade."[12] In the second instance, Barkow Leibinger had glulam wood cut into irregular cells and set again in steel frames in such a way that formed "a kind of infill webbing"; again the result was both varied and nuanced not only in appearance but also in function, since the cells could be "programmed as skylights, acoustic panels, or artificial lighting."[13] Even as the simple operations remain legible, the complex outcomes become resonant: the Seoul façade suggests a giant kaleidoscope, while the TRUMPF roof evokes a canopy of leaves.[14] In this way Barkow Leibinger make both materials and techniques respond to human invention and natural reference, which is to say that, just as they do not allow technology to be a black box that mystifies us, they also do not project it as a "second nature" that dominates us.

Another connection to Post-Minimalist Art might be mentioned here, one that involves not only a protocol of process but also a sensitivity to site. Again, like Serra, Barkow Leibinger understand work as embedded in a particular context, to be experienced there, bodily, under particular conditions. This is evident enough in the TRUMPF campus, for example, but even more in the Potsdam Biosphere, where the site helped to generate a structure that in turn articulates the site. Here the critique of "image making" is one with a commitment to "space making": buildings are not boxes dropped in an abstract space but rather interventions that extrapolate, demarcate and activate a specific field.[15] One of the strong suits of the Barkow Leibinger generation is to redefine architecture and

landscape in mutual terms, yet even more is at stake here for Frank Barkow and Regine Leibinger: a conception of architecture as an instrument to probe a site à la Serra, even to map a condition "where nature and technology are always in flux" à la Robert Smithson.[16] In effect, just as Post-Minimalists like Serra and Smithson critiqued Minimalist Art, so Frank Barkow and Regine Leibinger critique "Minimalist" architecture today, which, again, in its pursuit of atmospheric and affective effects, has tended not only to obscure structure and space but also to overwhelm subject and site.

Although Barkow Leibinger sometimes refer to architecture as "engineered structure," they always turn whatever engineering they employ to architectural ends.[17] In this way they avoid another great hazard in contemporary design, that of hypertrophic engineering presented as architectural art, which usually means architectural spectacle (e.g., Santiago Calatrava). Often enough, both materials and operations in the Barkow Leibinger repertoire are neither novel nor high-tech; some are not only traditional but also almost primordial in origin (e.g., wood, casting).

In the end Barkow Leibinger are *bricoleurs* as much as they are engineers. The *bricoleur*, Claude Lévi-Strauss writes in a famous definition, treats "a collection of oddments left over from human endeavors"; he or she "makes do with 'whatever is at hand,' that is to say, with a set of tools and materials which is always finite and is also heterogeneous."[18] Although sensitive to the materiality of these odds and ends, the *bricoleur* treats them as signs in which the signified turns into the signifying and vice versa, even as "operators" that represent a set of actual and possible relations."[19] This is the case with Barkow Leibinger. Often, they are inspired by found images and objects—a micro-photograph of a leaf, a snapshot of a stack of wood, a left-over piece of bubble wrap, an old toy like the Slinky (this cylindrical coil of wire is a miracle of tectonic elasticity), a picture of the sinuous brick walls designed by Thomas Jefferson for the University of Virginia campus, and so on. Sometimes they even make "frame-molds out of interesting junk lying around the office."[20]

This interest evokes a key aspect of Brutalist architecture as Reyner Banham almost sixty years ago: "valuation

of materials for their inherent qualities 'as found'." In fact, the two other elements in his definition of Brutalism also resonate with Barkow Leibinger: "formal legibility of plan" and "clear exhibition of structure."[21] "To make our mechanisms speak with our spaces is our central problem," Alison and Peter Smithson, the central protagonists of Brutalist architecture, once wrote, and Barkow Leibinger would agree.[22] "Brutalism tries to face up to a mass-production society," the Smithsons declared, "and drag a rough poetry out of the confused and powerful forces which are at work."[23] Barkow Leibinger update this ethical attitude of committed address for "a mass-customization society"; their architecture, which they label "prêt-à-porter," also extracts a rough poetry out of the complex forces of our time. In many ways Brutalism was an attempt to reclaim the values of the modern architecture of Ludwig Mies van der Rohe and Le Corbusier against its "degradation" as so much stylistic "veneer" after World War II.[24] Barkow Leibinger occupy a similar position in relation to an architecture given over to digital formalism and fetishistic ornamentation.

"The work of Barkow Leibinger comes to us from inside architecture," George Wagner has written, and it is true: theirs is a reflexive language, one developed recursively through building.[25] It is a language they always revise in accordance with the constraints of the program and the conditions of the site, and it is a language they always extend through other activities such as competitions and master plans, prototyping and archiving, teaching and exhibiting. It is a language in which architecture is an instrument, as complex or as simple as the case requires.

This brings us back to "design performance," from which I want to draw a final implication. There is always an element of inspired performance in *bricolage.* And as the greatest philosophers in German aesthetics tell us, such play (*Spiel*) is also essential to art; it opens up a realm for an imaginative response to any question. In the end, this is what Barkow Leibinger offer us all: *Spielraum*, room for play, space for invention.

1 Frank Barkow and Regine Leibinger, “Beyond Ground Zero: A Conversation with Frank Barkow and Regine Leibinger,” interview by Jan Otakar Fischer, in *Barkow Leibinger: Werkbericht 1993–2001*, ed. George Wagner (Basel, 2001), 23.
2 Ibid., 24; see Terence Riley, *Light Construction* (New York, 1995).
3 Barkow and Leibinger 2001 (see note 1), 22
4 In this respect Barkow Leibinger also acknowledge the guidance of Robin Evans at Harvard University, who, for all his interest in the representation of architecture, insisted above all on its *experience*.
5 Barkow and Leibinger 2001 (see note 1), 26.
6 Ibid., 21.
7 See Hal Foster, *The Art-Architecture Complex* (London and New York, 2011).
8 Frank Barkow and Regine Leibinger, *Barkow Leibinger: An Atlas of Fabrication* (London, 2009), n.p.
9 Ibid. The gatehouse at the TRUMPF campus in Ditzingen was the first Barkow Leibinger building to incorporate TRUMPF technology in the overall strategy.
10 Frank Barkow and Regine Leibinger, “Peripheral Vision,” in *Barkow Leibinger Architects*, ed. JaeHong Lee (Seoul, 2007), 11.
11 Barkow and Leibinger 2009 (see note 8), n.p.
12 Ibid.
13 Ibid.
14 Or perhaps a canopy of crystals. There is a way in which Barkow Leibinger here participate in the current shift in architecture from a biological paradigm to an environmental, even geological, one. See Stan Allen and Marc McQuade, *Landform Building: Architecture's New Terrain* (Baden, 2011).
15 See Aaron Betsky, “From Field to Form, With an Attitude,” in Lee 2007 (see note 10), 16–23, esp. 16.
16 Barkow and Leibinger 2001 (see note 1), 21, 20.
17 Similarly, Serra, who sometimes sees sculpture as “engineering structure,” always turns engineering to sculptural ends.
18 Claude Lévi-Strauss, *The Savage Mind* (1962; Chicago, 1966), 17, 19.
19 Ibid., 18.
20 Barkow and Leibinger 2009 (see note 8), n.p.
21 Reyner Banham, “The New Brutalism,” *The Architectural Review* (December 1955), 354–61, reprinted in *October* 136 (Spring 2011), 23.
22 Alison and Peter Smithson, *Without Rhetoric: An Architectural Aesthetic 1955–1972* (Cambridge, MA, 1974), 14.
23 Alison and Peter Smithson, “The New Brutalism,” *Architectural Design* (April 1957), 113, reprinted in *October* 136 (Spring 2011), 37. See also in the same issue Hal Foster, “Savage Minds (A Note on Brutalist Bricolage),” 182–91.
24 Theo Crosby, “The New Brutalism,” *Architectural Design* (January 1955), reprinted in *October* 136 (Spring 2011), 17.
25 George Wagner, “Matters of Fact,” in *Barkow Leibinger: Werkbericht 1993–2001*, ed. Wagner 2001 (see note 1), 11.

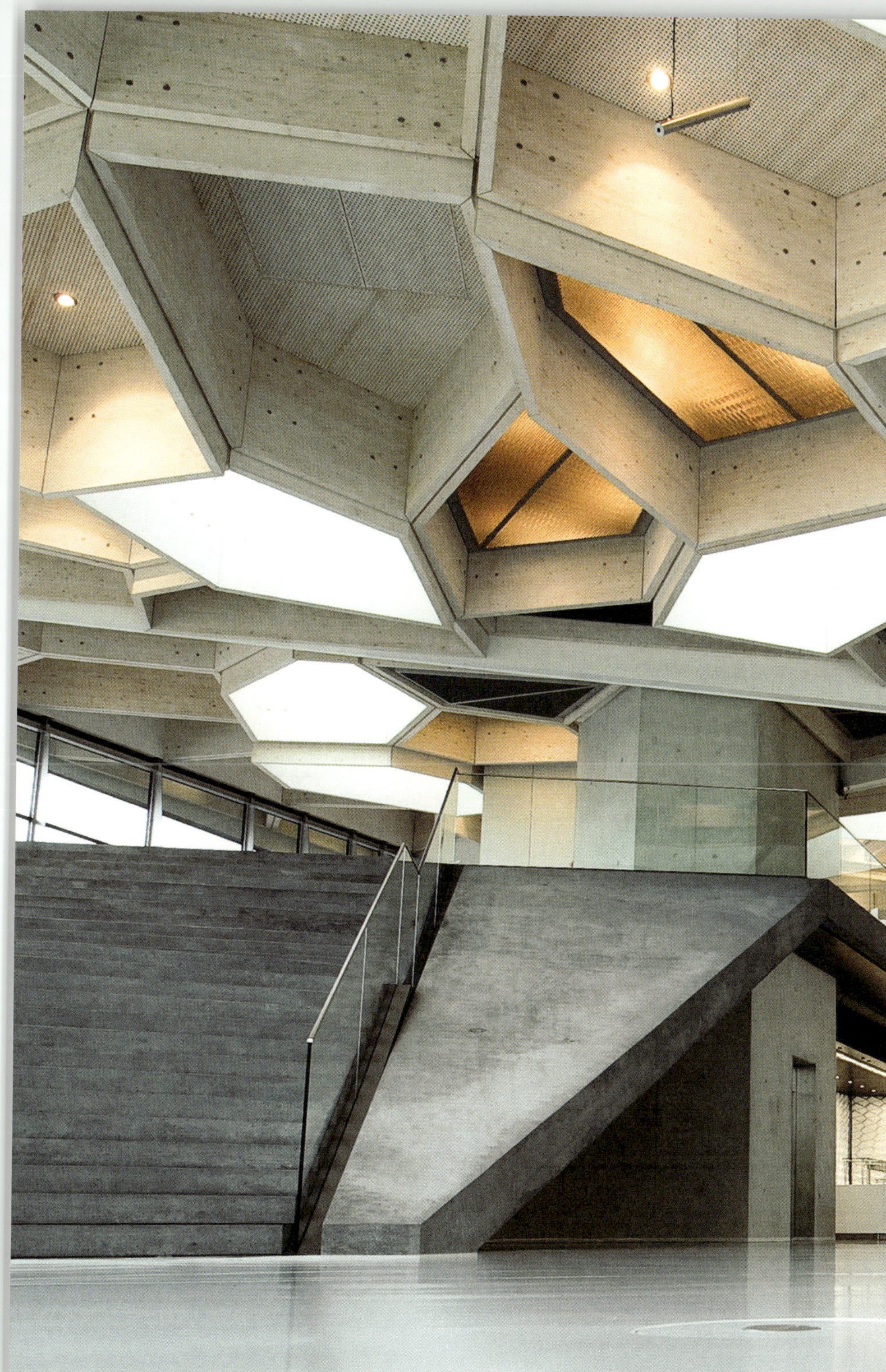

Discourse

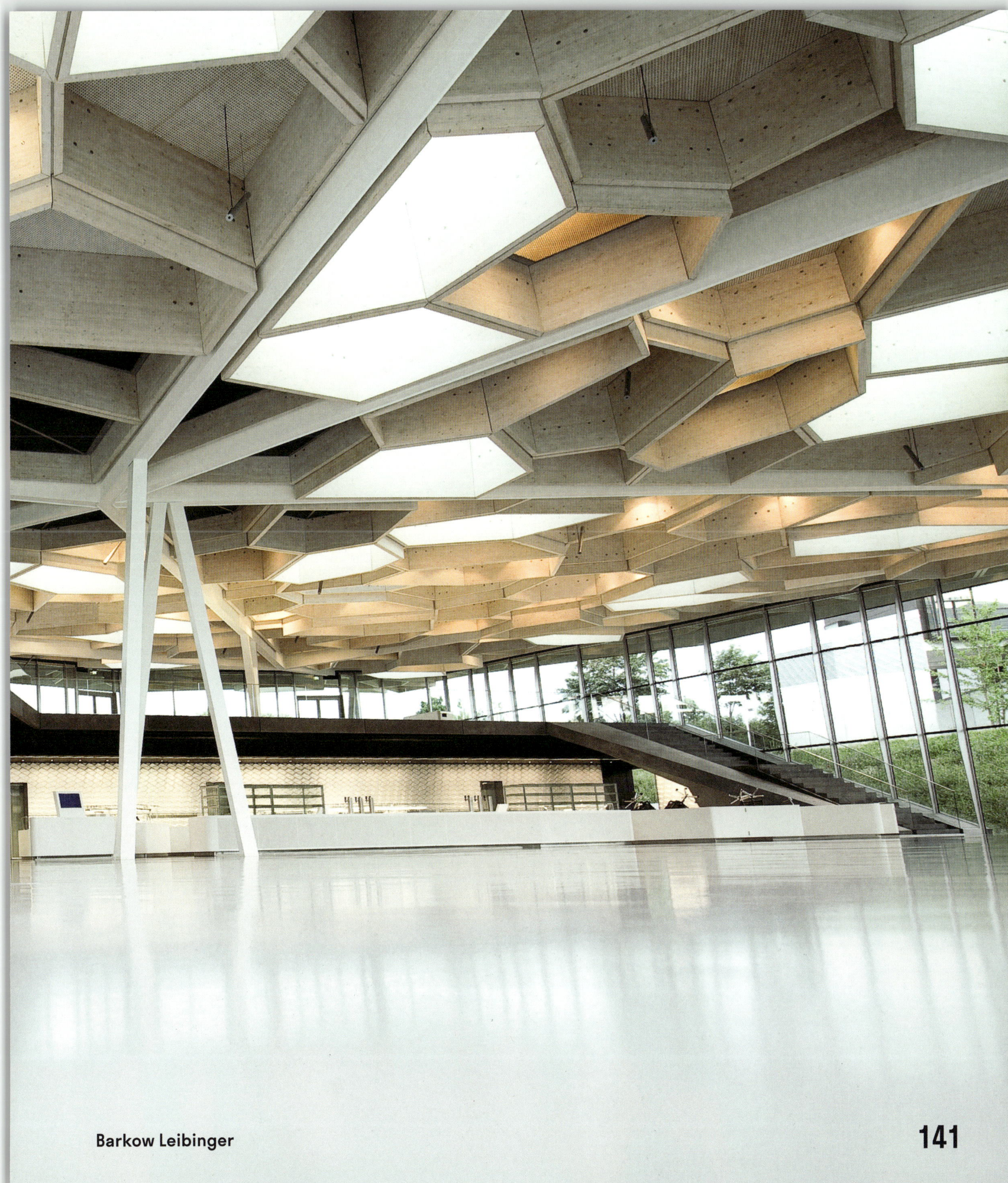

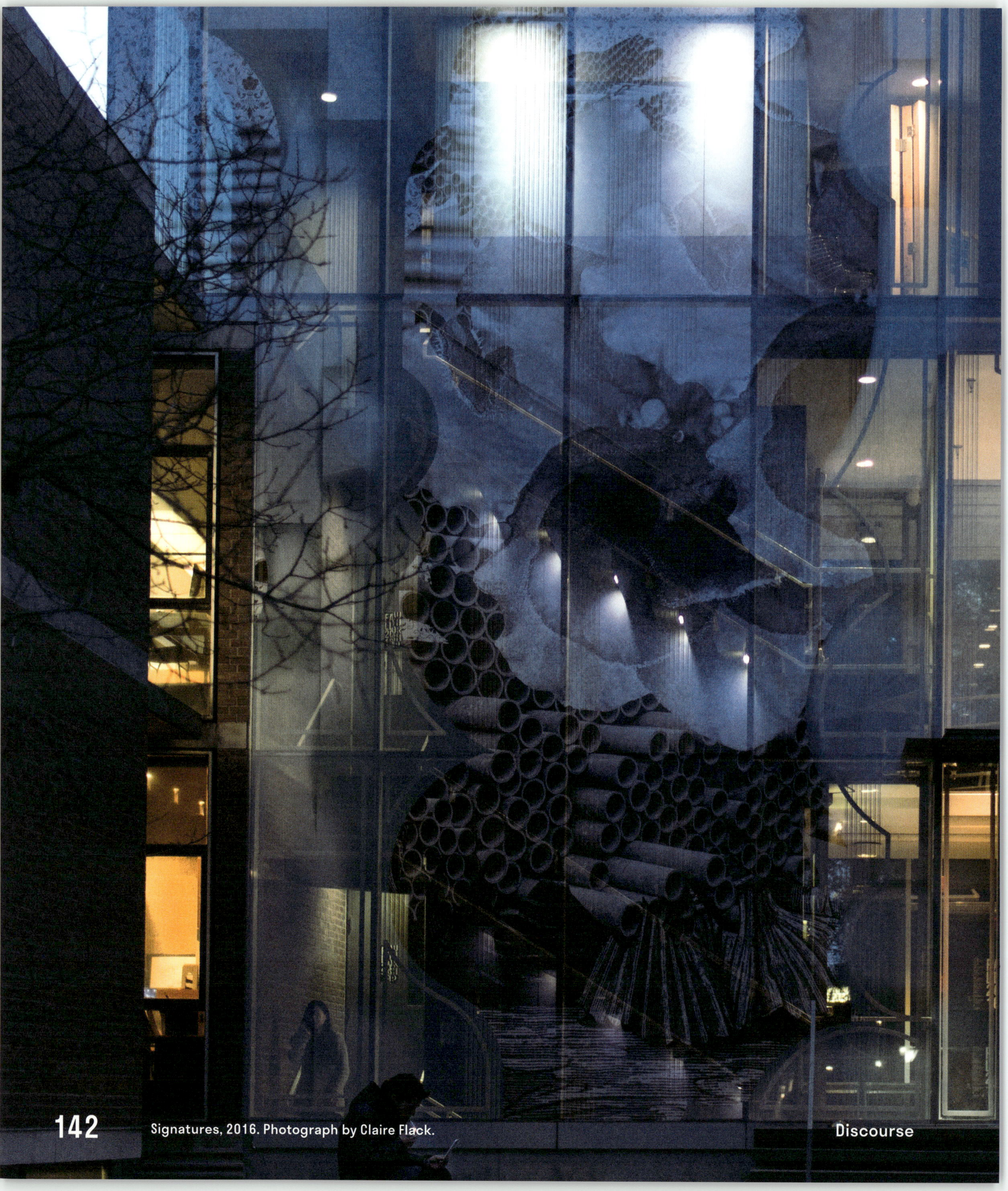

Signatures, 2016. Photograph by Claire Flack.

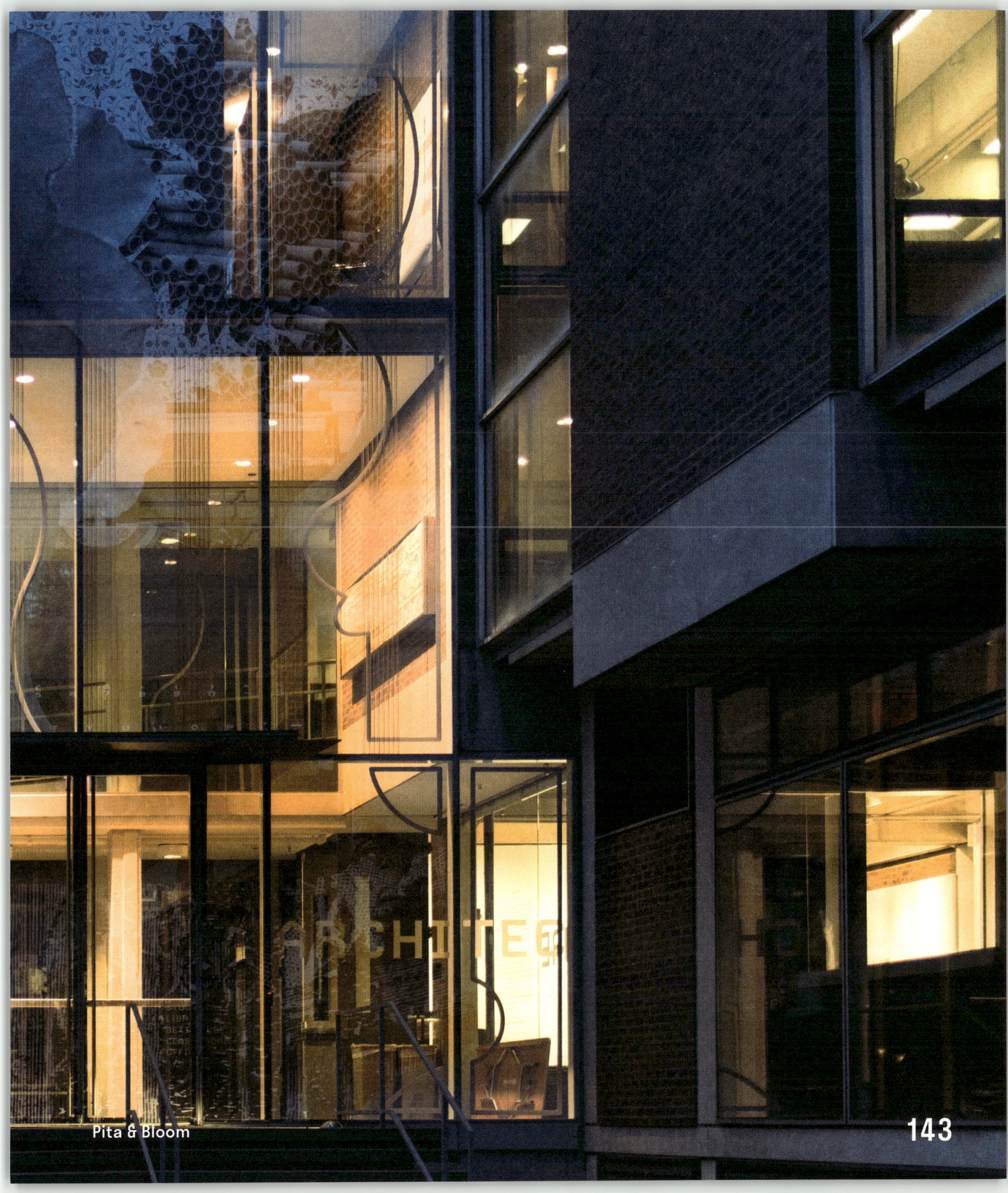

Pita & Bloom

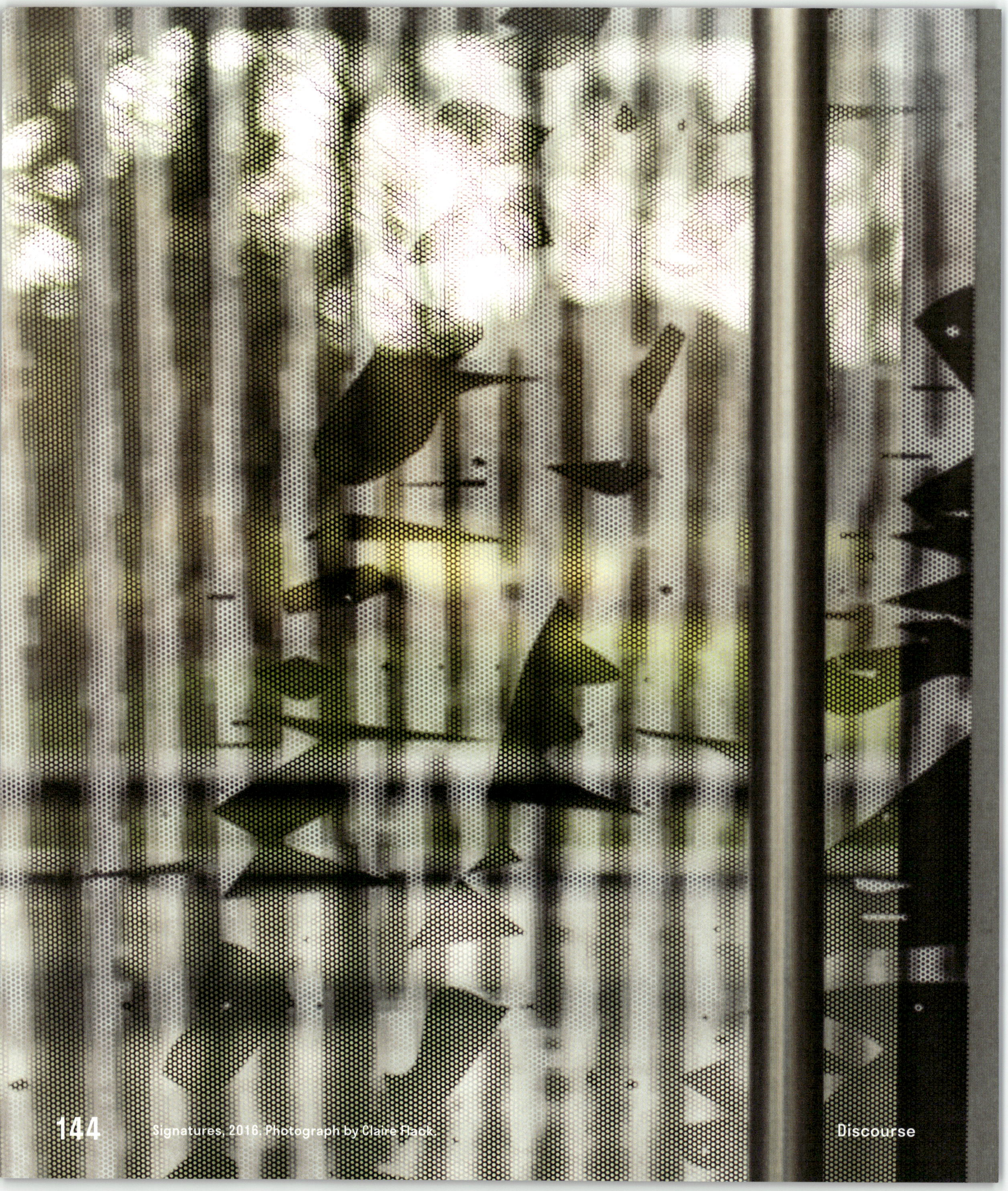

Signatures, 2016. Photograph by Claire Flack.

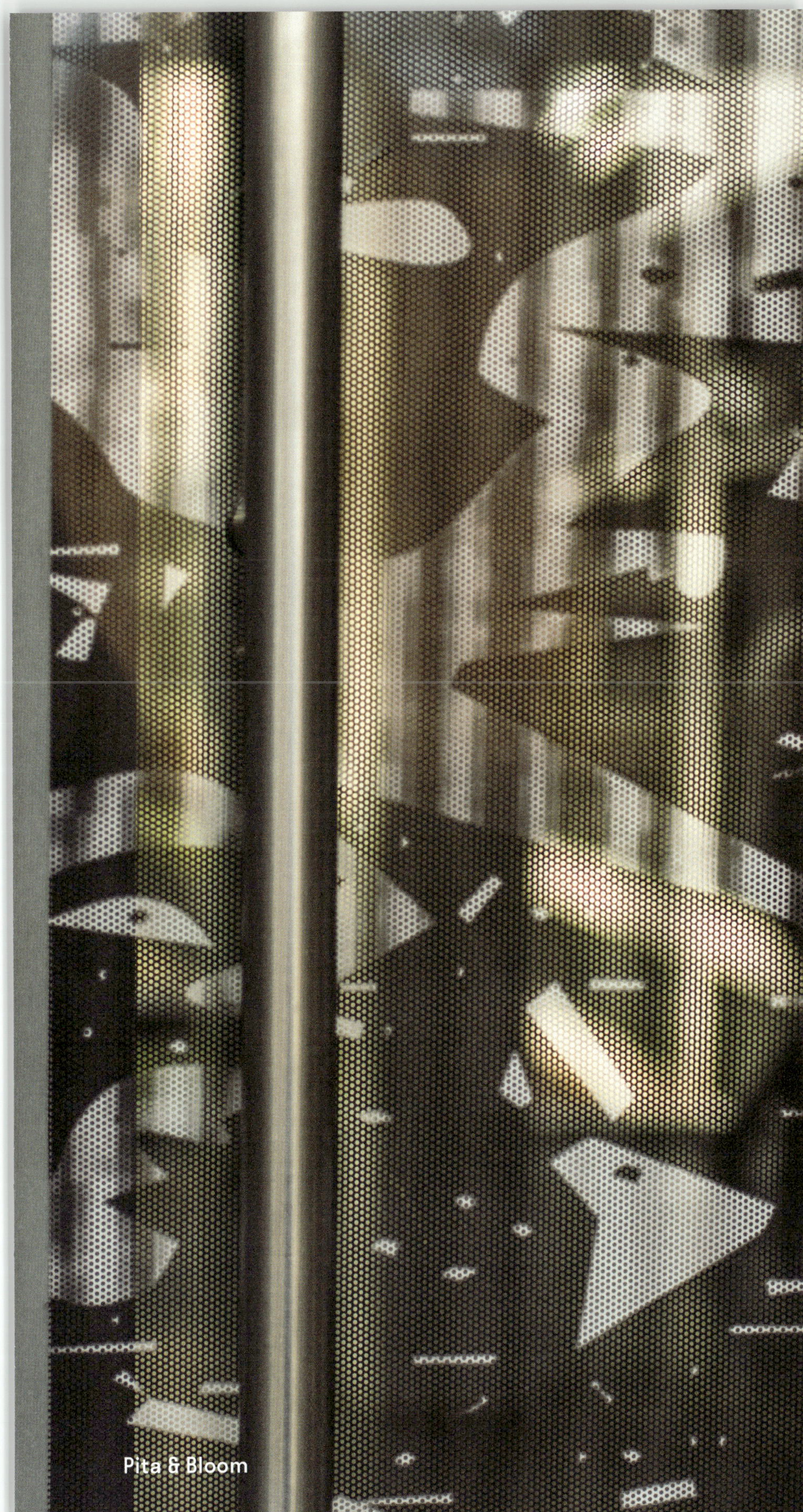
Pita & Bloom

Signature in the Age of Siri

Sylvia Lavin

Pita Bloom: an exotic flower, incandescently hued, rare and boisterous

Given Pita & Bloom's consistent use of alluring gloss, eye-catching color, Art Nouveau lineaments and Churrigueresque texture, stylistic traits that combine to mimic the strategy of a flower seeking to attract its mate and preserve life itself, the temptation to make the association between *Pita Bloom* and an imaginary blossom is overwhelming. It is difficult, in other words, not to assume that the name of this practice is not only a name but is also a signature, a stylized mark, a sign of a person or persons, proof of their identity and a manifestation of their own inimitable and singular style. *Pita Bloom*, like Palladio or OMA, portends significance and to be a name borne of a deliberate decision. *Signatures* promises to function as a Rosetta Stone for this name, unleashing its meaning and proving that no matter how obscured by time or translation, architecture, like language, signifies and can withstand the heavy burden that the notion of a signature has become. Yet the name of this practice is at best tenuous in relation to the biographies of the two principals. Jackilin Bloom was born Joung Min Hah, becoming Jacki Bloom by Americanization and marriage. Had Florencia Pita followed the same process as she moved to the U.S. from Argentina, she would have become Maria Florencia Pita de Diaz Alonzo. So, the name of their practice, if tied to the principals as persons or to the complex of global conditions that undergird the legality of their names—establishing such links as lawful being the most basic purpose of a signature—should have or at least might just as well have been Hah Alonzo or something else equally not aromatic or floral. In fact, under the sign of this name, would the roses of their design smell at all?

Pita Bloom, apparently so ripe with significance, so perfectly expressive of Pita & Bloom's *Signatures*, calls architectural signification into yet another crisis because this signature has been generated by the algorithms that autocorrect virtually every action of contemporary life. Rather than tie a person to a mark via the hand, which in the days before mechanical reproductions was why signatures were authenticating, the legal status of a signature today derives not from its physical connection with a person, but to the digital encryption through which it is encoded and transmitted, codes that are not visible even to the digital designer. Hence, rather than tie design to expression, a notion fundamental to almost all modern definitions

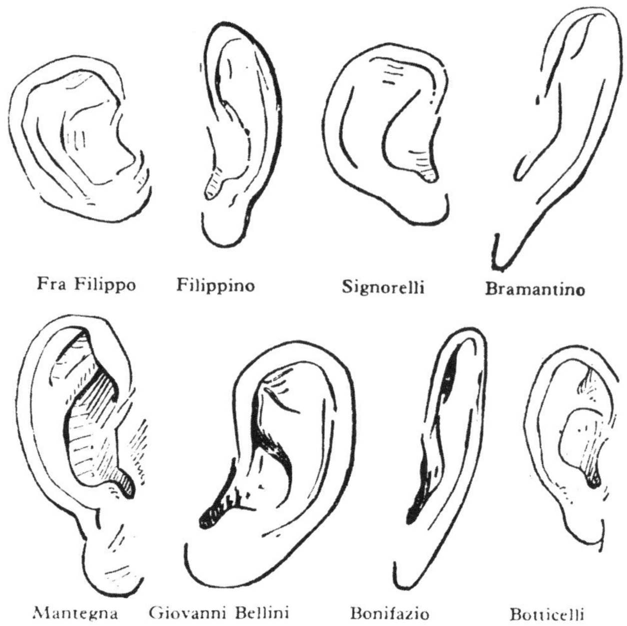

Kunstkritische Studien über italienische Malerei, 1890.
Image by Giovanni Morelli.

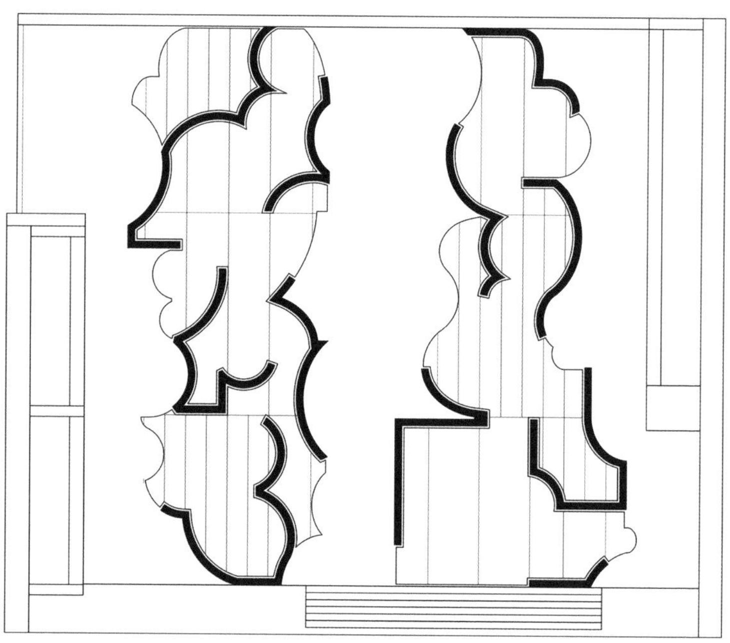

Signatures, facade mullions, 2016. Image by Pita & Bloom.

of stylistic signature, Siri and autofill will always make sure an architect's name is spelled in a standard way and appears in the appropriate Adobe font. Autocorrect—and all that for which it stands—has eliminated the possibility of the Freudian slip, the unintended truth, and the personal *je ne sais quoi* that has given modern signature its authenticating structure.

If Walter Benjamin was working today, he would be focusing not on photography but on algorithms and considering how they not only alter the means of production of specific works of art but change the ontology of art itself. Much of the modern history of art is rooted in a practice of reading signatures, not just of identifying names and maker's symbols or analyzing what they mean, but in the idea that every signature, whether a hand-written autograph or a general personal style, is a whole made of little bits and pieces of inadvertent marks, clues accidentally left by a criminal or neurotic slips of the paint brush. Codified as scientific connoisseurship by Giovanni Morelli in the late 19th century, seized as an analytical model by Sigmund Freud, and instrumentalized by Arthur Conan Doyle, connoisseurship turned the reception of art into a hunt for signs of the unconscious and therefore of a sphere of life that was both uniquely human and beyond human control. The detail—Morelli was particularly attached to how painters portrayed ears—was that which enabled signatures to affirm authorial authenticity because they were both too minor for a potential forger to notice but at the same time attributable only to one person because they were involuntary and hence idiosyncratic. The modern signature, therefore, became the very sign of authentic design and still serves this function precisely because it is a sign that cannot be fabricated—or designed.

Pita & Bloom's *Signatures* is composed of a surfeit of minor details—edges rather than the objects they delineate, pipes not yet assembled into structure, a typewriter rather than a text. As if to cover their tracks, Pita & Bloom left the connections between the references in the image tenuous, turning meaningful signs into meaningless clues scattered across a facade to lead the detective astray. Highly unstable, the image fades at night and from the interior is almost non-existent, like a message written in invisible ink. But at three stories high, these details are

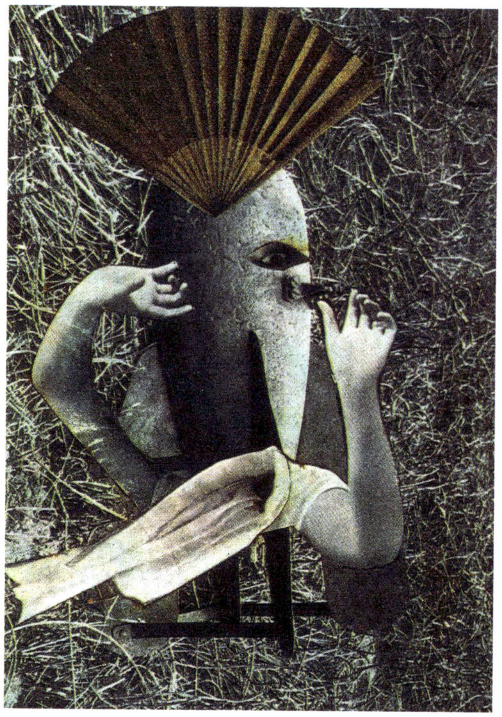

The Chinese Nightingale, Max Ernst, 1920. Image courtesy of the Museum of Modern Art, WikiArt.

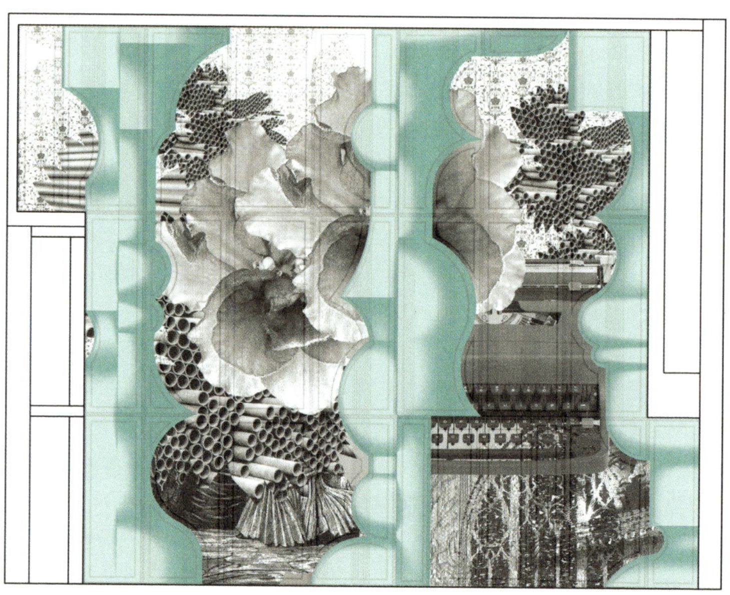

Signatures, exterior elevation, 2016. Image by Pita & Bloom.

not minor, and are so carefully and deliberately presented as stream of consciousness that they evidently cannot be expressions of the unconscious. The large-scale printing makes each detail appear as a blow-up that itself lacks detail. The more closely the massive sticker is scrutinized the more the image recedes into the prosaic facts of printing, vinyl and pixels. While *Pita Bloom* may appear to signify, *Signatures* appears instead to be the result of an operation, as if two architects followed Tristan Tzara's instructions on how to make a Dadaist Poem, but their newspaper had a URL rather than paper, scissors were a cut and paste icon and the only way to put words in order was to re-enter them into Word.docx.

> Take a newspaper.
> Take some scissors.
> Choose from this paper an article the length you want to make your poem.
> Cut out the article.
> Next carefully cut out each of the words that make up this article and put them all in a bag.
> Shake gently.
> Next take out each cutting one after the other.
> Copy conscientiously in the order in which they left the bag.
> The poem will resemble you.
> And there you are—an infinitely original author of charming sensibility, even though unappreciated by the vulgar herd.

No matter how conscientiously the architects copied the words, today's reader would receive their poem knowing full well that Siri's pervasive autocorrect function could have been invisibly at work without knowing exactly where and when: Siri is the new big brother of design, always in effect but without leaving tracks. Like Tzara, today's reader would recognize *Signatures* as the product of an infinitely original author of charming sensibility, but would no longer assume that author was uniquely human. *Signatures* has all the ingredients required to appear to be a signature, a signifying mark of identity and of personal style, but its conditions of production and reception belong to a system in which the struggle to resemble a self may be the last stand.

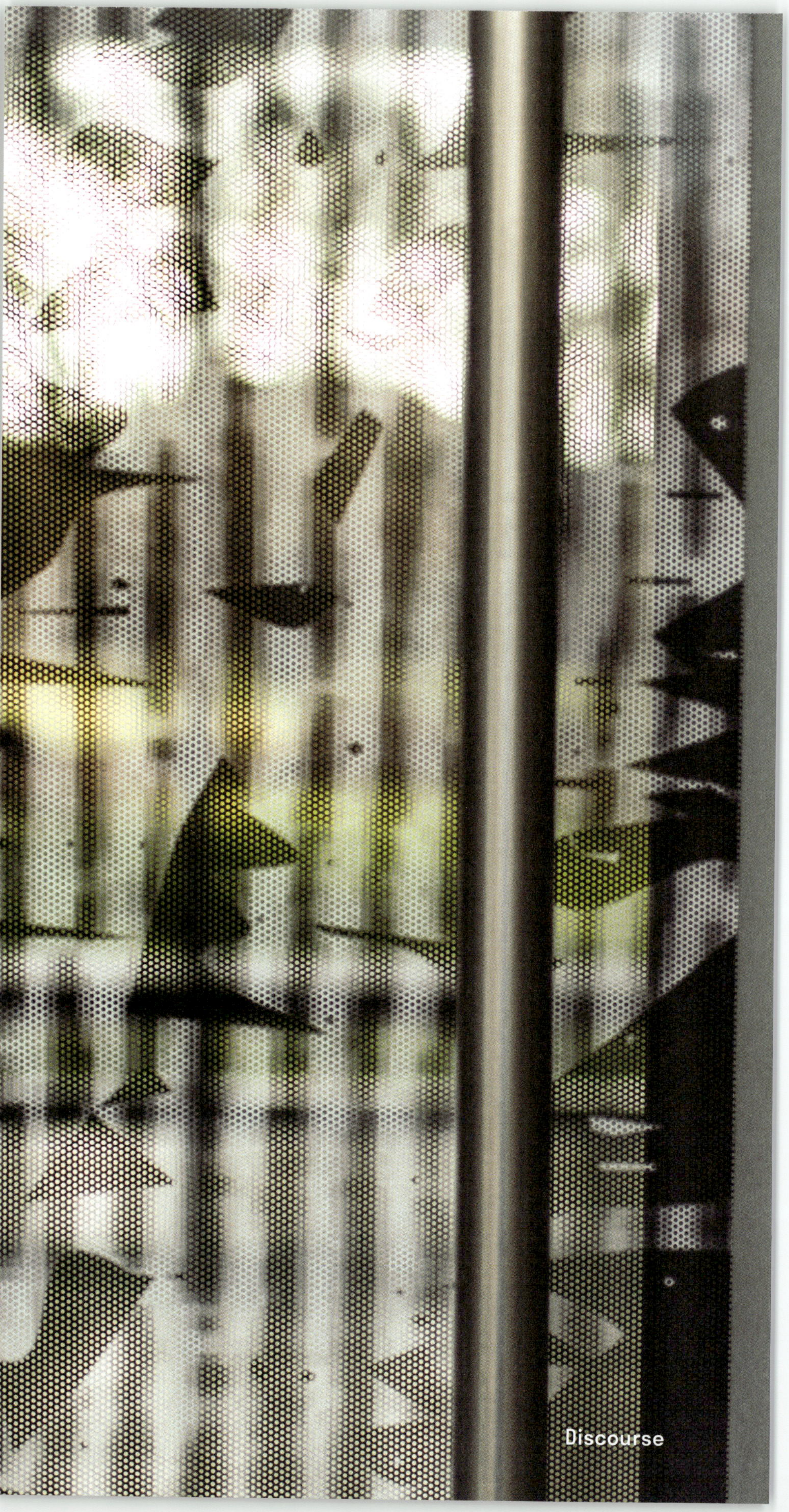
Discourse

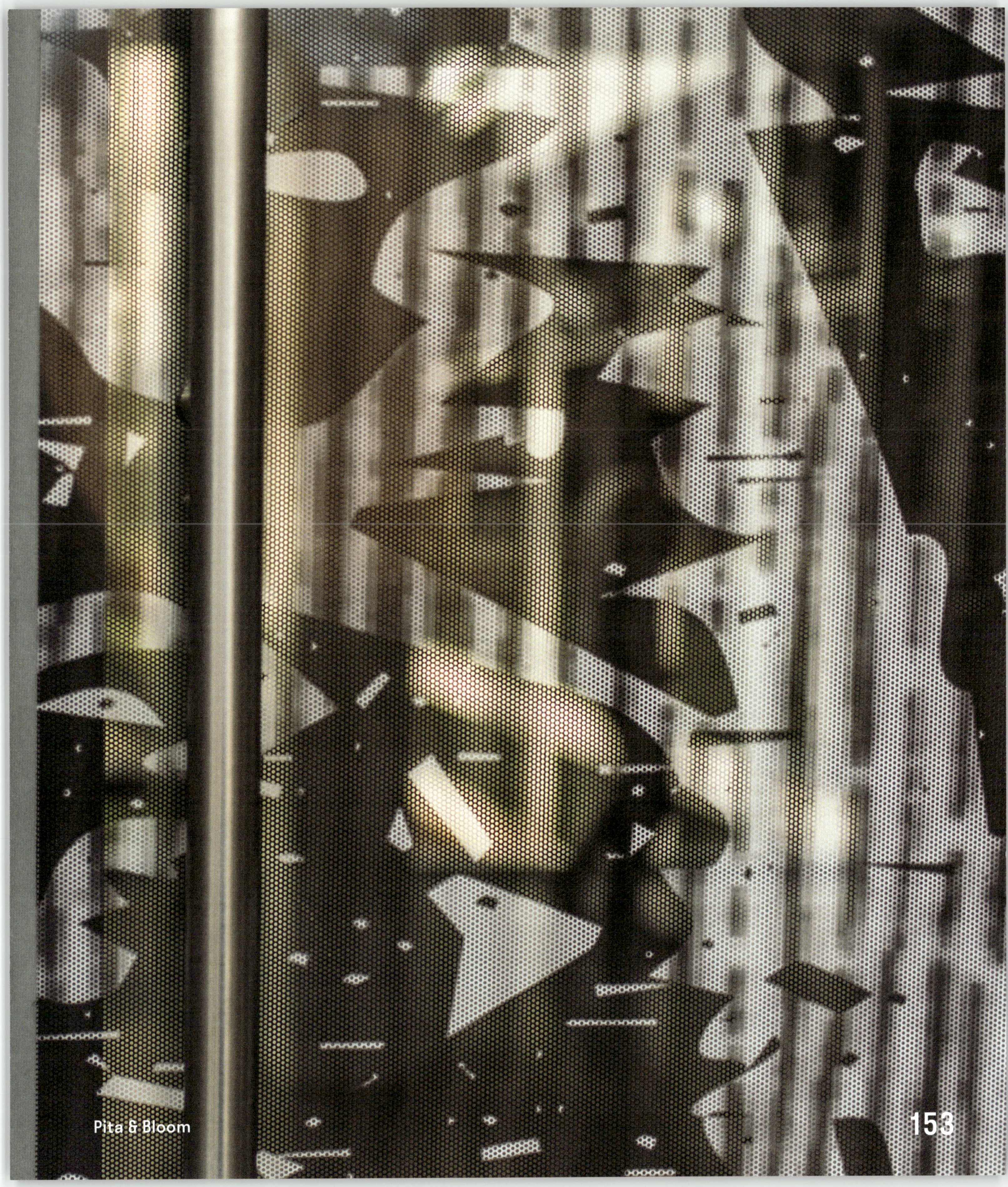

Authors

Ellie Abrons is a partner of T+E+A+M, an Assistant Professor at the University of Michigan's Taubman College of Architecture and Urban Planning, and a Visiting Lecturer at Princeton University School of Architecture.

Lucia Allais is Assistant Professor of Architecture at Princeton University, a member of the *Aggregate* Architectural History Collaborative, and an editor of *Grey Room*. Her forthcoming book, *Designs of Destruction*, is a history of monument survival and international bureaucracy in the 20th century.

Frank Barkow and Regine Leibinger are founding principals of Barkow Leibinger—an American/German architectural practice based in Berlin and New York—and visiting lecturers at Princeton University School of Architecture.

Marshall Brown is a principal at Marshall Brown Projects and an Associate Professor of Architecture at Princeton University. He also founded the urbanism, art, and culture think tank NEW PROJECTS in collaboration with curator Stephanie Smith.

Peter Eisenman is founder and design principal of Eisenman Architects in New York City and the Charles Gwathmey Professor in Practice at the Yale University School of Architecture. Among his many books are *Diagram Diaries* (1999), *The Formal Basis of Modern Architecture* (2006), *Ten Canonical Buildings, 1950–2000* (2008), and *Palladio Virtuel* (2015).

Hal Foster is the Townsend Martin, Class of 1917, Professor of Art and Archaeology and Program Director of Media and Modernity at Princeton University. Foster delivered the Mellon Lectures at the National Gallery in spring 2018.

Curt Gambetta is an editor for *Attention* audio journal and an architecture historian. His current research considers the history of architectural materials in 20th-century India.

Sylvia Lavin is Professor of Architecture at Princeton University and was Director of the Critical Studies program in the Department of Architecture and Urban Design at UCLA, where she was Chairperson from 1996 to 2006. Her recent exhibitions include "Architecture Itself and Other Postmodernist Myths" (CCA 2018), "Super Models" (Chicago Architecture Biennial and Princeton SoA 2016) and "Everything Loose Will Land" (The MAK/Schindler House, The Graham Foundation and Yale School of Architecture 2013–14).

Thom Mayne is founder of Morphosis Architects, co-founder of the Southern California Institute of Architecture and Distinguished Professor at UCLA Architecture and Urban Design. Mayne's distinguished honors include the Pritzker Prize (2005) and the American Institute of Architects Gold Medal (2013).

Antoine Picon is the G. Ware Travelstead Professor of the History of Architecture and Technology at Harvard Graduate School of Design (GSD). His most recent books—*Digital Culture in Architecture* (2010), *Ornament: The Politics of Architecture and Subjectivity* (2013), and *Smart Cities: A Spatialised Intelligence* (2015)—investigate the changes brought to cities and architecture by the development of digital tools and digital culture.

Florencia Pita (principal of FP Mod) and Jackilin Hah Bloom (principal of JHB Studio) are founding partners of Pita & Bloom—a design and research collaborative based in Los Angeles—and faculty at Southern California Institute of Architecture (SCI-Arc).

Jesse Reiser is a principal at RUR Architecture and a Professor of Architecture at Princeton University School of Architecture.

Julian Rose is a senior editor at *Artforum*, a co-founder of the design studio Formlessfinder, and a Visiting Lecturer at both Princeton University School of Architecture and Columbia Graduate School of Architecture, Planning and Preservation.

Eda Yetim is a designer and formerly worked on the U.S. Embassy in Beirut and Kolon Corporate and Research Headquarters as part of the Advanced Technology Team at Morphosis Architects.

Published by Princeton University School of Architecture,
1 Princeton University, S110 Architecture,
Princeton, New Jersey 08544
in association with Princeton University Press
Distributed by Princeton University Press,
41 William Street, Princeton, New Jersey 08540
In the United Kingdom: Princeton University Press,
6 Oxford Street, Woodstock, Oxfordshire OX20 1TR

press.princeton.edu

Library of Congress Control Number 2018936838
ISBN 978-0-9642641-0-6
British Library Cataloging-in-Publication Data is available

Publication of this book has been made possible by the
Betts Fund, established by Hobart D. Betts, Class of 1956.

Editor: Mónica Ponce de León
Managing Editor: Courtney Coffman
Design: Omnivore
Printer: Project-2

"Architecture as Instrument" by Hal Foster reprinted with
permission from Barkow Leibinger: Spielraum. Ostfildern:
Hatje Cantz Verlag, 2015.

This book has been composed in Stratos and Minion Pro
on Metapaper Extra Smooth White, Utopia U1X and
Cromatico Extrawhite.
Printed in Germany.

10 9 8 7 6 5 4 3 2 1